The Politics of Planting

University of Chicago Geography Research Paper no. 236

Series Editors

Michael P. Conzen
Chauncy D. Harris
Neil Harris
Marvin W. Mikesell
Gerald D. Suttles

Titles published in the Geography Research Paper series up to no. 235 are now distributed by the University of Chicago Press.

The Politics of Planting

Israeli-Palestinian Competition for Control of Land in the Jerusalem Periphery

Shaul Ephraim Cohen

The University of Chicago Press

Chicago and London

Shaul Ephraim Cohen is assistant professor in the
geography department at George Washington University,
and a research fellow at the Harry S. Truman Research
Institute for the Advancement of Peace at the Hebrew
University of Jerusalem.

The University of Chicago Press, Chicago 60637
The University of Chicago Press, Ltd., London
© 1993 by The University of Chicago
All rights reserved. Published 1993
Printed in the United States of America
01 00 99 98 97 96 95 94 93   5 4 3 2 1
ISBN 0–226–11276–4 (paper)

♾ The paper used in this publication meets the minimum
requirements of the American National Standard for
Information Sciences—Permanence of Paper for Printed
Library materials, ANSI Z39.48-1984.

Library of Congress Cataloging-in-Publication Data

Cohen, Shaul Ephraim, 1961–
    The politics of planting : Israeli-Palestinian competition for control of
land in the Jerusalem periphery / by Shaul Ephraim Cohen.
        p.   cm. — (University of Chicago geography research paper :
no. 236)
    Includes bibliographical references and index.
    1. Jerusalem Region—Politics and government. 2. Afforestation—
Jerusalem. 3. Jewish-Arab relations—1967–1973. 4. Jewish-Arab
relations—1973– 5. Afforestation—Israel.   I. Title. II. Series.
DS109.94.C65   1993
333.3'095694'4—dc20   93-18056
                                                              CIP

For Diane and Eliav

I will plant in the wilderness the cedar, the acacia tree, the myrtle, and the olive tree; I will set in the desert the cypress, the plane tree, and the larch together, that they may see, and know, and consider, and understand together. . . .

—Isaiah 41:19

Contents

Figures

Acknowledgments

Without the help of several individuals, this work would not have been possible. My wife, Diane Baxter, demonstrated that research not only could be conducted in the West Bank despite the Intifada, but that it was in fact more significant because of it. The success of her anthropological work in a Palestinian village encouraged me not to give up during difficult times. Initially she was my guide in East Jerusalem, during the writing phase she was a constant consultant and source of information, making the project both more interesting and more enjoyable.

Judeh Abdullah, an agronomist with the Palestine Agricultural Relief Committee, was a principal source of information concerning Palestinian agriculture, and was generous and patient with his time. The access to the villages which he arranged was invaluable, and without it the project could not have been begun, let alone completed. I appreciate his courage in supporting this research in the face of friction it could have caused him with both Israelis and Palestinians who may not have understood the basis of our cooperation.

Natan Sas was magnanimous in granting access to pertinent documents and employees of the Keren Keyemet L'Yisrael (the Jewish National Fund). The staff of that organization was open, helpful, and eager to educate me concerning their work. The members of the Forestry Division conveyed their conviction that care for the land can rise above politics, in spite of local conditions. Their help was also essential to my task, and I appreciate their cooperation.

Hassan Abu-Asala, a planner for the city of Jerusalem, is a gentle advocate of his village, eager to explore its history and relate the perspective of both the resident and the professional planner. His experience in both the Jordanian and Israeli periods was a valuable tool.

Awatif Alami and her children, Wa'el, Neiveen, Narmeen, and Shareen were an ongoing source of hospitality. They provided much needed insight for my attempt to understand Palestinian society, particularly in respect to Jerusalem, and were eager to unravel problems and help out with a variety of chores.

At the University of Chicago I was the beneficiary of the interest and support of Marvin Mikesell. His contribution to my education goes far deeper than our work on this project; the breadth of his geographical knowledge borders on the intimidating. Also providing intellectual stimulation were Marvin Zonis, Michael Conzen, and Rashid Khalidi. Each contributed a particular and important perspective, and provoked me to more sophisticated consideration of my topic. Alexander Murphy and Chad Emmett, of the University of Oregon and Brigham Young University respectively, were consistently prepared to share their thinking, and their input was always of use. Carol Saller, my editor, has improved the manuscript and taught me some important lessons. Also due thanks are those who reviewed the manuscript for the University of Chicago Press and offered many interesting comments. My parents and siblings have been my best teachers all along, and set me on a good path.

The research was supported in part by funding from the MacArthur Foundation's Committee on Advanced Studies in Peace and International Cooperation at the University of Chicago, which provided grants in 1988 and 1989, and the Harry S. Truman Research Institute for the Advancement of Peace at the Hebrew University of Jerusalem, which provided me with a fellowship and an intellectual home in the field. I offer my gratitude to both institutions and to the people affiliated with them, particularly Professor Naomi Chazan.

The list of those with whom I spoke in the course of the research is too long to detail here. I am grateful to one and all: for providing answers when possible, for helping to sharpen my questions when necessary, for opening doors, or showing me how to get around those that were closed in my face. I am particularly grateful to the villagers and the forestry workers, who spoke from their hearts. I wish them all well.

1

Introduction

A key element of the Palestinian-Israeli conflict—the struggle for land—is being played out with significant consequence in the area of Jerusalem. Because of the importance of the city to both peoples, as well as to others, the issue has implications at the national and international levels. Less appreciated is the portent that the changes resulting from the conflict hold for those involved locally. With the reunification of Jerusalem in 1967, efforts began to renew and expand the Jewish presence throughout and beyond the portions of the city which since 1948 had been under Jordanian control. A primary element of Israeli national policy was to consolidate an enlarged and permanent capital for Israel, and legislation was quickly passed enabling a change of the municipal boundaries which increased the area of Jerusalem by some 200 percent.[1] Both astride and beyond the new boundary, this policy brought the Israeli government into direct competition with existing Palestinian communities.

One element of the expanding Israeli presence was a plan to afforest open areas within the municipality and on the periphery of the city. A belt of forest had been planted in areas that had remained under Israeli control prior to 1967, and the postreunification plans called for an extension of this green belt[2] in such a way as to encompass the new municipal boundaries. As such, the extended green belt would touch upon the land of a number of Pales-

---

[1] Prior to 1967 the area of Israeli municipal Jerusalem was 37,000 dunams, and Jordanian municipal Jerusalem, 6,000 dunams. The area annexed to Israel to create the united and expanded Jerusalem municipality was 70,000 dunams. A dunam is approximately one quarter of an acre.

[2] "Green belt" is the term applied to the afforestation project by the Keren Keyemet L'Yisrael (called the Jewish National Fund, or JNF, in English). The role of the JNF will be discussed below.

tinian neighborhoods within the city, some sixteen villages bordering it, and the nonresidential areas that lay between them. This effort to encompass Jerusalem in an afforested belt caused and continues to generate significant conflict.

In fact, Israeli land policies, both in the territories and within the state, create a good deal of controversy and inspire abundant academic inquiry. Nonetheless, of the many elements of the Israeli-Palestinian struggle, the local dynamics of the land conflict have received relatively little attention. This is surprising in light of the importance of land control in the quest for state legitimacy at the national level, and for resource hegemony at the local level. That Jerusalem is the location for this study reflects an additional degree of significance and complication for both sides, each of which seeks to possess Jerusalem as its political capital and holy city. Sensitivities are thus heightened concerning the disposition of land, access, and rights in the area, thereby highlighting the issues involved. Though relatively contained disputes may have consequences for the participants alone, the outcome of the sum of these incidents has greater political overtones. Yet, despite the added sensitivity of the Jerusalem issue, the patterns of dispute occurring in the lands surrounding the city can be found throughout the area of the Palestinian-Israeli conflict.

Land as the core of the conflict is a common theme.[3] It is inevitable that land serve as a major object of contention in the struggle of two national movements over the same territory.[4] Though the groups have a different status—state-occupier and stateless-occupied—the goals, and often even the methods used to attain them, are similar. Baruch Kimmerling notes three elements in the struggle to control territory: sovereignty, ownership, and presence.[5] With sovereignty as the ultimate goal, each side strives for ownership of land wherever possible, along with as visible and constant a presence as practical, both on land owned and land disputed.

The tactic most commonly associated with Israel in what has been termed "creating facts," that is, establishing a presence, is the construction of Jewish settlements. While successful in creating a presence, at least in the

---

[3] Raja Shehadeh, "Some Legal Aspects of Israeli Land Policy in the Occupied Territories," *Arab Studies Quarterly* 7, nos. 2–3 (1985): 61; Usamah Halabi et al., *Land Alienation in the West Bank: A Legal Spatial Analysis* (Jerusalem: West Bank Data Project, 1985), p. 1.

[4] Indeed, the attempt to control territory seems to be a basic human characteristic. See, for example, Robert Sack, *Human Territoriality: Its Theory and History* (Cambridge: Cambridge University Press, 1986). For a discussion of how territorial claims are justified through historical arguments, a primary tactic in this conflict, see Alexander B. Murphy, "Historical Justifications for Territorial Claims," *Annals of the Association of American Geographers* 80, no. 4, (1990): 531–548.

[5] Baruch Kimmerling, "Sovereignty, Ownership, and 'Presence' in the Jewish-Arab Territorial Conflict: The Case of Bir'im and Ikrit," *Comparative Political Studies* 10, no. 2 (July 1977): 156.

short term,[6] the settlements occupy a relatively small amount of land,[7] require significant investment and continual human occupation, and are problematic in respect to both politics and security. Thus for a variety of reasons, Israel is unable and unwilling to settle in this fashion all the lands it wishes to dominate.

The history of landownership in the area of the former Ottoman Empire suggests that the most determinant factor in controlling land is that of presence. Ottoman land laws, which form the basis for the different legal systems pertaining to the area of the conflict, ascribe legitimacy of a sort to those who can demonstrate presence on the land. The method of establishing presence that concerns this study is not human occupation, but rather the planting of trees, and other agricultural activities that demonstrate land use.

The practice of planting capitalizes on the protection to which the trees and other forms of land use are afforded under Ottoman and ensuing legal systems, and the high level of effectiveness such use provides in preventing encroachment. In fact, it has been suggested that short of human occupation, trees are the most efficient way of preventing land alienation.[8] Trees also serve as an effective boundary demarcation, and in many cases planting is "a process of boundary building . . . trying to say where the boundary should lie between Arab land and Jewish land."[9] This tactic is thus intended to create or maintain, and demonstrate, a hold on the land.

In the context of the conflict, landholding confers the possibility of ownership, the legitimacy that ownership can ascribe, and the resulting position for claims to sovereignty over the area that both the Palestinians and the Israelis pursue. Lustick suggests that for the West Bank as a whole "the eventual disposition of the area will be determined by a series of small but cumulatively decisive political battles over provisional administrative and legal arrangements, the establishment of implicit and explicit precedents, and the imposition of faits accomplis."[10] For the Jerusalem area the small but cumulatively significant land disputes and their outcomes will have a decisive im-

---

[6] Ian Lustick suggests that the imposition of numerous settlements in occupied territories incites the local population to uprising. The unbalanced allocation of resources between settlers and Palestinians in the West Bank, along with the issue of land expropriation for settlements, is definitely a factor in the destabilization of the occupation. Ian Lustick, *State-Building Failure in British Ireland and French Algeria* (Berkeley: Institute for International Studies, University of California, 1987).

[7] The total land area of the West Bank is 5.5 million dunams. Total land area in Jewish settlements is only a small portion of that.

[8] Interview with Mordechai Ru'ach, head of Forestry Division, JNF, July 17, 1989.

[9] Interview with Sarah Kaminker, member, Jerusalem Municipal Council, August 28, 1989.

[10] Ian Lustick, "Israel and the West Bank after Elon Moreh: The Mechanics of De Facto Annexation," *Middle East Journal* 35, no. 4 (1981): 576.

pact on the creation and location of new political lines, ongoing settlement patterns, and the future landscape of the city.

Growth Following the 1967 War

The landscape of Jerusalem in 1993 is radically different from that of 1967. The range and pace of change has increased over the intervening period, and seemingly will continue to do so. Some elements of the transformation are natural and common to urban growth, others are particular to Jerusalem, while several result from a combination of the development of the city and the specific influences of the political-religious conflict surrounding it. As far as land issues are concerned, the most outstanding change of the past twenty years has been the expansion of Arab neighborhoods within and around the city and the creation of new Jewish neighborhoods. Growth has occurred in all parts of Jerusalem, but it is most evident in those areas not under Israeli control prior to 1967.

The growth in the Jewish sector has for the most part been planned, funded, and controlled by the state. It has taken place on land that has been expropriated, purchased, or declared state land, primarily but not exclusively at the expense of Palestinians.[11] The Arab growth during this time has been largely unplanned, individually funded, or supported by Palestinian organizations,[12] on private land, unclaimed land, or land of dubious title. In the landscape of 1993 this is visible in the form of new Jewish neighborhoods and greatly enlarged Arab villages. Despite this growth each side faces critical and increasing pressure for the construction of housing for their expanding communities.

During this same period various Israeli institutions and organizations have sought to impose a degree of control over the growth of both sectors, including efforts to regulate the use of land that, to date, has not been used for habitation. In fact, the agencies responsible for the supervision of the open lands have sought to gain as much control as possible in the Jerusalem area in order to preserve the status of the open lands. It is on such lands that the green belt has been planted in order to prevent any other form of use. It is on these same lands that Palestinians have been resisting Israeli expansion, and attempting to put the land into use.

---

[11] In 1970, for example, 1,405 dunams of land were expropriated from Jewish owners, necessitating the relocation of some 350 families. Meron Benvenisti, *Opposite the Closed Wall: Jerusalem Divided and Jerusalem United* (Jerusalem: Weidenfeld and Nicolson, 1973), pp. 295–296 [Hebrew].

[12] Housing construction loans of between $17,000 and $28,000, often ultimately forgiven, were provided by a joint PLO-Jordanian committee. In some cases this encouraged the construction of dwellings well in advance of their anticipated occupation in order to ensure a hold on the land in question.

Planting to Control Land

Often not visible are the planting efforts that each side has been employing to control land, and the various types of conflict—legal, administrative, botanical, and physical—that have accompanied them. While forests are a prominent feature in the western portion of Jerusalem (i.e., Israel since 1948), many of the 11 million trees planted by the JNF in the extension of the green belt are still too young to register their full impact. On the Palestinian side, though the effort has not been so massive, at many individual points there are recently planted groves of olives and other fruit trees, new or extended plowing of fields for cereals, and efforts to rehabilitate agricultural endeavors that had been abandoned during or prior to the period of Israeli rule.

There is a negative corollary to the planting as well. Since the outbreak of the Intifada in 1987, each summer has seen numerous instances of nationalistically motivated arson which have caused serious damage to both forests planted by Israelis, and those of natural growth. Indeed, one of the calls of the Intifada is to burn Israeli agriculture.[13] During this same period, and prior to it, there has been significant damage to Palestinian agriculture through a variety of means. Trees have been uprooted by both the army and West Bank settlers, crops have been damaged, and agriculture has been hampered by a range of administrative and legal obstacles. Thus the tactic of controlling land through planting draws direct attack from those in competition.

The Ideology of Land

The symbolic power of these measures must be seen within the cultural framework of the participants, in terms of both the significance of trees, and the meaning of land and the practices relating to it. For each side, both components have religious, historical, social, economic, and political significance. And while, as in this study, they are often related, each component has independent associations and characteristics that contribute to their importance and give them a status in the conflict quite distinct from that of other resources and tactics.

For Israelis a long-standing national goal has been to "make the desert bloom."[14] This is part of the landscape and nature consciousness that is an

---

[13] For example leaflet 31 of the United Command of the Uprising, which calls for Palestinians to "burn the land under the feet of the invaders." Taken from Shaul Mishal with Reuben Aharoni, *Speaking with Stones: The Words behind the Palestinian Intifada* (Tel Aviv: Ha-Kibbutz HaMe'uchad, 1989), p. 167 [Hebrew]. Nationalistically motivated arson preceded the Intifada, but since 1987 it has gained dimensions that brought it to public awareness in the form of crisis. It is seen as a systematic attack, rather than isolated incidents, as it was earlier characterized. New songs, available on cassettes sold in the territories, also encourage such arson in the fields and factories of Israel. For samples of the lyrics see "A Hit in the Territories," *Ha'Aretz*, May 25, 1989.

[14] See for example the remarks made by Ben-Gurion at the opening session of the second Knesset, which are quoted in chapter 4.

integral element of Israeli education and self-image, along with the sense of pioneering that accompanies it. The roots of this characteristic are found in the Bible, which Israelis—religious and secular alike—read as a history text of the Jewish people.[15] The Bible is replete with matters relating to the land, many of which have played a role in the development and current application of Zionist ideology. In fact, while the official name of the country is the "State of Israel," the location of the state is within "Eretz Yisrael," or the Land of Israel, a geographic term of biblical origin.[16]

Palestinians, Christian and Muslim, have a religious attachment to the land as well, originating with the same source of holiness ascribed to the land by Judaism. It is the Holy Land, with Jerusalem containing many of the significant locations from the life of Jesus. For the Muslims, the entire area falls within the land conquered in the early days of Islam. For them, land that has been a part of Dar al-Islam, or the land of Islam, can never be surrendered to those not of the faith. Both groups have, like the Jews, eschatological associations with the land in general, and with Jerusalem in particular.

The religious component will be explored more fully in relation to the land systems that have been developed by each side. For both Palestinians and Israelis, however, religion is only one element of the attachment. A concept that has a broader base on both sides is the claim to Israel/Palestine as a homeland for a nation. These claims, for the most part, are exclusive. It is true that in 1947 the Jewish community in Mandatory Palestine accepted a United Nations plan to partition the area, and that there are members of both communities who seriously consider such a solution today.[17] The fact remains, however, that neither side is generous in relation to the land needs and aspirations of the other, and, as a result, the land question is still frequently seen as a zero-sum situation.

Early Zionist tradition suggested that Palestine[18] would serve as the "land without a people for the people without a land." After an initial discus-

---

[15] For the sake of convenience, the use of the term "Israelis" refers to the Jewish majority of the state. This usage is not intended to ignore or insult Muslim and Christian Israelis.

[16] There is a lengthy debate as to what comprises the area of biblical Eretz Yisrael. That debate in its entirety is not relevant to this study. It should be stated however that the entire area under Israeli control today can be related to biblical Eretz Yisrael. This does have a role in motivating land activities in the West Bank, and it is certainly believed by Palestinians and the Arab world at large that this link is a primary cause of Israeli actions.

[17] United Nations General Assembly Resolution 181 of November 29, 1947, calling for the partition of Palestine, was opposed by all the Arab member states, as well as by representatives of the Palestinian Arabs.

[18] Palestine is the name given to this area by the Romans in the fourth century C.E. At no time was there a sovereign independent state of Palestine. The name however is the one of common use, and will be employed here for convenience when referring to the territory in question during the period subsequent to the Roman naming and prior to the establishment of the State of

sion of possible alternative sites, in the late nineteenth century Palestine was affirmed as the sole location for the renewal of a homeland for the Jewish people. In keeping with the belief of the times that the land was barren and empty, Zionist ideology took little account of the issue of an indigenous population. A component of Zionist ambition was to transform the urban Jewish communities of Europe into an agricultural, pioneering society. This was to be achieved through a return to their homeland in Palestine, and the establishment of an agrarian regime. Thus a socialist work ethic was often wedded to Zionist ideology. Settling and working the land were paramount in this pursuit.

Though that period has receded into the history of the state, its forms and images continue to hold influence in Israel, and pioneering is still an esteemed concept. Thus even though the Jewish population has become overwhelmingly urban, the notion of the land, of settlement, and of "Jewish agriculture" still has considerable power. Following the 1967 War it found expression in the settlement of the "new frontier," the West Bank. And, in a modern-day secular parallel of the religious concept of not relinquishing land, the government espoused—and legislated—an inalienability of land that is in their hands.[19]

Currently the Palestinians are a people without a state, but this certainly does not mean that they do not relate to Palestine as their homeland. Indeed Palestinians maintain a mental geography of a homeland which has not changed since 1948—they bear an image of Palestine as they believe it was, and should have been. Thus despite the displacement and encroachment that has accompanied the establishment of Israel, Palestinians nurture figurative attachments to the land as they believe it existed in 1948. Many in the West Bank, however, including those in the study area, have experienced a continuous presence on the land, rather than displacement, and this presence forms a key element in their identity, and the conflict with the Israelis.

The concept of a continuous presence on the land is one that is preached and supported by Palestinian organizations, and practiced, albeit usually without awareness of the guiding concept, by many villagers. Its name is *sumud*, or "steadfastness." For the Palestinians still living in the West Bank, even more important than a state is holding on to the land they own. Given a choice between statehood with displacement, or lack of enfranchisement but possession of the land, many Palestinians express an inclination for the latter. Because of the critical nature of the land issue, small parcels of land take on significance far beyond their economic value, and small dis-

---

Israel. From 1948 onward the area occupied by Jordan in that year will be referred to as the West Bank, with the exception of the area within the expanded Jerusalem municipality.

[19] The notion of inalienability of land is found in both Judaism and Islam, albeit in slightly different forms.

putes concerning individuals can collectively and, at times independently, become national battles.

The Role of Trees in the Land Conflict

It is with this background, and in the context of cultural values, that the trees play their role. For Israelis the individual tree is part of the greater forest. The forest is important in redemption of the land, a concept again based on biblical descriptions of Eretz Yisrael, and comprising a central theme in Zionist ideology. Since the declaration of statehood in 1948 Israel has planted some 200 million trees, mostly pine and cypress, thereby changing the landscape of the country. There is hardly a citizen of the state who has not planted a tree with his or her own hands, and each year on the Jewish holiday Tu B'Shvat (New Year of the Trees) alone more than half a million trees are planted. It is because of the goals of Zionism, individual participation, and the dramatic change in the Israeli landscape through afforestation, that the forest has become symbolic for the Jews of the redemption of the land.

Palestinians have a symbolic attachment to one particular variety of tree, the olive. The olive has been a major product of the area for thousands of years, and is a key component of Palestinian agriculture. Aspects of the olive tree which led to its symbolic place in Palestinian culture are its long life and ability to endure difficult conditions. The olive holds the land, and its produce supplies a living for those who maintain it. Olive oil, a main product, is a treasured commodity among Palestinians, and it is eagerly sought throughout the Palestinian diaspora, providing a link to the land. Palestinians believe their oil to be unique in its qualities, and it is considered essential in the diet for good health. The olive tree is a common feature of Palestinian art and poetry, and the trees are compared to children who have been tended by their parents, the Palestinians. Indeed, the Palestinians express the notion of having an intimate relationship with their trees, and their land.[20]

Participants in the Conflict

The participants in the land struggle, who act through planting on the one hand and damaging that which has been planted on the other, comprise vastly unequal forces. On the Israeli side, while individuals have strong feelings about trees, the prime executor of planting and implementor of land policy is an agency, the JNF, a quasi-governmental body. Frequent partners to planting projects, and often sponsors of them, are the Israel Lands Authority,[21] the Ministries of Housing, Agriculture, Justice, Treasury, Defense

---

[20] The symbolism of the olive is of course not unique to the Palestinians; the Bible and modern Jewish culture also draw upon the olive as a frequent symbol.

[21] The Israel Lands Authority (ILA) is a ministerial subunit, charged with formulating and executing land policy throughout Israel. The office of the ILA which deals with matters in the territories has technically been seconded to the Civil Administration.

(through the Civil Administration of the Territories), and Interior; the Inter-ministerial Committee on Jerusalem, and, for the green belt, a number of divisions within the Jerusalem municipal government.

On the Palestinian side the alignment is much thinner, with the local landowner or cultivator bearing most of the burden. Providing assistance are a number of Israeli and Palestinian legal aid organizations, agriculture and technical self-help advisory units, civil rights watchdog groups, and private lawyers who specialize in land cases, and, at the financial level, organizations such as the Palestine Liberation Organization and the European Economic Community. Through mechanisms that will be described below in case studies, the Palestinians also avail themselves of the Israeli High Court of Justice.

Research Aims and Difficulties

It was my intention to focus this research on the sector most underrepresented in academic work on the conflict, the Palestinian cultivators, or fellahin. The above list is an indication of the many actors, primarily institutional, who also have a role in the struggle. By necessity, the study then broadened to encompass at least some of these institutions. I originally hoped to concentrate on landholding patterns and their developments within the Palestinian community, a topic of inquiry for which there has been a lack of focus at the local level and a dearth of relevant fieldwork. Therefore the project initially called for an intensive examination of landholdings within a small number of West Bank villages.

One of the primary reasons for the change in the framework of the research and the shift to a study of the landholding dynamics of both sides in the green belt was the coincidence of fieldwork with the Palestinian Intifada. Under the best of circumstances the topic of land is a sensitive one for both communities, and inquiry is often met with suspicion and resistance. On the one hand, there is fear that the information is sought in the context of attempts to alienate land. On the other hand, there are many individuals—in both communities—who seek to prevent the details of their activities from being known.

On the Israeli side this is sometimes because of improprieties in the method of acquisition, or in order to prevent knowledge of the sale from driving up prices or, conversely, discouraging future sales. Within the Palestinian community there is a taboo on land sales to Jews, though not infrequently it is circumvented or disregarded. As a former occupier of the area, the government of Jordan passed a law making land sales to Jews in the West Bank a capital offense, though there is no record of official enforcement of this law.[22] However, during the data-gathering phase of this research more

---

[22] A Palestinian who served as a straw man in purchases by and for the Himnuta subunit of the JNF, Mohammed Nablusi, was shot on March 18, 1991. Nablusi had been sentenced to death (in

than ten Palestinians were murdered by other Palestinians, reportedly for land dealings. In the Gaza Strip a leaflet of the Islamic Jihad dealt directly with this issue, and, in the wake of an increase in the number of land-related killings, reaffirmed the prohibition on such deals.[23]

Another issue was the suspicion that any outsider might be an informant or member of the security forces. The presence of outsiders in a village was believed to presage a raid by the army, and thus almost all outsiders were viewed with mistrust and often hostility. This suspicion, whether or not substantiated, could result in serious complications for a Palestinian who played host to or was seen in contact with the stranger. The village that I identified as the best candidate for an intensive study was eliminated as a possibility, just prior to the initiation of fieldwork, when its mukhtar (village leader) was murdered for suspected sale of village land to Jews. Indeed, it soon became clear that an intensive study of a village or several villages was an impossibility.[24]

Even after the resulting shift away from an intensive village study, the Intifada continued to influence research opportunities, almost always negatively. In addition to the underlying suspicion, daily life was frequently disrupted. Villages were closed by curfew, military order, or Intifada strikes. Those assisting the research were sometimes arrested, or their ability to travel curtailed. It was also nearly impossible for an outsider to come to the village—by any mode of transportation—without being accompanied by a local resident. Even with this protection, stone throwing and other obstacles along the route to study sites prevented such visits from being a casual matter.

The Focus on Planting Activities

These difficulties I discovered in the course of trying to find a village for intensive study, and they influenced my decision to shift away from this goal. Prior to this, however, I had made on-site inspections from the periphery of many of the villages in the Jerusalem area. While doing so, I consistently observed one element of the landscape: where the agriculture of the

---

(in absentia) by Jordan nineteen years earlier for assisting in land sales to Jews. His name had arisen in connection with land conflicts that were being played out in Israeli courts at the time of the attempted assassination in 1991. *Kol Halyr*, March 22, 1991.

[23] *Jerusalem Post*, May 14, 1989; September 8, 1990. For examples of land-related attacks see the *Jerusalem Post*, November 17, 1988; and *Ha'Aretz*, August 8, 1988; June 30, 1989.

[24] In fact, with the progression of the Intifada, suspicion of all contacts with outsiders grew in the Palestinian community. This was especially so in regard to interactions with Israelis, and particularly those considered religious and thus automatically perceived by the Palestinians as the worst kind of citizen, the settler. Palestinians regard any bearded male as religious, and toward any such Jewish male there is an added measure of suspicion, and often violence. I resisted the repeated suggestion that I shave my beard, despite the assurance that this would make my presence in the village less problematic.

village ended, it was met by young pines planted by the JNF. Though initially
not obvious, once noticed this pattern was quite striking. A short distance
from the last furrow of plowed dirt or row of olive trees, and often immediately adjacent to or even intermingled with them, were the first trees of a future forest.

Further examination revealed an additional pattern. Where the JNF
trees were somewhat recently planted, or other forms of Israeli presence had
been initiated or expanded, there were signs of new or renewed use by the
Palestinians—such as plowed but not yet planted fields, new saplings of olive
and other fruits, or fencing and land reclamation. Each side had planting efforts underway adjacent to new neighborhoods or settlements, and this was
the case along new roadways as well. The picture in the landscape was one of
expansion, and competition.

In light of the presence of JNF trees throughout the area, it seemed
likely that material on landholding near the villages could be gained through
an examination of JNF activities, though traditionally the organization maintains an extremely low profile in regard to land matters in the West Bank. In
addition to this, there were policy and political questions related to their projects which needed to be addressed, within both the JNF and the other agencies involved. From the outset, the JNF proved to be open and cooperative. In
addition to providing access to the files of the Forestry Division, interviews
with senior staff members, and working maps for the areas in question, JNF
field supervisors led extensive on-site surveys, and revealed much of what
was taking place in the landscape.

It quickly became clear that the concept of the green belt served in great
measure to shape the afforestation policy for the JNF's Jerusalem district. And
while the concept of the green belt was not secret, and was in fact a matter of
pride for the JNF, the work was carried out with little fanfare. This differed
considerably from the attitude taken toward the green belt on the pre-1967
side of the city, which had been launched with pomp and ceremony, including speeches by the upper echelon of the JNF, the municipality, and the Israeli
government. The reason for this distinction is clear: prior to 1967 the afforestation was carried out in Israel proper, whereas the extension of the belt
would be carried out, at least in part, beyond the Green Line.[25]

If the green belt were entirely contained within the municipality it
would perhaps be somewhat less controversial. Technically there is no definition as to where the green belt ends and other afforestation projects begin.
Clearly, though, the belt extends beyond the municipal boundaries, and thus

---

[25] The "Green Line" is the name given to the armistice line between Jordan and Israel until
1967. The expanded Jerusalem municipality falls on both sides of the original Green Line,
though by Israeli law all of the municipality is sovereign Israeli territory.

enters the territory legally recognized as the West Bank.[26] It is primarily, though not exclusively, beyond the municipal boundary that this study focuses. It is an area rich in political and legal complications, and poor in detail and clarity.

The Research Area

The JNF files were used to identify locations of conflict—past, current, and future—within this area. Each year there is a working plan for afforestation, with the annual average composing roughly a thousand dunams.[27] The planting is carried out according to certain priorities, limited primarily by budgetary constraints and the availability of appropriate land. The purposes of planting include creation of parks, rehabilitation of existing groves, creation of greenery for new neighborhoods, and, prominent among the goals, a hold on open or disputed lands.[28]

Until recently such lands existed in abundance on Jerusalem's eastern periphery. The area to the west had already been afforested in the context of the green belt and associated projects. Connected with the green belt and continuing to the west is the Jerusalem Forest, one of the largest forest concentrations in Israel. Planting of parts of this forest by the JNF began prior to statehood, but it was in the early 1950s that it took the name "Jerusalem Forest" and was given high priority among national forestry projects.

North and south of the city there are some open spaces, but these are limited by the spread of the Palestinian cities of Ramallah/El-Bireh in the north, and Bethlehem/Beit Jalla/Beit Sahour in the south. The post-1967 Jewish neighborhoods of Ramot, Neve Ya'akov, Pisgat Ze'ev, and French Hill in the north, and Gilo and East Talpiot in the south have contributed to the lack of open land in these directions (fig. 1).[29] Thus the land now in competition is that which has not yet been built up—the agricultural and open lands adjacent to and beyond the city/village periphery. The Palestinian villages considered in this study are within or adjacent to the green belt: Beit Surik, Beit Iksa, Beit Hanina, A-Ram, Hizma, Shu'afat, Anata, Issawiya, Za'im, Azzariya, Abu Dis, Jabel Mukaber, Arab e-Sawachra, Sur Baher, Beit Tzafafa, Sharafat, as well as the neighborhood of A-Tur on the periphery of eastern Jerusalem.

---

[26] As I shall show, however, the legal distinction between municipal Jerusalem (i.e., sovereign Israel) and the adjacent West Bank territory is sometimes ignored in practical application.

[27] Interview with Tzvi Avni, director of JNF Forestry Division, Hill Region, January 30, 1990. See also JNF, 3307/425, July 28, 1987, p. 1. In peak years the planting covered several thousand dunams.

[28] "Discussion on the Topic of Planting around Jerusalem," JNF, 3307/701, October 1, 1986, p. 1.

[29] These direction headings are general, and reference should be made to figure 1 for exact locations.

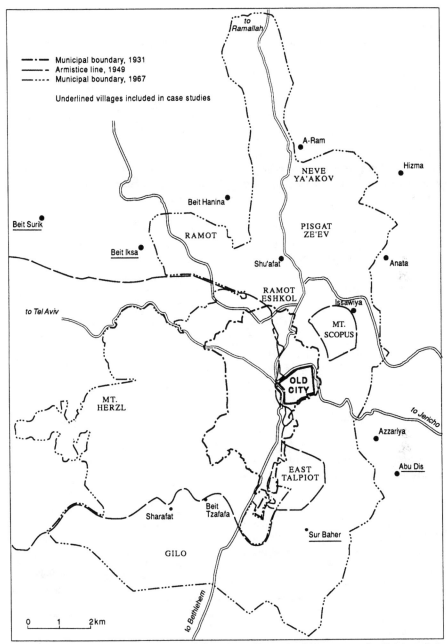

Fig. 1. *Changes in Jerusalem's municipal boundary. Shown in this map are the division of the city in 1948 and the expanded boundary created in 1967.*

Owing to the nature of landholding among the Palestinian community and the dearth of reliable documentation, it is difficult to provide a figure for the size of these villages. As a result of the unutilized spaces between them, and the practice of grazing carried out on the lands farthest from the village core, it is also difficult in some cases to delineate where one village ends and the next begins. Villagers often claim unworked land at the periphery of cultivated areas, while adjacent villages make claims for these same buffer zones. Often these lands are used for grazing alone, since cultivation is generally confined in its breadth and is located close to the built-up area of the village.

As distance from the village increases, the claims to land become more vague. In fact, much of the land throughout the study area can be categorized as ancestral land. As such the villagers may know the name of the land,[30] the general direction in which it lies, but not its borders or exact size. The one factor that is possible to determine is the size of the built-up area of each village, but this information is not pertinent to the question at hand. For total holdings, villages have been estimated at less than 200 dunams on the small end of the scale, to over 20,000 dunams at the large end. These figures however do not address the issues of actual use, documentation of ownership, or exact locations.[31]

Changes in Palestinian Land Use and Agriculture

One of the recent factors affecting the reliability of land information is the change in Palestinian land use that has occurred since 1967. During the first fifteen years under Israeli rule villagers tended to leave agriculture for wage-earning jobs in the Israeli economy.[32] Maintenance of village agriculture was left to women, the old, and the very young. A consequence of this was a break in the tradition of knowledge of the land. Older members of the Palestinian community learned the parcelization of landholdings by working in agriculture and grazing the flocks of the village, as well as by learning the traditions of their fathers. Today that information is rarely passed down with

---

[30] Land plots and tracts are customarily given names, generally relating to ancient owners of the land or prominent physical characteristics that mark it.

[31] Benvenisti provides what are often considered to be the most reliable Israeli statistics for matters in the West Bank; see Meron Benvenisti and Shlomo Khayat, *The West Bank and Gaza Atlas* (Jerusalem: West Bank Data Project, 1988). Palestinian sources generally disagree with Benvenisti's figures, often significantly, and indicate suspicion of both under- and overestimates. The Central Planning Department of the Civil Administration is creating blue lines to fix development zones for West Bank villages, but these correspond only to the area in which residential construction will be allowed, and do not, therefore, reflect the scope of village landholding or use.

[32] Interview with Judeh Abdullah, Palestine Agricultural Relief Committee, December 14, 1989.

accuracy.[33] Thus with the decrease in the scope of agriculture, and the passing of time, much information about local practice has been lost.

In most villages the area in cultivation is significantly smaller than that which is claimed in one way or another by the villagers. In the Jerusalem area crop type and quantity is restricted by the amount of water available, topography, and soil quality. For the most part, agriculture is rain-fed, and as a result the primary crop is olives, with other fruits grown as well. Wheat is sown after a rough plowing, but if there is insufficient rainfall to generate a good harvest, as is often the case, the field is opened for grazing by sheep and goats. Groves and fields generally abut the villages, but planting is also carried out farther away, along the slopes of wadi courses, where water tends to concentrate. East of the city such fields can run for a distance of seven to eight kilometers from the village, and they are visible only from a vantage point in or on the edge of the wadi.

It is the herding aspect of the village economy which leads to many of the land claims. Villages often combine their animals into large units and hire a bedouin to serve as a shepherd.[34] Moving primarily to the Judean Wilderness in the east, these flocks rarely maintain daily contact with the villages. As the young seek wage labor, and as the land available to the villages shrinks as a result of Israeli closure of large areas for military or settlement purposes, the size of the flocks decreases. In the past the villages had used the corridors mentioned above as exclusive grazing territories. Among the generation of Palestinian elders some still know the names of the subdivisions by heart. Again, it must be noted that the accuracy of such information is very problematic. Many sites are claimed by the people of a number of different villages, each proposing a different name and claiming to have supporting documentation.

Despite the generational decrease in familiarity with the land, the issue of land alienation is taken seriously by most Palestinians. During the Intifada there was, at least initially, a reawakened interest in agricultural pursuits, primarily among the youth.[35] Three reasons are suggested for this partial return to farming, all of them related to or heightened by the Intifada. The first reason is to supplement other forms of income. That agriculture has taken a secondary status in the Palestinian economy is related to a number of issues. In addition to the shift toward wage labor with the opening of the Israeli job

---

[33] Interview with Abu Yazzid of Abu Dis, December 26, 1989.

[34] Some of the villages in the green belt such as Arab e-Sawachra and Jabel Mukaber are populated by bedouin tribes who are no longer nomadic. These groups have adapted successfully to the agricultural practices of the area, and in fact prove no less attached to the land and their agricultural work than the traditional fellah villages.

[35] This phenomenon was picked up on quite early in the Intifada by geographer David Grossman of Bar-Ilan University: "Employment Potential of the Arab Agricultural Sector in the Occupied Territories," *Karka: Journal of the Land Use Institute* 30 (September 1988) [Hebrew].

pool,[36] competition from Israeli farmers and markets and the often stifling governmental regulation of Palestinian agriculture have decreased the return on time and effort invested in farming. Nonetheless, the money to be earned in agriculture gains in significance as other income sources are threatened.

The second reason for a return to agriculture—albeit as a part-time occupation—is the idleness that has accompanied the Intifada, both on account of growing unemployment caused by political unrest and economic recession, and by the significant number of strike days called by the Palestinian leadership. Both of these contribute to an increased amount of free time. Aggravating this situation is the displacement caused by the massive influx of Soviet Jews and the reallocation of jobs that prior to their arrival had been the province of the Palestinian labor force. A corollary of this factor is the attempt to increase self-sufficiency during a time of instability. Local or home production provides a hedge against job loss, strikes and their closure of markets, curfew, and the difficulty of resupply; and at the same time it creates a degree of independence from the Israeli economy, a key goal of the Intifada.

Political Land Use and Agriculture

The third reason for the increase in Palestinian agriculture is the effort to put as much land as possible into use in the attempt to prevent its alienation.[37] To this end Palestinians are planting trees and plowing fields in areas that recently had been unused, abandoned, or neglected. In this they have the support of the Palestinian agricultural organizations, who see the preservation of land as a priority of the highest order.

The need to put land into use is so pressing that Palestinian agronomists and economists encourage the planting of olive trees, knowing full well that the olive market is currently glutted, and that crop prices are dropping yearly. In spite of this, they support the fellah's inclination to plant the olive, a tree requiring relatively little labor beyond the alternate-year harvest. Another activity that ordinarily would incur the opposition of the agronomists is the continuous planting of cereals without allowing time for the fields to lie fallow. This is condoned by the agronomists because of the desire to fulfill the criteria of continuous cultivation used by the government to assess claims of ownership. Despite the detrimental effects of this practice for soil quality and harvest quantity, the risk in leaving the land unworked is considered to be a greater danger.

---

[36] Between 1970 and 1985 the percentage of the West Bank labor force employed in local agriculture dropped from 42 to 27 percent, representing a decrease in this work force despite the overall increase in the number of laborers. David Kahan, *Agriculture and Water Resources in the West Bank and Gaza (1967–1987)* (Jerusalem: West Bank Data Project and Jerusalem Post, 1987), p. 27.

[37] Interview with Judeh Abdullah, December 14, 1989.

In addition to providing technical support in bringing land into use, the agricultural groups attempt to organize marketing cooperatives and supply other means of making agriculture an economically feasible and attractive endeavor. One component of this effort is the subsidy provided for the purchase of olive saplings, a step that allows their acquisition at a price of approximately twenty-five cents each. The qualification for this price is that the land on which the trees are to be planted is in danger of encroachment by Israeli settlement efforts or the military. In 1989 small agricultural groups distributed over 70,000 trees to villagers with lands that met this condition.

Ironically, Palestinian attempts to preserve the land they consider their own come only after Israel has taken steps to prevent them from having access to much of the area in question.[38] Had they begun their planting activities ten years ago, the efforts would have been significantly more effective. Within the legal framework of the conflict one must plant and then wait a number of years in order to accrue rights. In most cases the test of ownership was put to the Palestinians before their preemptive or preventative planting took place.

Often though the fellahin are unaware of the legal technicalities concerning the land, and their actions to secure it may be independent of the timing of administrative challenges from the Israeli side. Attempts to prevent alienation may be initiated by outside encouragement, by growing suspicion of encroachment, or in response to Israeli actions visible in the field. Because of the connection between working the land and possessing the rights to it, each side tries to get a jump on the other, hoping to gain the advantage of time and preemption.

Growing Conflict, Instances of Accommodation

As the amount of land in current contention has decreased as a result of urban expansion, formalization of legal rights in some places, and the initiation of use through planting in others, the competition for the remaining space has grown in intensity. Both sides now conduct their planting within sight of the other, plotting each year to gain as much territory as their resources allow. Those who carry out the work speak of it in terms of a war.[39] The battle is conducted in the field through planting on the one hand, and a significant amount of uprooting, deliberate grazing, and arson on the other.

Supplementing these physical acts are a number of legal and administrative procedures. Some of these are designed to facilitate the acquisition of rights by Israel, others serve to decide the issues at hand on an ostensibly neutral basis. Surprisingly, both in the field and in the realm of the administra-

---

[38] Interview with Judeh Abdullah, January 29, 1990.

[39] Interviews with G. Sopher, area supervisor, JNF, November 8, 1989; and Ibrahim Abu Hilal, January 1, 1990.

tion, there has been found an inclination on the part of Israel to avoid conflict, and at times even to compromise with the Palestinians. The system is
overwhelmingly stacked against the fellah, both on paper and in outcome.
Nonetheless research reveals that the disposition of individual disputes cannot be surmised in advance. Decisions are made which are favorable to the
Palestinian cultivators. Those who fight for their land will, up to a point, take
help wherever it comes from, even if that entails explicit or implicit compromise with the government. Though many Palestinians feel that there is
no hope in engaging the system in an attempt to preserve land rights, those
who do, whether formally or informally, usually have a better chance.

Especially in the JNF there is a clear and pronounced policy to avoid
entering into dispute with those working the land whenever possible.[40]
Another guiding principle of the JNF and seemingly a number of governmental bodies is not to plant on privately held land.[41] As a result, much of
the active conflict is carried out on disputed state land, expropriated land, or
land sold under circumstances that leave its disposition unclear to one or
both sides. Especially on the state lands, Israel has been and continues to be
quite aggressive in its quest for control. Increasingly, the Palestinians are as
well.

Organization of the Study

Chapter 2 begins with an examination of the attachment to the land
motivating those involved in the multifaceted conflict over Israel/Palestine.
Beginning with the connections stemming from the formative period of the
respective religious traditions, the chapter quickly jumps to the land code developed during the period of Ottoman rule. It is this code which comprises
the basis of much of current land law in the region, and thus shapes the
forms and outcomes of current land disputes. Also addressed in chapter 2 is
the legislation pertaining to trees in particular, and some of the attachments
to them which are interrelated with sentiment concerning the land.

The next chapter attempts to convey an appreciation of the state of the
flora in Palestine prior to formal afforestation. The belief commonly held
abroad was that the country was lush and fertile. While the latter was true,
the former was much less so. Chapter 3 describes the growing discussion of
Palestine as a barren place, desperately in need of planting to restore it to its
former biblical glory. The primary endeavors in this regard, that is, the afforestation carried out by the British Mandatory authorities and the JNF, are

---

[40] City of Jerusalem, Division of City Planning, May 17, 1982, Summary of Meeting on Afforestation [from JNF, 3307, undated]; JNF, 3307/701, October 1, 1986.

[41] Interviews with Tzvi Avni, September 13, 1990; and Mordechai Ru'ach, January 22, 1990;
State of Israel, Ministry of Defense, Division of Planning and Infrastructure, 1015–2, October 10,
1985.

therefore related. So too is the British role in organizing the cultivation of olives in the Palestinian sector, an effort highlighting the long-standing importance of the olive tree in land matters in Palestine.

Chapter 4 expands on the theme first discussed in connection with the earliest days of afforestation by Jews in Palestine: the political use of tree planting. The forests are employed in the state-building effort in two primary ways: first, as a method of occupying land, such that its use is reserved for the state alone; and, second, by assisting in the process of providing employment for the massive wave of immigrants, thereby allowing for nationally planned population dispersal. The pattern of settlement correlates with security and land issues. The chapter concludes with a brief notation of the state of afforestation in the West Bank during the period of Jordanian rule.

With these three chapters providing background concerning land and afforestation issues, chapter 5 addresses a range of geographical factors related to the partition of Jerusalem in 1948 and its reunification in 1967. The chapter details the Israeli efforts to consolidate control of the city in the wake of the 1967 War, primarily through the expansion of the municipal territory and the subsequent construction of Jewish neighborhoods located to ensure demographic and strategic domination. With regard to the city's Arab sector, the chapter describes the stagnation and political frustration during the period of Jordanian rule, and the continuation of this situation under Israeli rule. Also detailed are some of the bureaucratic factors that set Palestinian Jerusalemites apart from their neighbors in the West Bank.

The next chapter looks at the land laws in the West Bank, and their influence on the disputes played out in the area around Jerusalem. An understanding of such laws is essential for any discussion of the mechanisms of the land regime and their application in the West Bank. It is the examination of these laws which places the dispute in its technical context, giving meaning to the terms and forms described in the case studies herein, and informs the discussion of the land conflict in general.

While describing the concept and execution of Jerusalem's green belt, chapter 7 also treats broader issues related to the political nature of trees and their use in the land conflict. Specifically, the chapter details the nuts and bolts of planting for political and other purposes, raising the issue of planting on private or contested land. Also examined are the actions taken by each side to impede the planting carried out by the competitor. On the part of the Israelis, these include primarily bureaucratic measures, along with the uprooting of trees for security reasons. On the Palestinian side, the acts include arson, uprooting, and destruction of trees through calculated grazing of flocks.

The next three chapters deal with particular villages, distributed in and around Jerusalem. The first village, Sur Baher, falls within the municipal boundary, and the chapter examines the conflict that arose when the JNF began afforestation on land that had been expropriated from the village in 1970.

This case is unusual in that it included cooperation between Palestinian villagers and Jews from the surrounding neighborhoods, together attempting to resist a bureaucratic and political mentality that sought to convert an area covered with olive trees—worked by the villagers—to one of forest. A wide range of actors is involved with the Sur Baher afforestation, and the chapter details the roles of the various bodies, and the ultimate disposition of the issue, influenced in part by a decision of the Israeli High Court of Justice.

The villages of Beit Surik and Beit Iksa, discussed in chapter 9, are in the West Bank, northwest of Jerusalem. They are both located just outside the Green Line along the corridor to Jerusalem, occupying strategic points on the approach to the city. Each of the villages is surrounded by different facets of the Israeli presence, including residential and agricultural land use, as well as JNF afforestation. This presence is spreading, and the villages will soon be almost completely encompassed. Here too there are legal issues involved, ongoing planting, and the willful destruction of trees. This dispute, however, unlike Sur Baher's, takes place in the West Bank; thus the villagers are confronted with a different constellation of adversaries.

The final case study deals with the village of Abu Dis. Though it is located in the West Bank, Abu Dis is facing afforestation efforts intended to mask the effects of a Jerusalem municipal dump created not far from the village. That same planting, funded in part by the municipality and the JNF, is intended to beautify the roadway leading to a new Israeli settlement, also located on land claimed by the village. The village is struggling against the afforestation by legal and illegal means; the settlement, it seems, has also engaged in illegal destruction of village trees.

My focus is on the practices that each side takes in the attempt to secure the land for its own purposes, whether in the present or for the future. In examining the creation of the green belt by the JNF and associated bodies, and the actions of Palestinians within that area to maintain or achieve control of this same land, I have tried to focus as much as possible on the local dynamics of the issue rather than exclusively at the level of policy planning and political decision making. Each side in the conflict has a deliberate, finite, and identifiable goal. Examination of the practices used in the pursuit of this goal reveals that the tactics are often common to both sides. This is evident through a study of individual conflicts, both past and ongoing, and areas wherein each side operates, at least for the meantime, without immediate friction.

While the land issue is broadly recognized as a central component of the Palestinian-Israeli conflict, insufficient attention has been given to the tactics invoked by each side, and their consequences for those immediately involved. Moreover, the common portrayal of the land struggle fails to note the incidence of compromise and accommodation, and the attempts to avoid conflict, which also characterize the dispute. In neglecting this element, an important opportunity for the study of possible conflict resolution is lost.

The political struggle for control of the city is accompanied by and in part based upon the battle for physical control of the municipality and its surroundings. During the Intifada this battle has become increasingly violent. However, the quiet struggle for control of the area's most important resource—land—long preceded the Intifada. Planting, along with the various measures against it, continues to shape future lines of conflict, and perhaps of accommodation. The green belt will increasingly set Jerusalem apart in the landscape. The visual impact of this will be great; how that translates into psychological and political influence remains to be seen. In the meantime, the trees—olive and pine—continue to grow.

2

Land and Trees in Historical Perspective

Throughout the area of the Ottoman empire legal technicalities of landholding were applied to actual practice only in a tenuous manner. Indeed, as Lambton asserts, "conformity with the legal theory was abandoned in practice at an early stage—if it ever existed—and once abandoned there was little check on arbitrary action, and the system that grew up in many respects bore little resemblance to the exposition of the jurists."[1] Despite this, current attitudes toward land are strongly influenced by underlying concepts that stem from earlier religious and legal constructs. While some of these are particular to one group or another, there is much in common throughout the region, and there is in fact an interweaving of religious and legal traditions from both Judaic and Islamic culture. As a result, even those aspects that are particular to the Jews or to the Arabs are often familiar, at least in a vague sense, to all concerned. The influence of these traditions, and the attitudes and atmosphere they create, contribute to the dialectic of conflict, and thus must be examined in order to understand the background and context that frame the land issues.

Land in Jewish Tradition

For Judaism the relationship between the community and Eretz Yisrael originates in the Bible, and is composed of theological and technical components that shaped and continue to influence issues in the current Israeli land regime. The two primary factors involved are the concept of the "promised

---

[1] Ann Lambton, *Landlord and Peasant in Persia: A Study of Land Tenure and Land Revenue Administration* (London: Oxford University Press, 1953), p. 53.

land," or that the land is pledged by God to the nation of Israel, and the notion that the land is given to national rather than to individual possession.[2]

The concept of a promised land comes from a variety of biblical
sources, and is subject to a host of conditions and geographical boundaries.
Genesis, the first book of the Bible, states that "the Lord made a covenant with
Abram, saying, Unto your seed have I given this land."[3] The implications of
this covenant were to become a determining factor in the geographic orientation of the Jewish people throughout their history. Whether residing in the
land or outside it, Eretz Yisrael has been viewed as the one and only homeland of the Jewish people.[4]

To those outside the land, whether or not by choice, Eretz Yisrael has
served as a focus of hope for return—physically and spiritually. This centrality, both actual and conceptual, is reflected in Hebrew terminology. One can be
"in the land," in Eretz Yisrael; or in Hutz L'Aretz, literally "outside the land,"
or the rest of the world. Further, to come to Eretz Yisrael from Hutz L'Aretz is
called *aliyah*, an ascent.

The bond between Jews throughout the world and Eretz Yisrael is
maintained through the liturgy and festivals that compose the organized religious aspect of Judaism. The lunar calendar that determines the cycle of Jewish worship is structured to reflect the seasonal progression within Eretz Yisrael. Some of the most significant Jewish festivals are related to agricultural
issues particular or appropriate to Jewish life in that land. Thus the seasonal
concerns, imagery, and liturgy of Jews in the Diaspora may differ strikingly
from those of the environment in which they reside.

For example, the festival of Sukkot, corresponding to the fall harvest,
marks a shift in the daily liturgy from a prayer for "bringing the dew" to one
of "making the wind blow and the rain to fall." This prayer for rain—in Eretz
Yisrael—continues until the festival of Pessach in the midspring, when there
is a return to the prayer for dew.

In addition to the yearly cycle being determined by events in Eretz Yisrael, the liturgy is replete with explicit references to life there, and a constant
refrain of hope for a restoration of the Jewish nation in the promised land on
the one hand, and a restating of the conditions for fulfillment of the promise
on the other. A passage in the daily prayer, taken from the Bible and repeated

---

[2] W. D. Davies, *The Territorial Dimension of Judaism* (Berkeley: University of California
Press, 1982), p. 8. The reference to Israel in the citation is in regard to the nation, rather than
the modern state.

[3] Genesis 15:17. The passage goes on to indicate borders for the promised land which far exceed
those related to this study.

[4] For a rare and controversial view suggesting a minimal role of Eretz Yisrael in the Jewish experience see Yeshiahu Liebovitz, *Faith, History, and Values* (Jerusalem: Hebrew University of
Jerusalem, Student Union, 1978) [Hebrew].

morning and evening as part of the core tenet of Judaism, that of a monotheistic god, states that if the commandments are observed, God will

> give [the Nation of Israel] the rain of your land in its due season, the first rain
> and the latter rain, that you may gather in your corn, and your wine, and your
> oil. And I will send grass in your fields for your cattle, that you may eat and be
> full. Take heed to yourselves, that you turn aside, and serve other gods, and
> worship them. And then the Lord's wrath be kindled against you, and He shut
> up the heaven, that there be no rain, and that the land yield not her fruit; and
> lest you perish quickly from the good land which the Lord gives you.[5]

The Bible serves not only to establish and remind the Jews of the
promise, but also dictates the basis for their association with the land. And
that it is an association rather than ownership clearly indicates that the land
belongs to God. As a result, there is a biblical stipulation that "the land shall
not be sold in perpetuity."[6] While this engendered an entire body of land
regulation during the biblical periods of Jewish administration in Eretz Yisrael, its most significant characteristic—then and now—is that land is considered a national rather than an individual possession. Indeed, the degree to
which God is involved with the land can be seen through the tribal boundaries that were established according to divine fiat, and the codes for land use
that were intimately connected to moral and social dictates.[7]

The land continued to play a central role in Jewish writing in the period subsequent to the conclusion of the Five Books of Moses. Fully one third
of the Mishnah, the explication on biblical laws, deals with the land and the
agricultural regulations pertaining to it. Even though these laws became less
relevant in periods of Jewish exile from Eretz Yisrael, they were studied, and
in some ways maintained, nonetheless.

In exile the Jewish community did not change its religious relationship
to the land, nor the centrality of it in their worship, yet in some aspects worship could not be as comprehensive in exile as it had been in the Land of Israel. There are commandments that can be fulfilled only in Eretz Yisrael, and
this creates for the community in exile, at least in religious terms, "an emaci-
ated life."[8] Clearly this would have greater impact on those more observant,
but it is safe to say that beyond the religious component, the exile had a de-
finitive influence on the life and character of the Jewish community. So too it
can be generalized that for the community as a whole, the promise of Eretz
Yisrael continued to play a significant role in religious and group identity,
and the return to the Land of Israel comprised one of the main elements of
religious and national aspiration.

---

5 Deuteronomy 11:13–21.

6 Leviticus 25:23.

7 See for example Ezek. 47.

8 Davies, p. 39.

Land and Islam

In part the Judaic connection to the land and its status as a holy place is also reflected in Islam, albeit with considerably less centrality. The Qur'an itself restates the promise: "Then We said to the Israelites: 'Dwell in this land. When the promise of the hereafter comes to be fulfilled, We shall assemble you all together." The Qur'an also addresses the history of Jewish presence and sovereignty in the land:

> In the Scriptures We solemnly declared to the Israelites: 'Twice you shall commit evil in the land. You shall become great transgressors.'
>
> And when the prophecy of your first transgression came to be fulfilled, We sent against you a formidable army which ravaged your land and carried out the punishment with which you had been threatened [i.e., the Assyrian conquest, 586 B.C.E.].
>
> And when the prophecy of your second transgression came to be fulfilled, We sent another army to afflict you and to enter the temple as the former entered it before, utterly destroying all that they laid their hands on [i.e., the Roman conquest in 70 C.E.].[9]

Islam suggests that the Jewish interpretation of biblical events is in error, and that the conduct of the Jews nullified their special relationship with God. Further, the promise of the land that originated with Abraham (Ibrahim in Islam), as in Jewish tradition, is asserted to have been given not to Isaac as the Bible relates, but rather to his older half brother, Ishmael. Each community recognizes the origin of its respective nation with these half brothers, though the recipient of the promise is of course disputed.

In terms of landownership, Islam had a concept similar to that of the community-holding found in Judaism. For Muslims, the world is divided into three areal categories: Dar al-Islam, Dar al-Ahd, and Dar al-Harb. Dar al-Islam is that area which has been subjugated or converted to the rule of Islam. Dar al-Ahd consists of an intermediate zone, under the influence of but not directly controlled by a Muslim regime. Dar al-Harb, or "the Land of War," is that area uninfluenced by Islam.[10] During the early period of Islam the land in the Muslim domain was viewed as the possession of God, and under the administration of the legitimate Muslim ruler. As such, it is suggested that ultimate individual ownership was not possible; rather the usufruct was the maximum right that could be attained and actual ownership remained with the state. The term for the state's right of possession is *raqabah*, literally "nape of the neck."[11]

This system was both religious and administrative in nature, since the conquest of the land was in itself a religious act, as was its subsequent admin-

---

[9] The Qur'an, sura 17, "The Night Journey."

[10] A. N. Poliak "Classification of Lands in the Islamic Law and Its Technical Terms," *American Journal of Semitic Languages* 57 (1940): 50.

[11] A discussion of differing opinions on ultimate ownership can be found in ibid., pp. 50–51.

istration.[12] One of the early distinctions in the Islamic land system was between Muslims and the People of the Book, that is, Jews and Christians, the tolerated minorities. Members of these communities were entitled to certain land rights, but these were not as full as the right of Muslims, and in addition Jews and Christians were compelled to pay a supplementary tax.[13]

Further, land that was a part of Dar al-Islam was expected to remain so. While that does not speak to the use of individual pieces of land or their transfer to non-Muslims, it does explicitly require the sovereignty of a Muslim government. For the Jews, the land could be lost as a result of communal misconduct, but the nature of the relationship to the land discouraged its transfer outside the Jewish community. For both Jews and Arabs however the sanctity of the land persisted, whatever the denominational character of its rulers.

Despite the termination of Jewish rule in Eretz Yisrael in the year 70 C.E., the land remained holy, the legal dictates concerning it remained in force, and, despite gradual dispersion, the Jews remained committed to the centrality of Eretz Yisrael in their religious life. For Muslims the area was irrevocably attached to Dar al-Islam from the moment of its conquest by Arab forces in the year 638 C.E., though the holiness of the land predated the advent of Islam through its Christian and Judaic roots, and its sanctity increased during the life of Mohammed. The sanctity was maintained during periods of non-Muslim rule, and during such interludes there was a strong drive to return the land to Muslim control.

Ottoman Land Practices

It is beyond the scope of this research to trace the development of succeeding land regimes in Israel/Palestine from the original days of Jewish and Muslim rule. Indeed to do so would be a monumental task.[14] Only the most recent of Muslim regimes, that of the Ottoman Empire, need be addressed, for its influence is widely felt in land issues of today. Directly this is because of the absorption and adaptation of Ottoman laws by the successor regimes, that is, the British Mandate, Israel and Jordan (in the West Bank), and Israeli mili-

---

[12] Ruth Kark, "Land and the Idea of Land Redemption in Traditional Cultures and in Eretz Yisrael," *Karka* 31 (December 1989): 25–26 [Hebrew]. Indeed, the Islamic resistance group Hamas has declared that all of Palestine is a holy trust, a notion adding to Palestinian attachment to the land and negating the idea of territorial compromise in a peace agreement with Israel.

[13] Farhat J. Ziadeh, *Property Law in the Arab World: Real Rights in Egypt, Iraq, Jordan, Lebanon, Libya, Syria, Saudi Arabia, and the Gulf States* (London: Graham and Trotman, 1979), p. 1.

[14] For a succinct overview of this period, however, see ibid. Though focusing on land issues in Persia, part 1 of Lambton's book deals with land regimes beginning in the seventh century C.E. and running up through the major dynasties. In general Lambton's work is one of most comprehensive treatments of land issues in the Middle East.

tary rule. Less directly, the patterns and particularly the problems of the Ottoman land regime have left their stamp on practices still current in Palestinian villages, as is the case in other former Ottoman territories as well.

The area of Palestine served a significant function in the Ottoman Empire primarily on account of its strategic location as a corridor for intercontinental transport, its proximity to the pilgrims' route to Mecca, and its religious prestige. Despite these elements, however, the area was considered a province of minor importance, and it contained no resource of particular value to Istanbul. Its economy, principally agricultural, was therefore drawn upon to support the empire only through its contribution to the imperial tax base. The interplay between taxation and the health of Palestine's agriculture provides the significant background to land issues in the twentieth century. The Ottoman period did almost nothing to advance the level of agriculture in Palestine, and villagers fell victim to a combination of ecological and administrative pressures. It must be noted that in the literature on this period the fellah plays a particularly anonymous role. It has been suggested that the peasant in the Middle East is "inarticulate and has been ignored for long centuries."[15]

In fact the fellahin, or villagers, are not ignored in the study of the Middle East in general, and the examinations of this period and location in particular. The difficulty lies in the predominantly top-down approach to the research. Thus while the literature is replete with studies of notables, politicians, military leaders, and other elements of the elite and merchant classes, the fellahin generally exist in the literature as a depersonalized class, represented primarily as an aggregate in statistical analysis. In part this is because "the population of the countryside was poor, illiterate and largely inaccessible, and as such left few records of its own."[16]

As a result, while information is available on the nature of the land regime as legislated, and its impact on government and elite society, we can learn little regarding the village level beyond general conclusions gained from statistical extrapolation and second-hand interpretation. In part the superficial treatment of the peasant stems from the difficulty in accurate representation beyond the confines of local practices.

> It need hardly be pointed out that the subject of Middle Eastern land tenure is one of overwhelming complexity. Not only did particular methods of allocating land, each with its own particular terminology, vary from province to province, and even from district to district [but in] the Middle East, as elsewhere, the attempt to create or define new forms of rural property was gener-

---

[15] Afif I. Tannous, "The Village in the National Life of Lebanon," *Middle East Journal* 3 (1949): 151.

[16] Rashid Khalidi, "Palestinian Peasant Resistance to Zionism before World War I," in *Blaming the Victims: Spurious Scholarship and the Palestinian Question,* edited by Edward Said and Christopher Hitchens (London: Verso, 1988), p. 208.

ally the work of men living in the towns. Whether or not they were successful depended on a whole host of conditions, among them the extent to which they had power to control events in the countryside and the skill with which they related their innovations to traditional or customary practice. . . . The result was often total confusion.[17]

In the case of the Ottoman rule in Palestine, from the perspective of the villager confusion was only one of the elements of the land regime that contributed to a difficult and often unstable existence.

For the greater portion of Ottoman reign in Palestine, the villagers did not enjoy full usufructuary rights for the land that they worked. In large part this was due to a combination of factors that kept the fellahin at a bare subsistence level, with fluctuations more often to the negative side rather than the positive. The two primary obstacles for the fellah were a difficult physical environment and an oppressive government, both local and imperial. These two sources of vulnerability interacted in a manner that virtually ensured the poverty of the fellahin, and thereby influenced their ability to maintain what land rights there might be. Added to this burden, and affecting the scope and location of agriculture, was the tenuous position of the settled population vis à vis a somewhat predatory bedouin population, a symptom of the often less than efficient Ottoman control of the territory.

The Ottoman Regime through 1857

Owen distinguishes between two categories of people in the Ottoman land regime, "those who controlled the land and collected the taxes" and "those who actually cultivated it."[18] While the current members of the latter category are the focus of this research, the roots of their condition lie in the actions and policies of the former. The study of the Ottoman land regime may be divided into two periods by the watershed Land Code of 1858. Prior to this legislation landholding in Palestine and elsewhere in the empire was a function of the revenue needs of the state combined with the efforts by local rulers to provide the imperial tax while making a significant, often enormous, wage for themselves as well. Thus the body of literature dealing with these issues fails for the most part to provide specific information about villages or villagers, and, as Hutteroth notes, "the presentation of earlier cultural landscapes seems to be vague and uncertain."[19]

What emerges, however, is a general picture of an economy that is roughly feudal in nature, though this classification remains somewhat quali-

---

[17] Roger Owen, *The Middle East in the World Economy 1800–1914* (London: Methuen and Co., 1981), p. x.

[18] Ibid., p. 33.

[19] Wolf Hutteroth, "The Pattern of Settlement in Palestine in the Sixteenth Century: Geographical Research on Turkish Defter-i Mufassal," in *Studies on Palestine during the Ottoman Period*, edited by Moshe Ma'oz (Jerusalem: Magnes Press, 1975), p. 3.

fied because of the above noted range of systems and types within the region, and the incorrect inclination to assume that a feudal Middle East would be equivalent to a feudal Europe. For the Middle East it is much harder to find an apt paradigm.[20] Nonetheless, an examination of land policies clearly reveals the plight of the Palestinian fellahin.

With the advent of Ottoman rule in Palestine in 1516 C.E., the sultan in Istanbul rewarded outstanding soldiers and others deserving of favor with land grants for their administration. The estates were called *timars* or *ziamets* (fiefs), and their rulers were *sipahis*, often from the Ottoman calvary. Within the fief the *sipahi* had free reign, contingent upon the remittance of taxes to Istanbul and the fulfillment of military obligations dictated by imperial need.

Toward the end of the sixteenth century a system called *iltazim* developed alongside and gradually replaced the *sipahis*. The *iltazim* was an imperial estate, rather than a fief, and was administered by a selected official called a *multazim*. Originally the *multazim* was granted something akin to a contract, usually lasting for only a few years. As a result, the *multazim* had no long-term interest in the health of the land or those working it. The motivation was for the extraction of maximum profit in minimum time.

In this system a fixed amount was due to the government, but this in no way corresponded to the tax taken from the subjects of the *iltazim*. Often a sum was set by the *multazim* for individual villages, and the villagers were required to meet this figure regardless of the condition of their harvest. Responsible for collecting from the villagers was the sheikh, or village leader. He too had a fixed sum to pass on, but no supervision or limitation on how much he collected. In these conditions the tax, intended to range between 10 and 50 percent of the value of the crop, often far exceeded this amount. Additional taxes and necessary bribes only made the plight of the fellah more severe. Within the system there was no recourse for the villager as the *multazim* could confiscate the crop, exact some other form of penalty, or even, according to Ma'oz, impose corporal punishment.[21]

Though not originally intended as such, the *multazim* came to be an inheritable position. As a result the "state received the [tax] but had no power

---

[20] Lambton, p. 53. See also Peter Sluglett and Marion Farouk-Sluglett, "The Application of the 1858 Land Code in Greater Syria: Some Preliminary Observations," in *Land Tenure and Social Transformation in the Middle East*, edited by Tarif Khalidi (Beirut: American University of Beirut, 1984), p. 409, citing A. L. Udovitch, "Technology, Land Tenure and Rural Society: Aspects of Continuity in the Agricultural History of the pre-Modern Middle East," in *The Islamic Middle East 700–1900*, edited by A. L. Udovitch (Princeton: Darwin Press, 1981), p. 18. Also Peter Beaumont et al. *The Middle East: A Geographical Study* (Chichester: John Wiley and Sons, 1976), p. 142.

[21] Moshe Ma'oz, *Ottoman Reform in Syria and Palestine 1840–1861: The Impact of the Tanzimat on Politics and Society* (Oxford: Clarendon Press, 1968), p. 159.

over land that was nominally its own. *Iltazim* came more and more to resemble full private ownership, though this was never officially recognized."[22] The system continued to move away from state control, and power devolved to local elite families who were disinclined to pass on to outside sources the revenue they extracted. The result was "a fierce competition for access to rural economic wealth, a competition that itself ensured that much of the wealth was invested in unproductive strife."[23]

The siphoning off of funds led to decreasing revenue for Istanbul, which in turn led to greater taxation and pressure on the fellahin. The competition for funds contributed to the disruption of agriculture, resulting in less produce to provide for the increased taxation. Often the only way for the peasant to avoid defaulting on taxation was to leave the land. Facing the loss of the labor pool, some *multazims* forced their fellahin to remain in the villages, working the land.

At times those who could not or chose not to leave nevertheless abandoned their fields and orchards, since after taxation there was no real reward for their efforts. By the end of the eighteenth century these two factors had led to the abandonment of perhaps as much as one quarter of the land previously cultivated in Palestine, with a corresponding decrease in harvests and revenues, and in measure of unrest. Indeed, it has been suggested that "of all the *sancaks* in Palestine, the *Sancak* of Jerusalem was the most unruly and recalcitrant."[24]

Gibb and Bowen assert that the spread of tax farming "accounted more than any other cause for the disruption of the former order that had ruled in the provinces" adding that "what rendered the pursuit of agriculture difficult, and in many cases impossible, was the provincial anarchy that resulted from the weakening of control by the central government."[25] A symptom of this anarchy leading to the further disruption of agriculture and the instability of village life was the vulnerability to attacks and pillaging by the bedouin population of Palestine, which was by no means confined to the desert. Increasing the damage caused by the bedouin was their ability to rob or extract payment from those transporting produce (and other things) along the routes between points controlled by the Ottomans. This vulnerability was felt, directly or indirectly, by those bearing the tax burden. The physical and financial vulnera-

---

[22] Gabriel Baer, *A History of Land Ownership in Egypt: 1800–1950* (London: Oxford University Press, 1962), p. 2.

[23] Owen, p. 13.

[24] Amnon Cohen, *Palestine in the Eighteenth Century: Patterns of Government and Administration* (Jerusalem: Magnes Press, 1973), pp. 203, 171.

[25] Sir Hamilton Gibb and Harold Bowen, *Islamic Society and the West: A Study of the Impact of Western Civilization on Moslem Culture in the Near East* (London: Oxford University Press, 1950), 1: 256.

bility led to the contraction of the fellahin to areas that were more secure, and the abandonment of agriculture in areas prone to attack.[26]

In effect this was expressed by a withdrawal of the rural population to the area in the proximity of the larger towns and cities. Primarily that meant a return to the high ground of the hills, an area running north-south between Nablus and Hebron. Much land in the western plain and the eastern desert was given up. So too was land at some distance from villages, even in the more secure zone. For defense the villages were located on hilltops, and agriculture was conducted on the slopes and in nearby wadis.

The decreasing area of cultivation exacerbated the difficulties for both the fellahin and the government. In essence the situation had become intolerable for Istanbul. The combination of decreasing tax revenues in the face of increasing taxation, competition—at times violent—between local officials marginally loyal to the state, the disruption of agriculture and the abandonment of land, and the threat posed by the bedouin all necessitated drastic change.

Land Registration, Taxation, and the 1858 Code

The primary goal of the Land Code of 1858 was to ascribe and register the rights of individuals to specific plots of land in order to reform the method of taxation, thereby producing greater revenue for Istanbul. In theory the reform was intended to streamline the collection system, cutting out the intermediaries between the fellah and the central government who had been siphoning off much of the revenue. The assignation of land rights was a profound and usually frightening concept for the village population. The fellahin, often illiterate and justifiably wary of any attempt by the government to establish a formal relationship with them, suspected that the reform was an attempt to impose taxation (which it certainly was) and facilitate conscription. Thus from the outset they were ill-disposed toward the changes that the code proposed. This isn't to imply that they had any particular grasp of the new code, or indeed of the Ottoman laws that had preceded it. Simply, they were against any rule that came from the outside.

It is difficult to imagine how their situation could have been made worse. Yet despite the fact that in theory the code could have assisted them, this was rarely the case in any direct sense. In essence, with the formalization of a procedure for registering land rights, the fellahin now officially had something to lose. What often transpired was the transfer of the newly declared rights from the hands of the fellahin back to the hands of the elite

---

[26] On this topic see Owen, pp. 78, 81, 184, 264; also Charles Issawi, *The Fertile Crescent 1800–1914: A Documentary Economic History* (London: Oxford University Press, 1988), p. 269; and Israel Kimche et al., *The Arab Settlement in the Metropolitan Region of Jerusalem* (Jerusalem: Jerusalem Institute for Israel Studies, no. 16, 1986) [Hebrew].

(albeit frequently a local and indigenous elite), either voluntarily or under compulsion, but rarely with the fellah's full comprehension of the consequence. Thus many practices detrimental to the fellah, as described below, followed the land reform.

Owing to the fear of an official existence and all that that could entail, the fellahin endeavored to remain off the books of the Ottoman administration. When it came to land it was easy for the fellah to avoid registration, and thereby at least some of the taxation. There was almost always a local notable, whether related to the clan or not, who would be willing to have the land registered in his name—if not the village mukhtar, then a local merchant or landowner was available. Of course the tax burden could still be passed on to the fellah. In many cases, to minimize the tax as much as possible, the amount of land being worked was grossly understated, sometimes to the extent that one dunam in ten was reported.

As a result the opportunity was created for the accumulation of land in the hands of those with flexible scruples, and this was a common occurrence. Usually the result of the false registration became apparent at times of transaction, when questions of ownership or plot size were regularly clarified to the detriment of the fellah. Often bewildered by the documents, and in any case intimidated by the officials and those manipulating him, the fellah had little recourse.

At times the manipulation was assisted, and honest transactions impeded, by the lack of clarity in the way of plot description. The landmarks employed in identifying land were taken from the daily experience of the village, but, as memories and landscape features changed, they lost whatever utility they may have had. Such references as "near the pile of stones" or "to the side of the path" served as often to obfuscate as to indicate.

In many villages a communal form of landholding contributed to the difficulty of registration. The *musha'a,* or share system, was prevalent in the nineteenth century throughout Palestine. Under *musha'a* the village lands were divided into plots according to their value, which was based on proximity to the village, soil quality, slope, and other factors. The parcels were assigned on a temporary basis—usually two to three years—according to a lottery system. One method for the lottery was an equivalent share based on the number of males per family, while another allocated according to the number of draught animals each family possessed.

The *musha'a* system hindered registration in two primary ways. First, it held land collectively, and if the plots were registered at all, it was usually in the name of a village elder; the registration was not changed with each parcel rotation. The second factor affecting registration was the nature of plot delineation under *musha'a.* Each sector of village land was divided many times in order to give each family its share of the varying qualities and worths. As a result plots were often quite small and oddly shaped. The difficulty of locating plots by colloquial description, as suggested above, was compounded by the profusion of odd-shaped parcels within a very confined space. When *musha'a* landholding was outlawed under the 1858 code[27] these problems remained.

A more pervasive threat to the rights of the fellahin was debt. With some regularity climatic conditions prevented a harvest sufficient to provide seed for planting the following year.[28] In such circumstances money was often borrowed for the purchase of seed, or even to buy food in the interim. The terms of interest on these loans, combined with the limited opportunities for saving money, insured that the loan could not be repaid.[29]

As a result of loan default the fellah was pushed farther and farther down the ladder of the agrarian social structure. From subsistence owner/ cultivator, he was pushed by debt foreclosure to sell part of his land and eventually to become a lessee. From there, again as a result of debt, he was reduced to sharecropper. As such, he remained on land previously worked as his own, but now was entitled to even less of the crop than before. In addition to the ever present tax burden, this smaller share insured that the fellah would continue to decline in terms of economic standing, even without the assistance of natural disaster. The next step down could come either in the form of a smaller percentage of the crop as compensation for the work, or in the dispossession from share rights, and the reduction to wage labor. Even so, in this situation the fellah could often maintain the tie to the land that had once been his own. The final step was to the status of itinerant laborer, not connected to any particular piece of land. The only alternative was the military— not a popular option—or migration, either abroad or to the urban underclass.

Provisions of the 1858 Land Code

The Land Code of 1858 was intended to "consolidate and retrieve the [land] rights which the state had lost in earlier times."[30] In the attempt to at-

---

[27] Ottoman Land Code, book 1, chapter 1, article 8. "The whole of the lands of a town or village cannot be granted *en bloc* to the whole of the inhabitants nor by choice to one, two, or three of them. Different pieces of land are given to each inhabitant, and title deeds (*Tapu sened*) showing their possession are delivered to them." This and other quotations from the land code are taken from F. Ongley's translation of the *Ottoman Land Code* (London: William Clowes and Sons, 1892). *Musha'a* landholding persisted in many villages well into the twentieth century despite the Ottoman ban.

[28] Doreen Warriner, "Land Tenure Problems in the Fertile Crescent in the Nineteenth and Twentieth Centuries," in *The Economic History of the Middle East 1800–1914*, edited by Charles Issawi (Chicago: University of Chicago Press, 1966), p. 77.

[29] This situation, at least as an intentional policy of the landowner, is part of what has been described as "rent capitalism," rather a benign term, given the consequences. Hans Bobek, "The Main Stages in Socio-Economic Evolution from a Geographical Point of View," in *Readings in Cultural Geography*, edited by Philip L. Wagner and Marvin W. Mikesell (Chicago: University of Chicago Press, 1962).

[30] Sluglett and Farouk-Sluglett, p. 413.

tach parcels to taxpayers, streamline the system of taxation, and return fellahin to agriculture, the code delineated five principal categories of land, which
included in their subunits all possible land types. Though with this code too
there was some gap between theory and application, current land laws relate
to these basic categories, and thus their outline merits attention.

The first land category is *mulk*, or land held in fee simple. This category has relatively little significance in the area of this study in that *mulk*
land was found primarily within cities and towns. It extended to villages and
rural areas only for the actual house plots and immediately adjacent gardens
of limited size. The second category of land is *miri*, or land of the emir. As it
is the most pertinent it will be discussed further below.

The third category is *waqf*, or land held in religious trust or dedicated to
a religious institution. Land dedicated as *waqf* was not entirely for the use of
the religious community, however, and, in fact, the donor of the land often
set the terms of the relationship of the land to its recipient institution. As
such, *waqf* could be used to provide an income for the original holder of the
rights to the land, as well as a degree of charity. The advantage of this was that
waqf land could not be alienated, divided, or, for the most part, seized by the
state. Holders of a deed could dedicate land as *waqf* from the time of their
own death, or the deaths of their children, and so on. Thus those vulnerable
to land loss often engaged the *waqf* status as a way of protection. To confiscate
waqf land contravenes Muslim law.[31]

A fourth category of land is *matruka*. This classification encompassed a
number of different public usages, primarily in and around the village. Within the village itself *matruka* land was that upon which community institutions were located, including schools, courts, and other administrative buildings. Common areas such as village roads, pastures, and groves also fell into
this category.

The final class of land is *mewat*, or "dead land," which is not in use for
cultivation. A geographical standard for *mewat* land held it to be "distant
from town or village so that the loud voice of a person from the extreme inhabited spot cannot be heard, that is about a mile and a half to the extreme
inhabited spot, or a distance of about half an hour."[32] Except for what little
bedouin agriculture there may have been beyond this point, for the most part
it consisted of the area not being cultivated. *Mewat* also included pastures,
groves, and places too stony for cultivation "which are not in the possession
of anyone by [deed], and which *ab antiquo* are not assigned to the inhabitants
of towns and villages."[33] *Mewat* land could be domesticated through culti-

---

[31] For a detailed discussion of *waqf* issues in the study area, see Yitzhak Reiter, *The Waqf in Jerusalem* (Jerusalem: Jerusalem Institute for Israel Studies, 1992) [Hebrew].

[32] Ottoman Land Code, preface, article 6.

[33] Ibid., book 2, chapter 2, article 103.

vation, but rights to it were granted by authority of the state. If this land was worked without permission, the deed value of the land was taken, and the deed was granted. Often this was conditional on continuous cultivation of the land, usually for three years. When all the requirements were met, *mewat* land changed to the status of *miri*. Because of climatic and social reasons described above, much of the land in Palestine qualified as *mewat* land.

The code focused heavily on *miri* land, which was the largest revenue-producing land category. This was logical in that the vast majority of agricultural land was *miri*, and with *mewat* land as a reserve, it stood to be the category with the greatest potential for growth. The code dictated that *miri* land also included all that which had been held as *timars* and *ziamets*, and all that had been the possession of the *multazim*.[34] In an attempt to assure that *miri* land produced a continuous income, the code stipulated that *miri* land that was left unworked for a period of three years reverted to the state for the purpose of re-leasing to those interested in cultivating it.

Though *miri* was technically no more than a usufructuary right (with the *raqabah* remaining with the state), in effect it was barely distinguishable from outright ownership. The *miri* right could be sold or transferred, leased, divided, and inherited. The primary functional difference between *mulk* and *miri* was that *miri* land could be confiscated in the case of prolonged absence of agricultural work. In addition, as *miri* land was intended for crop production, there was a restriction on construction on such land. Structures erected without the permission of the government could be legally demolished.[35]

The Special Status of Trees

Significant attention is given in the code to the subject of trees growing on *miri* land. In some respects the regulations concerning trees were independent of land rights, but in other respects they played a determining role in such matters. They touched upon issues of planting, grafting, harvesting, cutting down, and transferring individual trees as well as groves, differentiating between different types of trees, and those growing naturally as opposed to those being cultivated.

The most striking element of these rules was the complexity of official regulation of the planting and cutting down of trees. Though trees could be owned by individuals, property rights governing their use were limited by the state. Complicating matters further was that trees could be owned by an individual who did not possess the rights to the land on which they grew. Thus a system of obligations and privileges was ascribed to both the owners of the trees and the owners of the land.

---

[34] Ibid., preface, article 3.

[35] Ibid., book 1, chapter 1, article 31.

In order to supervise this sector of rural life the 1858 code ordered that:

> without the permission of the official a person cannot make into a garden or vineyard the land he possesses by planting vines and different kinds of fruit trees. [If] he has done so without permission the government has the power during three years to make him pull them up. *If three years have passed, and the trees have arrived at a stage to be a source of benefit to him, they should be left as they are . . . the freehold property of the owner.*[36]

Particular attention should be paid to the latter part of this clause, which indicates that trees planted without permission (i.e., illegally) could be legitimized if they were undisturbed for a period of three years and they had the ambiguous potential "to be a source of benefit." The only requirement was that the yearly tithe on their produce be taken. This lenience is a clear indication of the Ottoman desire for increased agriculture and a broadened tax base.

In light of the separation between the right to own trees and the right to own land, if a landowner did not interfere with the trees planted by another on his land, the same legitimation of the tree rights as indicated above would apply. The status of the trees also provided their owner with an inside track to acquiring land rights. When land was sold by one party, trees that had been planted on that land by another remained the possession of the planter, while trees growing naturally were considered part of the land transaction. Further, a landowner could not sell or give to a third party property on which another had tree rights "while the owner of the trees . . . is willing to take it for its [deed] value." This right of preference continued for an additional ten years beyond the initial sale.[37]

Trees growing naturally on *miri* land were the property of the landowner, but here too there was a restriction in that tax had to be paid on them. In addition, they could not be "cut down or pulled up by the owner or by a stranger."[38] If trees were planted on land by its owner, subsequent sale of the trees implied a sale of the land as well.

The motivation and intention of these regulations were primarily economic in nature. It is logical that this be so in light of the fact that olives were the primary agricultural product of Palestine during the time of Ottoman rule. While other fruit trees and timber for firewood played a role in the home and market economies, the olive tree was clearly the principal source of livelihood for much of the region, particularly in the hill district in which Jerusalem is located.

Along with its role as a staple in the daily diet, the olive was used for one of Jerusalem's main industries, namely the production of soap. Even

---

[36] Ibid., book 1, chapter 1, article 25. Emphasis added.

[37] Ibid., book 1, chapter 1, articles 48, 44.

[38] Ibid., book 1, chapter 1, article 28.

more important was the function of olive oil in the Palestinian economy. While by law tithes on fruit trees were to be collected in kind—and in fact sometimes fruit was taken—the product taken from the olive was oil, rather than the raw fruit itself. Often olive oil was substituted for produce from other types of fruit trees, so that the oil, which was easier to preserve and transport than fruit, served as currency. To further increase the ease of preservation and transport, it was often transferred in the form of soap. Eventually soap and gold coin became the two primary methods of paying taxes.[39]

The Ottomans were by no means the originators of legislation concerning trees in this region. Laws and legends concerning trees go back to biblical times, and prior to the advent of the monotheistic tradition trees were worshiped by indigenous cultures.[40] Since the conflict is often cloaked in religious terms, it is instructive to examine some of the earlier laws and traditions that contribute to current attitudes concerning trees and forests.

The Tree in Religious Sources

The Bible and other Jewish sources are replete with references to trees, both as descriptive features of the landscape and as metaphors for the people and their nation. Trees are also subject to some regulation in terms of their economic capacity, and in regard to the function of their fruit in the sacrificial ritual of the temple in Jerusalem.

The fate and fortune of the trees is commonly used to represent the condition of the Jewish nation in relation to the Land of Israel. The image of trees being uprooted, burned, or withering in drought is used to convey God's displeasure to the people. Nonetheless, trees are a positive symbol, and they convey attachment to the land. The book of Isaiah states that "as the days of a tree shall be the days of my people," following the dictate that the people shall rejoice in Jerusalem (following their return from the Babylonian exile in 536 B.C.E.) "and they shall plant vineyards, and eat the fruit of them. . . . [T]hey shall not plant and another eat."[41] The promise that others shall not eat of the fruit planted by Israel is seen in contrast to the passage in Deuteronomy which notes that the Jews were given in their coming to the promised land "vineyards and olive trees which you planted not and you shall eat and be full."[42]

---

[39] Amnon Cohen, *Economic Life in Ottoman Jerusalem* (Cambridge: Cambridge University Press, 1989), pp. 71–79.

[40] To this day some rural populations ascribe holiness to trees based on local traditions. For the most part though these practices are based upon some human association with a tree or a wooded site, rather than the divine association of ancient times which was present even in early Israelite culture.

[41] Isaiah 65:19–22.

[42] Deuteronomy 6:11.

The destruction of trees, either by natural causes or through the actions of an enemy force, was perceived by the nation as a divine punishment, again as a metaphor for the people. "Thus says the Lord God; behold I will kindle a fire in thee, and it shall devour every green tree in thee, and every dry tree; it shall not be quenched; it shall be a burning flame, and all faces from the south to the north shall be burned."[43] Despite the fact that trees were used as a symbolic victim for the nation, the tree itself had a protected status among the people.

> When you shall besiege a city a long time, in making war against it to take it, you shall not destroy the trees thereof by wielding an axe against them: for you may eat of them, but you shall not cut them down, for is the tree of the field man that it should be besieged by you? Only trees of which you know that they are not for food may you destroy and cut them down, that you may build bulwarks against the city that makes war with you, until it falls.[44]

The notion that people are like the trees of the field has been a source of discussion in both religious and secular forums. In modern Israeli culture it is taken as a metaphor at face value. In early religious sources, however, the discussion was somewhat deeper. Some commentators also accepted the statement at face value, and indicated that if the tree was to be treated with care, so much the more so the people on the battlefield. Others suggested that the biblical intention was the opposite, to indicate that people are not like trees, and therefore are to be treated with higher respect. In either case, the connection between conduct toward trees and human behavior is suggested.[45]

That trees have a lesser role in the writings of Islam is not surprising, inasmuch as the Arabian peninsula, the source of the religion, does not lend itself to an arboreal description in the way that Palestine does. Indeed, exaggerated conditions were projected onto the holy land: "Jerusalem . . . is surrounded with flowing rivers and fruit bearing trees."[46] In a similar vein, "Filastin [the Arabic pronunciation takes an *f* rather than *p*] is watered by the rains and the dew. Its trees and its ploughed lands do not need artificial irrigation. . . . Filastin is the most fertile of the Syrian provinces."[47]

---

[43] Ezekiel 21:2–3.

[44] Deuteronomy 22:19–20. Emphasis added.

[45] The religious discussion reemerged recently when Jewish settlers openly destroyed roadside groves in the West Bank that had been used as a hiding place for attacks on Israeli traffic. Their justification for the destruction was also religious, in that saving a life takes precedence over other laws, such as those protecting trees.

[46] Helmut Gatje, ed., *The Qur'an and Its Exegesis: Selected Texts with Classical and Modern Muslim Interpretations* (London: Routledge and Kegan Paul, 1971), citing the twelfth-century commentary of the Persian-Arab scholar Zamakhshari.

[47] Quoted from Istakhari and Ibn Hankal, in Guy LeStrange, *Palestine under the Moslems: A Description of Syria and the Holy Land from A.D. 650 to 1500 Translated from the Works of the Medieval Arab Geographers* (1890; reprinted Beirut: Khayat, 1965), p. 28.

Though there is scant mention of trees in the Qur'an, here too there is a sense that they have a special status. Sura 24 says that "God is the light of the heavens and the earth. His light may be compared to a niche that enshrines a lamp, the lamp within a crystal of star-like brilliance. It is lit from a blessed olive tree neither eastern nor western. Its very oil would almost shine forth, though no fire touched it."[48] Peasant interpretation of the Qur'an also makes a link between discussion of fruit trees and the human works. "When the Qur'an swears by the fig and the olive, it is as if it swore by Damascus and Jerusalem,"[49] those cities being associated with the two fruits respectively.

Despite the status that trees nominally held in the tradition and in the law, their fate on the land was determined by more practical concerns. As a result the condition of the forests in Palestine declined markedly in the waning years of Ottoman control. A review of the landscape in the late nineteenth and early twentieth centuries, and the actions taken by various governments and agencies to influence the situation, reveals the immediate backdrop to the current conflict, and the crystallization of many of the patterns that persist to this day.

---

[48] The Qur'an, sura 24 (35).

[49] George Adam Smith, *Jerusalem: The Topography, Economics, and History from the Earliest Times to A.D. 70* (London: Hodder and Stoughton, 1907), p. 299, citing Ritter, *Comparative Geography of Palestine* 4, 184 (no further information provided).

3

Afforestation in Palestine from the Turn of the Century through 1948

While biblical sources contribute to an image of Eretz Yisrael flush with forests and other flora, many of the descriptions proffered by pilgrims and tourists in Palestine during the final decades of Ottoman rule are of a land barren and waste. And while these reports are to some degree problematic—in terms of reliability or relevance—their description indicates that the landscape of Palestine, at least in those places discussed, was often contrary to expectations based largely on reading of the Bible. Relying solely on biblical description, Eretz Yisrael was believed to contain widespread forests including twenty different species of trees, among them pine, oak, cedar, cypress, olive, and myrtle.

Many of the travelers' accounts of visits to Palestine, however, describe a state of decline in the vegetation of the land, often to the degree of devastation. One of the most well known of these commentators was the author Mark Twain, who described his visit to Palestine in *The Innocents Abroad*, which was published as a book in 1869, but had earlier been featured serially in newspapers in the United States. The account is extreme, yet important, owing to its wide circulation and the frequency with which it appears in descriptions of Palestine as it was believed to be in the nineteenth century. In part playing off the biblical expectations held by himself and his readers, Twain wrote that

> nowhere in all the waste around was there a foot of shade, and we were scorching to death. "Like unto the shadow of a great rock in a weary land." Nothing in the Bible is more beautiful than that, and surely there is no place we have

wandered to that is able to give it such touching expression as this blistering, naked, treeless land.[1]

Twain's comments related to the northern part of the country. Moving south, Twain seemed to pay attention to the quantity of trees visible, as well as other natural elements of the landscape. He indicated that there was "no dew here, nor flowers, nor birds, nor trees," such that "no man can stand here . . . and say the [biblical prophecy of desolation] has not been fulfilled." On the matter of trees, Twain contradicts himself a number of times, reporting at various points the existence of oak, olive, lemon, and other trees, on the one hand, and saying that there were no trees at all, on the other.

Particularly bleak is Twain's description of the journey from the area of Beit-El to the city of Jerusalem:

> The further we went the hotter the sun got and the more rocky and bare, repulsive and dreary the landscape became. There was hardly a tree or a shrub anywhere. Even the olive and the cactus, those fast friends of a worthless soil, had almost deserted the country. No landscape exists that is more tiresome to the eye than that which bounds the approaches to Jerusalem.[2]

In sum Twain's commentary on the land must be seen as hyperbolic. Even his positive remarks about elements of the landscape are mitigated by the caveat that they are "mere toy gardens set at wide intervals in the waste of limitless desolation."[3] Nonetheless, his remarks cannot be dismissed as those of a "cynic."[4] For all that they may be exaggerated, his descriptions indicate that the landscape was sharply different from that anticipated from the images drawn from the Bible. And, as noted, they are far from unique.[5]

The Changing Perception of Palestine in the West

With the accumulation of such travelers' reports, the common public perception of Palestine—at least in the West—underwent a change. There, the biblical image of a land flowing with milk and honey gave way to one of a land barren and desolate. The phenomenon of contradicting reports was already discussed by Smith in the early eighteenth century, well before Twain. In an attempt to explain the wide discrepancies in the descriptions coming from Palestine, Smith wrote:

> It is curious what opposite appreciations have been given of the neighbourhood of Jerusalem. The City has been described as lying "upon barren moun-

---

[1] Mark Twain, *The Innocents Abroad; or, The New Pilgrims' Progress* (New York: Heritage Press, 1962), p. 365.

[2] Ibid., p. 422.

[3] Ibid., p. 465.

[4] Edward W. Said, *Orientalism* (New York: Random House, 1979), p. 63.

[5] Examples can be found in Yehoshua Ben-Arieh, *A City Reflected in Its Times: New Jerusalem—The Beginnings* (Jerusalem: Yad Izhak Ben-Zvi, 1979) [Hebrew].

tains," as "the centre of a stony waste," as "having a few fertile spots within sight," but the rest "dry and arid," "a great plain, part stony, part of good soil"; as "the most fertile portion of Filastin," "a country where on the hills are trees, and in the plains fields [sic], which need neither irrigation nor the watering of rivers, . . . 'a land flowing with milk and honey.'"

Such differences of opinion are explicable partly from the different economic conditions during which the writers quoted visited the City; but principally from the fact that the favourable opinions are those of Mohammedans accustomed to the more desert regions of their world, while the unfavourable are by travellers, ancient Greeks or mediaeval pilgrims, fresh from the greater fertility of Europe.

Observing the olive, fig, and grape cultivation in the Jerusalem region, Smith commented that "they form the full, bright vestitures of all but the desert landscapes of Judea."[6] Concerning particularly the non–fruit bearing trees, Thirgood suggests that "those woodland patches that survived received special notice," and that "despite the paucity of forests to travellers from densely wooded countries, there were more forests in the country at the beginning of the nineteenth century than at the end of Turkish rule."[7]

The Destruction of Palestine's Natural Forests

Supporting this description is a forestry professional's summary of the nature of the forest in Palestine in the latter half of the nineteenth century and in the early part of the twentieth century, which suggests that it was primarily

unfit bushes gnawed by goats, shortened by hewing, eaten by fire, dense and entangled in one place, spread out and isolated in another: few tall trees, lacking adornment, damaged by axes and struck by the wind, and at the same time in the Judean Hills, the Samaria and the Galilee deep in the earth and in places sheltered by stones the roots battle for vitality. In their growth they sprout to be groves, if they do not have the capacity to grow to forests, and there is no affinity for forests among the poor population.[8]

The last of these comments, concerning the lack of affinity for forests among the local population, deserves comment.

One of the themes of the discussion concerning the competition for political hegemony in Palestine in the twentieth century has been the condition

---

6 George Adam Smith, *Jerusalem: The Topography, Economics, and History from the Earliest Times to A.D. 70* (London: Hodder and Stoughton, 1907), pp. 297–299.

7 J. V. Thirgood, *Man and the Mediterranean Forest* (London: Academic Press, 1981), p. 114.

8 Yosef Weitz, *Forest and Afforestation in Israel* (Israel: Massada, 1970), p. 67 [Hebrew]. This work and others by Weitz, particularly his multivolume *My Diaries and Letters to My Sons* (Israel: Massada, 1973) [Hebrew], serve as primary sources on afforestation in Israel and the activities of the JNF. They contain a large number of documents, letters, and maps from a plethora of sources directly related to the issues under discussion. Weitz served as head of afforestation in the JNF for many years, and through this and other positions was a main architect of Israeli land policy.

of the land under the respective control of Muslims and Jews. The main premise of this issue is the Zionist contention, supported by many sources such as the traveler reports cited above, that the land was barren, and that Jewish rehabilitation brought the area into hitherto unrealized or renewed productivity. From the Arab side, the argument is made that descriptions of the debilitated state of the land in late Ottoman times are exaggerated, and that the accomplishments of the Zionists are a result of their monopolization of the best resources. There is also testimony that the denuded state of the land was not the desire of the local inhabitants, but rather a consequence of the difficult conditions they faced. Thus, a British expert in afforestation commented that

> the will to plant is here, but the means are limited by poverty. The barren hills of Judea sadly need to be planted. Their rain washed slopes are bared of humus. The struggling peasant farmer scratching a poor existence from the soil looks up to the hills for forest protection for his crops. If only these hill tops could be planted it would make his task of reconstruction the lighter.[9]

It is not within the focus of this research to decide the question of whether one side or the other put the land to better use, and if so, why. Suffice it to note that the dispute exists, and that an exact picture of the situation at the turn of the century cannot be attained. From research conducted with the advent of the British Mandate, however, it is clear that the condition of flora in Palestine, and, in particular, that of the forests, was very poor. In this, there is no reflection of the earlier fertility of the land or suggestion as to the nature of its stewardship during the period of the Jewish Diaspora. There is, however, a consensus that a number of human factors contributed to the destruction of much of the natural flora in Palestine in the late Ottoman period.

The Decline of the Forest in the Late Ottoman Period

Several causes are seen as primary in the destruction of the natural forests and groves of Palestine. Four of them relate to the quantity of natural resources and the state of the local economy. In light of the difficult environment, there was pressure on local resources long before the advent of the current political conflict. The forest suffered at the expense of other activities involving the maintenance of rural life and the greater economy. For example, the wood of the forest was used as the primary source of fuel in the region. Thus, stands of trees closest to places of habitation (and most likely to be in the areas observed and described by travelers) were gradually reduced. Commenting on the situation, a French diplomat wrote at the time that

---

[9] From *Proceedings of the First Meeting of the Men of the Forests: Palestine*. The remarks are those of the founder of the parent organization, Men of the Forests in Britain, Richard St. Barbe Baker. The *Proceedings* can be found in the Israel State Archive [ISA] collection of mandatory files: ISA, 641/AG/30, 1931.

regulations for forest conservancy exist, but are defeated by corruption, as is the case with the magnificent woods in the Aleppo [Syria] district, which are being destroyed by charcoal burners and oak-bark strippers, despite governmental prohibition, and under the eyes of the officials. In Syria and Palestine forests no longer exist.[10]

On the village periphery the extension of cultivation to new lands often encroached on whatever forest had not fallen prey to earlier needs or misuse.

Farther from the villages, the goats, both those of village herds and those of the bedouin, grazed in the forests. Overgrazing of this sort damaged mature trees and eliminated much of the natural regeneration and spread of the forest, as saplings were particularly vulnerable. These challenges to the forest were by no means unique to Palestine. The phenomenon of forest abuse has been documented throughout the lands of the Ottoman Empire. The island of Cyprus had a situation quite similar to that in Palestine, and, in fact, the damage to the forests of that island paralleled, in many ways, much of what happened in Palestine.[11]

Also common throughout the Ottoman Empire was the difficulty in maintaining trees that was brought about by Ottoman tax practices. This situation is well described by a late nineteenth century resident:

> Taxation was extravagantly disproportionate, and the burden of it fell chiefly on the defenceless poor. A man was assessed on what his vineyard or olive grove could bear in an exceptionally good year, no matter what the actual harvest might be. One man whose two or three olive trees yielded him in a good harvest twenty francs was assessed one year at thirty francs and had to pay that to save his trees from being cut down before his eyes. Trees were taxed as they stood, and the fellaheen levied upon what might have been growing on the ground occupied by the tree itself, as well as for what could not grow under its shade. To escape the tree tax, the men from a village in the Hebron district one winter cut down some five hundred trees, in all stages of growth and promise, and left them lying where they fell.[12]

A statement by a different observer relates to one of the most famous sites in Jerusalem, known for and named after the trees that have grown there since biblical times:

> When trees died they were never replanted because of the Turkish law taxing fruitbearing, or indeed any tree from time of planting. A prominent example

---

[10] "Note sur la situation économique de la Syrie," August 1897, France, Ministère des Affaires Étrangères, Correspondance Commerciale, vol. 12, 1897–1901, cited in Charles Issawi, *The Fertile Crescent 1800–1914: A Documentary Economic History* (London: Oxford University Press, 1988), p. 311.

[11] J. V. Thirgood, *Cyprus: A Chronicle of Its Forests, Land, and People* (Vancouver: University of British Columbia Press, 1987), p. 44. The case of Cyprus also has many interesting parallels at the political level, and forest arson in Cyprus was similar in some respects to that described in chapter 7.

[12] Thirgood, *Man and the Mediterranean Forest*, p. 113, citing Miss Blyth, *When We Lived in Jerusalem* (London: n.p., 1880).

was the summit of the Mount of Olives. Originally covered with apricot trees these trees were demolished by a scourge of locusts in 1864 and were never replanted because of the severity of the Turkish law.[13]

It seems, however, that the principal damage to the forests of Palestine occurred during the period of the first World War.[14] In the war years, trees were cut down in huge numbers to provide firewood for the military and to provide ties for railroad lines extended in Palestine, as well as for other military purposes.[15] Under the Turkish administration, no reforestation was carried out; thus the damage was left unrepaired.[16] The planting of forest trees that had been carried out was on a small scale, and, for the most part, undertaken by European families stationed in Palestine for organizational or political purposes, as well as by resident members of the clerical communities.

The Beginnings of Jewish Afforestation

In the late nineteenth century, with the advent of the increased Jewish settlement that accompanied the growth of the Zionist movement, tree planting in Palestine took on a systematic character that it had previously lacked. The first deliberate planting of trees, for a purpose other than fruit and nut cultivation (and with the exception of small garden groves here and there), employed the eucalyptus, imported from Australia.

The initiative for the importation came from foreign Zionist supporters, and experimentation by Palestinian Jews with different strains of eucalyptus revealed that the trees could well serve their intended purpose, that of assisting the drainage and drying of swampland. Reclamation of such land was a significant element of the Zionist effort to acquire and work land that, owing to its seeming lack of utility, was cheaper and more readily sold by Arab owners. In the 1880s, the eucalyptus was pressed into service in the area of Hadera (on the central coastal plain), but subsequently its use was copied

---

[13] Ibid., citing the account of the American Vester family (1950), missionaries resident in Jerusalem from 1881. The account is somewhat curious in that it ignores the famous olive trees on the mount, some of them well over a thousand years old.

[14] Meir Garon, "Changes in the Face of the Forest in Eretz Yisrael from the Beginning of the New Jewish Settlement and until Today" (M.A. thesis, Hebrew University of Jerusalem, 1971) [Hebrew]. Garon makes this suggestion on the basis of comparison of German maps of Palestine from the 1880s and mandatory maps produced immediately after the war.

[15] This seems to have been the case in Jordan as well, where some forests survived until 1900 or later "after which [they] suffered severely from the cutting of fuel to supply the Hejaz Railway." H. F. Mooney, "Southwestern Asia," in World Geography of Forest Resources, edited by Stephan Haden-Guest et al. (New York: Ronald Press Co., 1956), p. 436.

[16] Ben-Arieh (p. 84) writes "At the beginning of the twentieth century the Ottoman authorities planned the planting of new forests in the Jerusalem surroundings, following the decrease in the natural vegetation." It seems that these plans were not fulfilled. Thirgood notes that "Although French foresters were brought in by the Sultan to organize forestry in the Empire in the 1860s and an Ottoman Forest Law was promulgated, these developments seem to have passed unnoticed in the Levant." Thirgood, Man and the Mediterranean Forest, p. 115.

elsewhere, particularly in massive reclamation projects in the northern valleys. The use of the eucalyptus spread, and soon became so clearly identified with (and at that stage limited to) these efforts that the Arabs called it *Sajarat il-Yahud*, the tree of the Jews.[17]

In light of the limited scope and resources of the settlement movement at the turn of the century, no thought was given to afforestation for the purpose of creating a timber industry, or for any use not related in some way to fostering agriculture. Even at this stage, however, the planting of trees was an act that expressed a certain symbolism concerning presence on the land. Theodore Herzl, popularly credited with being the founder of modern Zionism, participated during his first and only visit to Palestine in a tree-planting ceremony in the village of Motza, just outside Jerusalem.

During that visit Herzl realized how far off the mark his impression of the Palestinian landscape had been prior to the trip. His earlier view was that there were abundant forests in Palestine, and that it looked something like his native Austria.[18] Following the trip, Herzl called on the Jews of the world each to donate a tree or more, that is, to provide the money for planting in Palestine, with 10 million trees as the goal.

Interestingly, a few years after his death in 1904, the cypress tree planted by Herzl was deliberately damaged, and subsequently perished. Suspicion fell upon a segment of the ultrareligious Jewish population in Jerusalem that was opposed to Herzl's ideology, and the act caused considerable distress in the Zionist community. In a response that predated a current tactic for responding to nationalistically motivated forest arson, the Zionists planted more than two hundred trees on the site in a ceremony attended by officials of the movement.

The Keren Keyemet L'Yisrael (JNF)

Around the time that Herzl was planting his symbolic cypress, efforts were being made to find more practical applications for tree planting. A way to do so was found through the agency of the Keren Keyemet L'Yisrael, formally founded in 1901. Familiarity with the JNF is essential for an understanding of land and particularly afforestation issues in both the prestate and state periods.

The idea that gave birth to the JNF was the product of the congresses of the World Zionist Organization held in Europe in the last years of the nineteenth and early part of the twentieth centuries. Jewish immigration to Palestine had increased in the 1880s, as noted above, but without any formal

---

[17] Weitz, *Forest and Afforestation in Israel*, p. 69.

[18] Tzvi Shiloni, "The Keren Keyemet L'Yisrael as a Factor in Shaping the Colonized Landscape of Eretz Yisrael from the Time of Its Foundation to the Outbreak of World War I, 1897–1914" (Ph.D. thesis, Hebrew University of Jerusalem, 1987) [Hebrew].

framework by which immigrants could be absorbed. The Zionist congresses suggested that, in order to facilitate Jewish renewal in Palestine, there was a need to provide and fund a mechanism for purchasing land. Since the goal was to develop an independent Jewish community, emphasis was placed on the purchase of rural land to be used for agricultural purposes.

The JNF was then one of a number of land acquisition bodies, but it soon became the paramount institution for purchasing land in Palestine and developing it for settlement by the Jewish community. At that time, there was no official governing body for the Jews, but the World Zionist Organization held de facto control of Jewish affairs in Palestine, and the JNF was subject to its authority. Of course as a private institution it had no tax base to finance its activities. Rather, it was funded through donations from Jewish communities throughout the world. At the sixth Zionist congress in 1903, a special fund was created for "donations for olive trees in Eretz Yisrael" to be planted on land purchased by the JNF.[19] Within a year, the activities of this fund and responsibility for it were absorbed by the JNF itself.

The first afforestation project directed by the JNF took place on land purchased from Arab effendis near the village of Lod. The total amount of the purchase, executed in a number of phases and carried out over several years, came to 2,158 dunams. Initially, there was some confusion as to how best to use the land. While the decision was pending, the area was rented to Jewish farmers for a period of three years, thus avoiding the Ottoman reclamation clause for land left unworked for that time period. Eventually a decision was made to plant the land with olive trees, and name the forest after the by then deceased Herzl.

The work of planting the Herzl Forest began in 1908. For the most part, the labor was done by hired Arab workers living in the area. This aroused the anger of the Jews in Palestine who advocated "Hebrew labor," particularly on land purchased for the good of the Jewish community. A delegation of Jewish workers arrived at the site and uprooted the olive saplings that had been planted by the Arab laborers. They then prepared the soil and themselves planted trees for the Herzl Forest.[20] On a number of dunams pine trees were planted, and elsewhere eucalyptus as well, such that the forest was more than just a commercial olive grove.

The financing for this project came in large part from the Donate an Olive Tree fund-raising in Europe. Donors were told that, for six German marks, an olive tree would be planted in Palestine. Those supervising the Herzl Forest project came to realize that the cost of each tree was significantly greater than six marks, and as a result fewer trees were planted than had been paid for by European donors. An additional factor contributing to the concern

---

[19] Weitz, *Forest and Afforestation in Israel*, p. 82.

[20] Ibid., p. 83.

of the project managers was that the olives took longer than expected to produce fruit, thus delaying and decreasing income from the investment.[21]

The Shift to Planting Forests to Hold the Land

In light of its experience in this planting, the JNF realized that it was uneconomical to rely to such a degree on the cultivation of olives, which, while not demanding a great amount of labor, were nonetheless not the easiest trees to work with. The goal was to find the simplest and cheapest method of planting in order to hold the land purchased. The JNF, therefore, made the shift to planting primarily forest trees. In 1913, the Donate Olive Trees fund had its name modified to Donate Trees, as other species were brought into increased use. This change constituted an explicit recognition that tree planting would not be a profitable enterprise. Rather, its contribution came through the provision of jobs and the improvement of Palestine's landscape and environment.

Afforestation was also perceived to have a role in the primary goal of the JNF, the acquisition of land, and forests were planted to this end:

> It quickly became clear that the very fact of planting and care of these groves was a good solution to the question of exploitation [of the land purchased], especially the question of possessing those types of areas that belonged to the JNF, which otherwise would be left as natural grazing areas, which, as unused land and in light of their legal standing in Ottoman law, would constitute an opening that called to the Arab neighbors to come onto the land with their flocks and claim possession. As a result, among those dealing with settlement, recognition rooted and grew that the forest was of value, both as a sign of Jewish settlement and as a tool for maintaining possession of Jewish areas not given to other use.[22]

In 1914, two thousand dunams were purchased near Kfar Dalib (today Kiryat Anavim) and slated for planting with pine trees. According to Zogorodski, the chief agronomist of the Zionist Federation, the location of the site was important: "I chose a place exposed to all passers-by in order that the neighbors [i.e., the Arabs] as well as the passers-by will see that the Jews are reclaiming the land."[23] The spot was intended to be visible to all, and as it was adjacent to the route between the coast and Jerusalem, it would, in fact, be commonly observed. As a result of budget difficulties, however, work on the site was not undertaken during the war years, and local Arabs resumed cultivating the land. With the conclusion of the war, the Jewish presence was reasserted, and the land planted with pines.

In addition to the temporary holding of land acquired by the JNF, afforestation began to be used for other purposes. On land that was unsuitable

---

[21] Shiloni, 1: 144.

[22] Ibid., 2: 7.

[23] Weitz, *Forest and Afforestation in Israel*, p. 93.

for agriculture, its main function was still to provide utility in the face of Ottoman regulation. Afforestation was also employed for the purpose of draining swamps in the coastal and northern areas of Palestine, as discussed above, while in other coastal areas trees were used to slow the drift of sand dunes. Throughout the hill region, afforestation was considered a method for preventing slope erosion while increasing hydrologic infiltration. Trees were also used to decrease wind erosion and crop damage through the planting of windbreaks. The planting of orchards, despite the experience in the Herzl Forest, was not entirely abandoned.[24] Despite this variety of tasks, however, afforestation was still only in its inception. A significant boost to afforestation efforts in Palestine came with the advent of the British Mandate.

Afforestation and Olive Planting under the Mandate, 1922–48

Though the JNF continued to be the primary planter of new forests, the Mandatory government took the lead in forest regulation and administration. A special Forestry Service was organized to this end, with the intention of protecting the resources then extant.[25] In their role as caretaker in Palestine, the British were responsible for the amelioration of the situation left in the wake of World War I. This was essential in the broader effort to foster the local economy, as dictated by the terms of the League of Nations Mandate. Though the Mandate was different in constitution from other British administrations throughout the world, the physical conditions faced and the tools brought to the task were familiar. Two main planting efforts evolved as goals of the British authorities. The first was standard afforestation. The second was the development and supervision of the olive industry, in part through the widespread distribution of olive saplings.

One of the first projects undertaken by the Mandate authorities was to assess the condition of existing natural forests and groves as well as orchards in Palestine, with the intention of preserving and improving them. Though this was approached in part in terms of physical care for the trees, the main focus of the attempt was legislative in nature. In seeking to bring the forests under governmental control, the British were attempting to prevent the dilapidation of a resource that was subject to increasing demand. Like the JNF, the British advocated the role of afforestation in the fight against soil erosion, in the stabilization of dunes, and in other uses, such as the need to meet the demand for timber that would come with an expanding economy. Thus, their afforestation policy was conservational and utilitarian at the same time. Hav-

---

[24] Indeed there was a call in 1913 by one of the directors of the JNF to develop a "Jewish Jerusalem, around which would be different fruit-tree orchards and growth of forests." M. Shenkin, cited in Shiloni, p. 144. Citriculture expanded rapidly during this period in the coastal plain.

[25] Esco Foundation for Palestine, *Palestine: A Study of Jewish, Arab, and British Policies* (New Haven: Yale University Press, 1947), 1: 307.

ing a more immediate impact on the population, however, were the steps taken for development of the olive industry.

Growth of the Olive Industry under Mandatory Supervision

The olive was, and remains, a significant element of the Palestinian Arab diet, and played a further role in the economy through trade in olive oil and soap. Though less central in the market than in Ottoman times, the olive, nonetheless, had a special place in Palestinian agriculture.[26] Following World War I, the main consumer of the Palestinian olive crop was the soap industry, with a concentration of presses and factories in the area of Nablus.

The demand from this industry exceeded the local supply, and oil was thus regularly imported from Syria. With a seemingly firm market, the fellahin began replanting olive trees as soon as possible following the conclusion of World War I.[27] British censuses of the olive tree population in Palestine relied upon local reporting of numbers, and were of questionable accuracy. The problem was the same as it had been in the Ottoman era, the under-reporting of holdings in order to avoid, as much as possible, the tax burden.[28]

Olive cultivation in Palestine is subject to significant fluctuation in annual yield owing to the biennial cycle of the fruit, and the influence of rain and other climatic factors such as wind and temperature. The shift in the market from year to year caused enormous changes in the price that olives would bring for the fellahin. In many respects, the nature of the market favored large cultivators, who could survive the down trends and even use them to advantage. The pressure felt by the smaller-scale cultivators often led to poor agricultural practices, such as premature harvesting to capitalize on the early market prices. The British sought to improve the condition of these small-scale cultivators through regulation and education.

Responsible for this effort was the Olive Oil Committee, a subcommittee of the Mandate's General Agricultural Council. This committee initiated rural education efforts by the local agricultural inspectors, and followed closely the rise and fall of the market from year to year. In an effort to study the issue the committee toured rural areas and saw

> many kilometres of country which showed all the signs of having been once before covered with olive trees but were now treeless and void of cultivation. Their conviction that much of these regions afforded further areas for olive growing—for which they seemed most particularly suitable—would seem to be

---

[26] ISA, 672/AG/38/1/2, "The Olive Oil Industry," report of the Olive Oil Sub-committee, November 10, 1941.

[27] Ibid.

[28] ISA, 627/AG/3/1, September 9, 1937.

borne out by the desire expressed by villagers everywhere to increase plantations where possible.[29]

In addition to contributing to the economy of Palestine, both through
the olive crop and through the taxation on trees and produce, it was suggested
that the expansion of olive cultivation would lead to better use of and care for
the land, since "the plantings in many cases necessitate terracing and other
soil conservation practices and there is no doubt we [the Mandatory authori-
ties] should do whatever possible to encourage the present desire for increased planting of olive trees."[30] To facilitate the expansion of olive cultivation, the government sold trees to the villagers at a subsidized price. The
popularity of this move was confirmed when the supply was consistently
short of demand, and the British were compelled to establish limits on the
number of trees that individuals could purchase at the discounted price.

In the latter half of the 1930s, the amount of land under olive cultivation increased by 100,000 dunams, in addition to some 475,000 dunams previously being worked for olives. On this land, there were some 2 million trees
that had not yet begun to produce fruit, a portent of tremendous growth in
the size of future harvests.[31] Though the olive was ranked third in terms of
the income it generated in Palestine—following citrus and wheat—it was
clearly the crop of preference among the fellahin, and it was considered by
British agricultural experts to be the soundest investment a villager could
make.[32] This despite the fact that the olive took eight years to bear first fruit,
and reached maximum production only after approximately twenty years.

In order to deal with this enlarged sector, in 1943 the British passed the
Olive Control Ordinance, which dictated the creation of the Olive Control
Board. The spread of olive cultivation and the increase in the amount of individual harvest did not eliminate the vulnerability of the peasants, or the
variability of the market. Indeed, with millions of additional trees, there was
danger that the market would be flooded. The Olive Control Board, therefore,
began to develop foreign markets for Palestinian olive oil, primarily in the
Arab lands to the east, while supervising production and setting standards for
quality. The danger of overproduction seems not to have deterred the Palestinian population, or affected their affinity for this crop, and olive cultivation
continued to proliferate throughout the period of the Mandate.

The British Role in Forest Planting and Protection

The main tool in the British effort to protect, improve, and increase
both the remnants of forests in Palestine and the creation of new ones was the

[29] ISA, 672/AG/38/1/2, November 10, 1941.

[30] ISA, 664/AG/38/1/2, no. 1358, April 26, 1944.

[31] ISA, 672/AG/38/1/2, November 10, 1941.

[32] ISA, 639/AG/26/3/7–AJ/29/1, April 5, 1942.

Forest Ordinance of 1926. This measure formalized a direct government interest in every forest in Palestine, whether on private or public land, and was related as well to the use of fruit trees on agricultural land.[33] The British treated trees, first and foremost, as a resource, and, as such, sought to regulate their use and ensure their protection. Of course, this often put them at odds with agriculturalists and others who desired unrestricted access to the forests and unrestrained control over the orchards. With a view to improving the situation in Palestine, however, the British took the broader view of the function of trees, and considered the overall land use and water conservation role that they fulfilled. To this end, forest reserves were established throughout Palestine and use of the existing forests was licensed and monitored. A main problem in the establishment of such reserves was finding

> the best method of obtaining control of the land which needs treatment. Title deeds are at present obscure, and land settlement must in some regions be long delayed. If the condition of the country is to be improved, it seems inevitable that legislation must provide for state control of certain land, both public and private.[34]

The Issue of Private Property

A. Y. Goor, conservator of forests for the Mandate, explained the function of the forest reserves, and his description serves to highlight a number of issues that relate to ongoing land and forestry problems:

> The Forest Ordinance of 1926 provides for the demarcation and proclamation as a forest reserve of any waste forest land not being private property. In a forest reserve no cultivation is permitted and no grazing nor cutting except by a license issued by the Department [of Forestry]. In practice, all local villagers are permitted to graze and cut, but not to cultivate, *so that no new claims to ownership based on cultivation are allowed to arise.* As a result, with the minimum of disturbance to the life of the villagers, the rights of the state have been safeguarded, and the state still has the chance of afforesting and developing these uncultivated lands at some future date when circumstances permit.[35]

Before continuing with Goor's description, a number of points need to be made concerning this first paragraph. Regarding the nature of "waste forest land," there was some dispute within the government, with forestry officials

---

[33] Trees listed as protected by the British included olive, carob, oak, pistachio, pine, tamarisk, poplar, willow, acacia, eucalyptus, cypress, laurel, and others. Cutting of such trees was permissible only with a license obtained from the government. The 1926 Forest Ordinance (section 19) set a six-month jail term and/or a £50 fine for breech of this regulation. The 1947 Amendment of the Ordinance doubled the punishment for infraction. To this day, cutting down a mature tree in an urban area is regulated by permit. To receive the permit a fee must be paid, and an inspector comes to verify the location of the tree and the justification for its removal.

[34] ISA, A324/AF/41/39, Department of Forests, *Report on the Period 1936–1939* (Jerusalem: Government Printing Press, 1940), p. 4.

[35] ISA, A403/F/26/12/4, A. Y. Goor, "Forest Reservations in Palestine," December 31, 1946, sheet 1 (emphasis added).

maintaining a definition of wasteland somewhat broader than others. This difference of opinion simmered throughout the Mandate years, and found sharp expression when the Forest Ordinance was reconsidered in 1946.

The 1926 ordinance provided for the inclusion in forest reserves of land that was deemed "uncultivable." The 1947 amendment to the ordinance went even further, allowing the high commissioner to "authorise a forest officer to take under his management and protection lands known or believed to be private property, for the afforestation of such lands, or the improvement of vegetation existing on them," if it was determined that such action was, "in the public interest, in order to protect water supplies, prevent flooding or soil erosion, or to ensure the continuity of supplies of forest produce."[36] The explanatory notes for the amendment contained in the working papers of the amendment draft indicate that "this section allows the High Commissioner to include in a forest reserve *any land even if devoid of vegetation.*"[37]

The director of the Mandate's Land Settlement Department, R. F. Jardine, objected to these broad definitions and vociferously opposed their formalization through the amendment to the Forest Ordinance. He commented, in part:

> I also feel a little surprise that consideration should be given to the enactment of such a Bill without further consultation with the Arab inhabitants. I mention the Arabs particularly because it is their land which is mainly to be found within the category described as "uncultivable land" in the Rural Property Tax Ordinance.[38] I am not aware whether there has been any consultation with Jewish land interests, but they are also entitled to their views, although the area of Jewish owned land classed as category 16 in the Rural Property Tax Ordinance is less than 200,000 dunams as compared with the figure of nearly five million dunams of Arab land in that category.
>
> There is much that I disagree with in the Bill, but my chief objection is to the legalization of the contention that all uncultivable land is forest land.[39]

The broad range of land that could be included in a forest reserve, and the extent of the governmental power that could bring this to pass, cast a different light on Goor's contention that there would be a "minimum of disturbance to the life of the villagers." In fact, the forestry service was not highly regarded by the villagers of Palestine.[40] In no small part, this was because the villagers were enjoined, "not to cultivate, so that no new claims to ownership based on cultivation are allowed to arise."

---

[36] ISA, A115/F/51/6, Department of Forests, "Proposed Amendment to Part VI of the Forest Ordinance, Control over Private Land," November 14, 1944.

[37] Ibid. (emphasis added).

[38] This ordinance set a tax schedule for land based on its use, with uncultivable land falling near the bottom of the scale in tax category 16, subject to minimal taxation.

[39] Letter from Jardine to the chief secretary, ISA, G/2(31), March 11, 1948.

[40] ISA, AF/1C/46, December 29, 1947.

Some of the lands used or designated for use by the British remained undeclared because of the inability to protect the forests on them from retaliatory action by the villagers, making the declaration a "dead letter."[41] At least in theory, however, by virtue of the Forest Ordinance, the government could prevent the extension of agriculture anywhere in Palestine through the declaration of a forest reserve, whether it be on public or private land.[42] In fact, this often was not the case, and the British found that

> the local attitude towards land tenure is such that a cultivator is considered to have a very good claim to the land on which he works, unless other persons, or the state, can conclusively prove that they have a prior and better title. This being so, the rapid clearing and ploughing of suitable plots within the forest reserves has become a common practice, the offenders then pleading that they have cultivated there for generations, and thereafter being very hard to dislodge.[43]

The Declaration of Forest Reserves

Goor continues his description with an explanation of the process of locating and declaring the forest reserves:

> Early attempts at demarcation had failed . . . and it had been left to the coming of Land Settlement to define the forest boundaries and to save the remnants of the natural vegetation. By 1926, however, it became clear that, if nothing else were to be done, the vegetation would all disappear long before the arrival of the Settlement Officers. . . .
> The need for immediate action was so keenly felt that in 1926-28 166 forest reserves with a total approximate area of 644,000 dunams were gazetted with the vaguest of boundaries. This step may have been justifiable at the time for tactical reasons, but it has proved no permanent value. In practice the only satisfactory method is the survey and demarcation of the boundaries of the forest land, and the cultivated enclaves.[44]

Here Goor indicates generally what some of the problems were with the declaration of forest reserves. His characterization of the boundaries as vague is quite accurate. The boundary descriptions are much closer to the indigenous or colloquial system than to that customarily used by the British. Stones, cultivated patches, and village landmarks are intended to document the areas closed off or restricted by the Mandate.

---

[41] ISA, A324/AF/41/39, p. 6.

[42] Justification was of course expected for the declaration of forest reserves, and when objections were entertained by the mandate to such declarations each side was expected to prove its case. Until the claimant made his case, however, the inclusion of the area within the forest reserve, and all the restrictions that accompanied it, remained in place. ISA, A403/AF/4/46, April 15, 1946. The British power under this ordinance should be compared with Israeli policy and practice as described in chapter 5 and onward.

[43] ISA, A324/AF/41/39, p. 11.

[44] ISA, A403/F/26/12/4, Goor, "Forest Reservations," sheet 1.

And, while the accuracy of forest demarcation improved over the years, the issue of land settlement, a crucial component of British land policy, played only a limited role in afforestation and related issues. In great part, this is because the British land settlement program began in the north, and only gradually worked its way through the area later to become the West Bank. In lieu of formal land settlement, the government used the forest reserve as one method of establishing or maintaining land rights. Goor writes:

> The demarcation and gazetting of forest reserves were intended to safeguard state forest land and the vegetation thereon until unassigned Land Settlement could provide for the registration of all rural state Domain [referred to currently as state land], after which it was believed that the state could surely manage and develop the forests found on its own property. The system of reservation has more than fulfilled all expectations; in many localities Settlement Officers have recorded as state Domain the whole of a forest reserve and nothing else. . . . There are many newly registered state Domains with precisely the same boundaries as the old forest reserves, while *all the unassigned lands outside those boundaries have been occupied and claimed by private owners in whose names it is* [sic] *now registered.*
>
> If all state Domain had been lost, as seemed likely at one time, Government would merely have been a powerful outsider, but since the registration of those unassigned lands in the name of the state, Government is one of the largest landowners in many villages.[45]

Goor's statement has profound significance in light of the patterns of the current dispute. He indicated that land that remained unafforested was put into use by surrounding villagers. At the same time, through afforestation, the government had become a significant owner of village lands. Of course, in some cases, the Mandatory actions were contested, and, as indicated, only land settlement served to clarify matters to such a degree as to end the disputes, at least in terms of their legal disposition. Thus, the director of land settlement recommended that the British "should endeavour to 'settle' certain areas where there are or there are thought to be important Government . . . interests."[46]

The total area falling within forest reserves was never particularly significant in relation to the amount of land within the Mandate, nor was the number of new trees planted by the government particularly great. Out of a total of some 26 million dunams in Palestine, the British classified approximately 850,000 dunams as forest reserves.[47] Of these, fewer than 40,000 du-

---

[45] Ibid.

[46] ISA, SD/1/8(4), January 1, 1947.

[47] ISA, A403/AF/2/47, Department of Forests, "List of Forest Reserves by Categories as of December 31, 1946," 1947. This document lists the land categories of Palestine as 11 million dunams climatic desert, 9 million dunams in use for agriculture, 4.5 million dunams wasteland and grazing ground, and, in addition to the forest reserves, 644,573 dunams of "ruined forest not reserved."

nams were in the Forest Department's Jerusalem District.[48] In the area that became the West Bank only 8,000 dunams were afforested during the Mandate years.[49] What is significant, however, about the period of Mandatory afforestation is the aggressive attitude on the part of the government, and the widespread application of afforestation for a variety of broad-ranging yet focused goals. It is also important that the British determined that "it is clear that fire protection must form an integral part of the management of the forests, which are small, isolated, with long boundaries, and special hazard [sic] due to land disputes," because in most cases of forest fire, "the usual causes have been sabotage."[50] That this is so indicates that the relationship between afforestation authorities and the villagers, as well as Arab nationalists, was marked, in part, by competition and antagonism.

Jewish Afforestation during the Mandate Period

As noted above, the primary agency for Jewish afforestation in Palestine was the JNF. Early in the Mandate period, the JNF completed the shift from the planting of olives to a policy favoring forest trees, especially the pine and cypress. This was a logical outcome of the soil conservation and land-use goals that were the primary reason for Jewish afforestation. Experience confirmed that the pine was easier and cheaper to work with, and sufficiently quick-growing for the task.[51] For the Zionist movement, afforestation was seen as one of the tools in the broader settlement effort. Its contribution to settlement came in the form of improving land and living conditions, and in providing employment for new immigrants. Indeed, immigrants were, at times, directed to afforest the area around the land on which they would create their homes.

At the same time, the JNF undertook forest projects that were intended for the benefit of the community as a whole. To this end, a number of tree nurseries were created in the early 1920s, several of them in Jerusalem. The seedlings cultivated in the city—75,000 by 1921—were, for the most part, planted outside Jerusalem, though some were given to the newest of the city's Jewish neighborhoods. One of the uses of the nursery seedlings was the planting of trees funded through the donations of the Jewish communities outside

---

[48] This district included Hebron, Jerusalem, Jericho, Bethlehem, and Ramallah, and a breakdown of the distribution within these areas is not provided. As of December 1946 the total for the Jerusalem district was 34,556 dunams. ISA, A403/ F/26/12/4.

[49] Thirgood, *Man and the Mediterranean Forest*, p. 118.

[50] ISA, AF/41/39, Department of Forests, *Report on the Period 1936–1939*, p. 11.

[51] Two types of pine are used primarily in the planting by the JNF. Through the early 1960s the most commonly planted tree was the Aleppo pine, *Pinus halepensis.* The name is something of a misnomer in that this species is not found in the area of Aleppo, Syria, for which it is named. Rather, that area supports the Brutia pine, *Pinus brutia,* the second most common tree planted by the JNF. In Hebrew the Aleppo pine is referred to as the "Jerusalem pine."

Palestine, such as the planting of the Herzl Forest discussed above. The trees there had fallen victim to the needs of the Ottoman and British armies during World War I, and the JNF felt an obligation to its donors to replant the area.

For the most part, the major afforestation efforts of the JNF in the Mandatory period were in the Galilee, along with a number of locations in the foothills and the coastal plain. The two primary sites in the Jerusalem region were Sha'ar HaGai, at the foot of the ascent to the city, and Kiryat Anavim, which was the site of Dilab. Within the city itself, planting was carried out by the JNF and the government at locations of historical or religious significance, as well as near important public institutions. This effort was small in scope, however, and easily matched by the planting of private citizens, often with trees procured from the nurseries belonging to the afforestation agencies.

The amount of planting by the JNF increased dramatically in the latter half of the 1920s. In 1927, nongovernmental planting of trees in Palestine (the vast majority of which was carried out by the JNF) covered some 5,000 dunams. The area afforested expanded annually until a peak in 1936 when nearly 44,000 dunams were planted. However, this number was not matched again until the advent of the state period. The cause for the drop in planting following the 1936 peak was the outbreak of the "Arab Revolt," the Palestinian Arab uprising against the Mandatory authorities. The destabilization of the countryside inhibited the JNF in its activities. So, too, did the sharp upswing in the occurrence of arson, and in "private forests, mainly in Jewish [i.e., JNF] hands, political sabotage accounted for most of the damage done."[52] Interestingly, the attacks on the forests stimulated donations from Jewish communities abroad, and as a result, during this period the JNF had a larger disposable income than in any previous year.

The forests planted by the JNF corresponded in location with the areas of Jewish settlement activity, for the reasons stated above. For the most part, this meant that these forests were within the area that came under Israeli control in the wake of the war in 1948. There had been a nursery established in the town of Hebron in the 1920s. However, this endeavor was abandoned when the Jewish population of the city fled in 1929, following Arab violence that claimed some sixty lives. The only other significant activity in the area, which was later to come under Jordanian control (i.e., the West Bank), was planting in the area of the Etzion settlement block in the Hebron Hills. This area, of course, passed out of Jewish control in the years 1948–67.

The primary significance of Jewish afforestation during the Mandate period was the role it played in the creation and application of Jewish land ac-

---

[52] ISA, A324/AF/41/39, Department of Forests, *Report on the Period 1936–1939*, p. 11.

quisition and settlement policies. While the total amount of land afforested by the JNF was not great, the method of planting on land that was unfit for agriculture, or that temporarily had no other utility, contributed to the domination of key points in the overall land scheme, particularly in the attempt to create continuous areas of Jewish control. Along with the actual land use, afforestation was a tool in population distribution and overall economic development. These factors constituted a fundamental strategy in the attempt to create as broad an area of control as possible in the effort to establish a viable state.

At the same time, the experience of the Mandate period prepared the JNF for a major role in the functioning of the Jewish state. In terms of both its professional expertise and the coordination between it and governmental agencies, the JNF matured into a powerful and pragmatic body, completely devoted to the realization of Zionist goals in Palestine/Israel. The Mandate years were a time of experimentation, and the lessons learned were applied with vigor once the authority and resources of the new state were directed toward the afforestation efforts of the JNF.

4

Afforestation as a National Enterprise, 1948–67

At the opening session of the second Knesset in 1951, Prime Minister Ben-Gurion spoke of the importance of afforestation and its role in building the state:

> We must plant many hundreds of thousands of trees on an area of five million dunams, a quarter of the area of the state. We must wrap all the mountains of the country and their slopes in trees, all the hills and stony lands that will not succeed in agriculture, the dunes of the coastal valley, the dry lands of the Negev to the east and south of Baer Sheva, that is to say all of the land of Edom and the Arava until Eilat. We must also plant for security reasons, along all the borders, along all the roads, routes and paths, around public and military buildings and facilities. . . . We will not be faithful to one of the two central goals of the state—making the wilderness bloom—if we make do with only the needs of the hour whose return is close and not do in our generation projects which will be a blessing for all the generations to come. We are a state at the beginning of repairing the corruption of generations, corruption which was done to the nation [i.e., the Jewish people] and corruption which was done to the land. We must enlist for this all the professional strength we have in the country . . . we must come in time to plant a half million dunams per year.[1]

While Ben-Gurion's call to afforest a quarter of the area of the state was somewhat exaggerated, the role of afforestation and its symbolism were to be major elements in the foundation of the country, and a primary factor in the transformation of the landscape. Yosef Weitz, who directed afforestation for the JNF, was the chief architect of the use of trees in the state-building effort. It was his vision and effort that led to many of the forests, and forest policies, which are significant to this day. His prolific writing, therefore, provides a

---

[1] Yosef Weitz, *Forest and Afforestation in Israel* (Israel: Massada, 1970), p. 295 [Hebrew].

primary source for tracing the evolution of forestry and afforestation in the period following the 1948 War of Independence.

Weitz's estimate for potential afforestation in Israel was somewhat more modest than that of Ben-Gurion. An appreciation for the variety of tasks that afforestation could accomplish, however, was held by both men. Though the primary purpose of planting was to create forests, for the variety of reasons discussed above, afforestation also had a significant role in the settling of the country and the absorption of the massive wave of immigrants that came in the early 1950s. Tree planting was of use in this effort through the creation of employment for new immigrants, and through the provision of basic training in agricultural skills that were expected to serve as the basis for the economy. The experience of the prestate period demonstrated the tremendous potential of the JNF in this regard.

The total area within the armistice lines following the creation of the state was some 20.5 million dunams, of which roughly 8.5 million dunams were fit for cultivation of some sort. Of the remaining 12 million dunams, Weitz estimated that 3.5 million were appropriate for afforestation. Of this number, 427,000 dunams had been afforested during the prestate period or were covered with natural growth, leaving 3,073,000 dunams for future afforestation.[2] With only 2 percent of the country covered at that time by trees, the call for increasing the coverage by nearly 750 percent was quite ambitious, even if not up to Ben-Gurion's expectations.

New Purposes in Planting

With the creation of the state and the transfer of the governmental afforestation enterprise to Israeli hands, a number of new purposes and goals were added to those that had been carried over from the Mandate era. One of these was the planting of "security groves," stands of trees that either sheltered roads from the view of observers and soldiers in the hostile neighbor states, or provided a marshaling point for Israeli military forces, again out of the view of hostile eyes. This use proved particularly important in Jerusalem, where much of the city was within the proximity of Jordanian snipers, and in the north, where roads were exposed to the Syrians on the Golan Heights.

The use of trees to shelter the roadways immediately met with opposition from different sectors. Road builders were concerned that the tree roots would damage the road itself. Safety engineers were concerned that the patterns of sunlight and shade would be a hazard that would negatively affect driver vision. The Israeli public was opposed on esthetic grounds, complaining that the narrow corridor of the security lanes destroyed the view of the surrounding area. Ultimately, most of the trees were removed from the roadside as a result of pressure from those opposed to this use.

---

[2] Ibid., p. 297.

A second new purpose (actually, the massive expansion and institutionalization of a previous use) was the planting of trees, as well as complete groves and even forests, as memorials to individuals and communities. The two most prevalent memorials were for those who perished in the Nazi Holocaust, and those who fell in battles and attacks in Israel. The projects were sponsored by donors from abroad, citizens in Israel, and the government, in conjunction with the JNF.

A third purpose, in fact the evolution of an earlier tactic, was that of planting to hold the land. Subsequent to the creation of the state, there was of course no need to fear the loss of state land to an external authority, such as the Mandatory government or the Ottoman Empire. There was, however, a need to protect the land from the citizens of the state. For the most part, this meant the prevention of land use by Arab citizens of Israel who had lost their lands in the 1948 Arab-Israeli War or in its aftermath.[3] As in the prestate period, planting of forests was used as a method for the prevention of grazing or cultivation on land that the government (and the JNF) did not want to fall into or return to the hands of Arab agriculturalists and pastoralists.

The Initial Division of Labor

With the variety of goals and the tremendous aspirations for afforestation, it was clear that the mechanisms for carrying out the work needed to be expanded and institutionalized. The basic dichotomy between the government and the JNF, nonetheless, remained. The Mandatory Forest Department was replaced by the Forestry Division of Israel's Ministry of Agriculture, while the JNF retained its semi-independent status. In theory, there was to be a clear division of tasks between the two.

The government's Forestry Division reserved for itself a number of the more technical elements of forestry. Research addressed the most efficient method of planting trees, problems that arose in afforestation, and the most appropriate type of tree for different areas and purposes, and included experimentation with planting in arid regions, primarily in the Negev and the Arava. Also a responsibility of the government was the exploration and creation of a timber processing and supply system, an attempt to address the undesir-

---

[3] The subject of how this land, often termed "abandoned property," was legally removed from Arab hands and placed at the disposal of the state is an interesting and serious topic, deserving much broader coverage than can be given here. The land in question is primarily that belonging to those classified as "absentees" or "present absentees," whose property is controlled by the Custodian for Abandoned Property, totaling 5,793 square kilometers; Ephraim Orni, *Land of Israel: History, Policy, Management, and Development* (Jerusalem: HaKeren Keyemet L'Yisrael, 1980), p. 29. Information on this topic can be found in several sources. See for example Aharon Liskovski, "The 'Present Absentees' in Israel," *HaMizrach HeHadash* 10, no. 3 (1960): 186–192; Bakir Abu Kishk, "Arab Land and Israeli Policy," *Journal of Palestine Studies* 11, no. 1 (1981): 124–135; Sabri Jiryis, "Domination by the Law," *Journal of Palestine Studies* 11, no. 1 (1981): 83–90.

able need to import the bulk of the country's timber, which was a problem already in the Mandate era. The government was also to operate tree nurseries that would supply cheap or free seedlings to the public and private sectors in an effort to stimulate planting around the country. A further task of this division was the planting of the trees that contributed to security interests, as described above. The government also undertook to educate the country's youth concerning the contribution of afforestation in order to instill an appreciation for trees and forests.

For its part, the JNF was responsible for the major share of actual afforestation work. From the outset, this included the improvement and completion of tasks that were carried over from the Mandate period. The primary goal in new planting was to improve soil conditions and provide employment in areas designated for settlement. The JNF thus focused on the hill region of the center of the country and in the Galilee, on areas where sand dunes were a problem, and, in the Negev, on the planting of windbreaks to assist agriculture.[4]

The immediate increase in the scope of JNF planting can be seen by a comparison of the attainments in the years 1949 and 1950. In the former, a total of 2,910 dunams were planted throughout the country. In the latter year, this number had more than quadrupled to 12,650 dunams, with 56,400 dunams planned for 1951. Most of this work was carried out by new immigrants, including 252,000 trees planted in the Jerusalem Corridor.

The Jerusalem Corridor

The Jerusalem Corridor—that part of the route between the coastal plain and Jerusalem which ran from Sha'ar HaGai to the city's western entrance—was one of the most fiercely contested areas of the 1948 War. In the course of the war, and in fact prior to it, the Arab villages on the heights above the road to Jerusalem had been a constant source of pressure on Jewish attempts to maintain a link with the city. Israel, therefore, decided to clear the corridor of its Arab inhabitants, and those who did not flee in advance of or during the battle for the area were subsequently directed to leave.[5]

One of the villages in the corridor was Deir Yassin, site of an infamous massacre of Arabs in 1948.[6] In the planting season 1950–51, work was begun

---

[4] Weitz, *Forest and Afforestation in Israel*, p. 300.

[5] For information concerning the movement of this population see Benny Morris, *The Birth of the Palestinian Refugee Problem, 1947–1949* (Cambridge: Cambridge University Press, 1987). The village of Abu Gosh, known for its cooperation with the Jewish community, was evacuated, but residents were later allowed to return. Together with its subunit Ein Nakuba, Abu Gosh constitutes the only Arab presence in the pre-1967 Jerusalem corridor.

[6] Deir Yassin was attacked on April 9, 1948, by troops of the Irgun, a semirival of the official military arm of the Jewish community. In the attack 250 Arab civilians were killed. The reasons for this and details of the battle are disputed; the results are not.

on the afforestation of the village's southern-facing slope. As a result of the battle for Deir Yassin, the village was no longer inhabited by Arabs, and the afforestation was part of an effort to provide employment for and settle new Jewish immigrants in the Jerusalem neighborhood named Givat Shaul, which was being created on the site. The work on the slope continued for four years, though at the end of this period a fire destroyed nearly all of the 400 dunams that had been planted.

In the corridor some fourteen communities were established, most of them kibbutzim or moshavim, working primarily in agriculture. Afforestation carried out during the Mandate period covered 1,800 dunams within this area.[7] Weitz divides the corridor into two sections, that to the south of the Tel Aviv–Jerusalem highway, and the section to the north of this road. In the entire corridor there are 230,000 dunams, of which 150,000 were fit for afforestation. Since 20,000 dunams were already covered, a goal was set of planting much of the remaining 130,000 dunams.

Among those forests begun in the early 1950s were six blocks on the outskirts of Jerusalem. They were the forests of Mevasseret Yerushalaim (440 dunams), Ora-Aminadav (380 dunams), Kaplan (470 dunams), Canada-Sataf (3,340 dunams), American Independence (3,045 dunams), and the Bar-Kochba Forest (855 dunams).

The Martyrs' Forest

The largest project in this area, indeed one of the largest in the country, was undertaken in 1950, that being the Holocaust Martyrs' Forest. In addition to the significance of its size—ultimately totaling 30,000 dunams—the Martyrs' Forest was significant for its importance in the eyes of the Jewish community in Israel, and abroad. Indeed, the Martyrs' Forest served as a transition in the participation of the Diaspora communities in the creation, through donation, of forests in Israel. Part of the dedicatory scroll of the forest reads:

> Thus the Judean Hills and Jerusalem will again be rooted and afforested, again the branches of the Tree of Israel, those that were hewn in the great Holocaust and those that fell for the freedom of the nation and the land, the souls of our holy ones and our heros will live eternally with the green trees, abundantly living—to reawaken the barren land and to fertilize the exiled of the nation.[8]

The official announcement of the forest said in part:

> The memory of our six million holy ones will be eternalized in the trees which will be planted in the earth closest to the heart of each and every Jew. Their names will be sanctified for eternity by the tree which is renewed time after time with the passing of the year. "Forest of the Holy Ones" will rise in

---

[7] Weitz, *Forest and Afforestation in Israel,* p. 386.

[8] Ibid., p. 392.

the Judean Hills at the entrance of the capital of Israel and thus will serve as a practical contribution to the resuscitation of this important area.[9]

Of course Jerusalem and its environs, with their primacy, were not the only parts of the country considered important. Significant land and planting issues were being played out in the Galilee, the Triangle—an area with a heavy concentration of Arab population—and border locations, and they merit a short discussion before returning to the topic of the Jerusalem area.

Planting for Containment and Border Supervision

In the role of assisting settlement, the location of afforestation projects was often determined by security needs. In Israel's strategic thinking the security issue was paramount, and settlement was a key element in holding and guarding both internal areas and the nation's borders. Settlement was, therefore, directed to strategic sites, and often afforestation was undertaken to provide employment for the settlers of these sites. In order to facilitate settlement and achieve a Jewish majority in the various areas of the country, Arab growth was also limited.[10] This was partly achieved by the domination of land that had been declared abandoned and land that was categorized as state land. Large amounts of such land were found in the Galilee and the Triangle, some of which was put at the disposal of kibbutzim and moshavim, while other parts were afforested.

The JNF saw itself as a guardian of land that was turned over to it for any of a variety of purposes, though particularly that which was slated for afforestation. The amount of land in the care of the JNF was considerable. The status of public ownership (that is, not owned by individuals) applied to more than 90 percent of the land in Israel.[11] Since 1948, some 1,330,000 dunams had been transferred by the state to the JNF, both for preparation for settlement, and for afforestation, serving the purposes previously described. Another 500,000 dunams were being supervised by the JNF on behalf of governmental agencies. The JNF felt that its task was to preserve this land for the use of future generations.

> Preserving state land is one of the most important things. . . . When you say "preserving land," that isn't only against Arabs who would take it. Jews too can find an area, and it's happened more than once that Jews take over something that isn't theirs. We guard the national land.[12]

---

[9] Ibid., p. 386.

[10] This is primarily in reference to areal growth. There is however a link between the amount of land available to a population and its ability to grow numerically. Land shortages also contribute to out-migration, which was a factor in the balance between the groups.

[11] Ephraim Orni, *Agrarian Reform in Israel* (Jerusalem: HaKeren Keyemet L'Yisrael, 1975), p. 28 [Hebrew].

[12] Interview with Mordechai Ru'ach, director, JNF Forestry Division, January 22, 1990.

In the period following the 1948 War, there was great uncertainty as to the ownership and disposition of much of the land in the state, a situation persisting from the Mandatory reign in Palestine. Thus, at times there existed a free-for-all that was not approved of by the government, which preferred to control the disposition of this resource rather than have it grabbed by the first squatter to establish a claim. As noted, the JNF felt that trees were "the best guards of the land. There is no better. Walls and fences can be cut down. A tree says 'we are here.' If you plant a tree, that's your land."[13]

More important under such circumstances is that the tree, in the company of a forest, prevents others from using the land no matter who the owner is. While the "other" in the view of the JNF could be either Arab or Jew, more often the prevention of use is directed against the Arab population. The forest is, therefore, employed as a barrier to expansion, whether it be agricultural or residential. In many places in the Galilee and the Triangle, "The Arab villages end where the forest begins," and the forest serves as "a clear sign to the villagers."[14] And whether the forest borders on residences or on agricultural land, the sign is that there is no room for expansion, as the adjacent land is off-limits.

With border areas, the planting is not to prohibit land use, indeed often it is to promote it. Israel has attempted throughout its history to disperse the population, hoping to foster growth on the sparsely settled periphery at the expense of the densely populated center. This has been accomplished through the construction of agricultural settlements, or through the provision of employment for the occupation of town residents. The planting of security groves and boulevards, as discussed above, served this function for townspeople as well as for the temporary labor camps constructed by the government to help absorb the wave of immigrants of the 1950s. Forest planting provided work for agricultural or semiagricultural communities along the armistice lines with Lebanon in the north, and Jordan (i.e., the West Bank) in the east. Work was also provided for the Nachal units of the Israeli army, whose bases were frequently part of or converted to new civilian settlements.[15]

Often the planting and settlement came on border land that had been closed for security reasons. Arab land in these areas was often forfeit by virtue

---

[13] Ru'ach, July 17, 1989.

[14] Ibid. Also, *Jerusalem Post*, August 4, 1976, cites Sharon Weitz, head of JNF Forestry Division, as indicating that the JNF would "protect State lands not with fences but with trees." This was in reference to 10,000 dunams of Galilee land to be planted in order to prevent the creation of land rights by either Arabs or Druze.

[15] Nachal units combined active army service with periods of work in agriculture, the name of the unit being an anagram for "Pioneering Fighting Youth." They were used by the government to create new settlements or augment young ones, especially in the early years of the state. They fulfilled this role too, albeit to a lesser degree, in the West Bank after 1967.

of this form of closure. According to Jiryis, "It later emerged that . . . regulations had been specially drafted to allow the authorities to confiscate lands on the frontiers or the adjacent areas so that they might be sold to the Keren Kayemeth."[16] In a number of places the land just over the Green Line remained as a no-man's-land between Israel and Jordan. In the wake of the 1967 War, when this land became accessible, much of it was quickly afforested, in an effort by the government and the JNF to "create facts," thus preventing resumption of use by former landowners.[17]

Setting Jerusalem Apart in the Landscape

Prior to 1948 no significant afforestation had been carried out in Jerusalem or on the city's immediate periphery. Most of the seedlings grown in the nurseries located in the city during the Mandate had been planted in the corridor, though some had been used in the new Jewish neighborhoods. The forest planted in Deir Yassin/Givat Shaul marked the beginning of serious afforestation in Jerusalem. Following the destruction of that forest in 1956, plans were drawn up for afforestation on a much larger scale.

The man responsible for the details and implementation of the plan was Yosef Weitz of the JNF. His intention was to plant a belt of forest—a green belt—along those parts of the municipal border that were adjacent to open areas. Of course, with the city divided since the 1948 War, this meant primarily the western-facing edge of the city. Much of this area was composed of exposed stony slopes, making it a candidate for afforestation according to the normal operating criteria of the JNF. The purpose of the proposed forest, however, was the beautification of Jerusalem, the provision of an open recreational area for its residents, and the physical distinction of Jerusalem from the surrounding landscape. This final goal was an attempt to preserve and commemorate the uniqueness of Jerusalem, as perceived by those responsible for the future of the city. It was thought that the green belt would make the city stand out for anyone viewing it from the western approaches (which for Israelis was the only approach, as long as access from the other directions was controlled by Jordan). It was also felt that a green belt on the municipal periphery would prevent future expansion of built-up areas that would lead to a merging of Jerusalem with surrounding communities, thus negating the status that the city had had since biblical times as "the city that sits alone."

---

[16] Jiryis, p. 89. Jiryis bases this claim on the words of Yosef Weitz, who wrote, "We [the JNF] continued the clarification with the [ILA] legal advisor. It was agreed, that the principle is legislation that will certify the government to confiscate lands in border areas for security reasons." Yosef Weitz, *My Diaries and Letters to My Sons* (Israel: Massada, 1973), 6: 373.

[17] Weitz, *My Diaries and Letters to My Sons*, p. 258. The planting along the armistice line, both before and after the 1967 War, has led to the mistaken notion that the boundary was called the Green Line because of the forests that were planted by Israel, and that were coterminous with Israeli sovereign territory.

The idea of setting the city apart did not originate with Israeli planners, nor was it first discussed in 1956. British plans for Jerusalem had strongly favored the creation and preservation of open and green spaces in and around the city. A 1944 British plan called for the creation of a belt around the city that would, in one hemisphere, be composed of agricultural land, that being primarily the eastern side of the city. In the other hemisphere, there would be afforested land.[18]

The Western Segment of the Green Belt

The interest of the JNF in the creation of an open or agricultural area in the Jerusalem environs also predated 1956, and was prior even to the establishment of Israeli control in part of Jerusalem in 1948. The development of agricultural villages in the corridor was seen as a significant contribution to the creation of the greater Jerusalem landscape.[19] It was with the plan for the green belt, however, that the JNF gained a primary role in the creation of the landscaping of the city. The green belt planting program also served as the foundation upon which the interministerial, municipal, and JNF cooperation for projects of this type would be built. It is interesting to note the fanfare that accompanied the project of planting the green belt, and to compare this with the amount of attention given to the extension of the green belt to those areas conquered by Israel in 1967.

In 1956–57, the first planting season of the green belt, 130,000 seedlings were planted on the city's periphery. With the conclusion of the season, a ceremony was held to herald the green belt that was in progress. On that occasion Weitz said:

> The Keren Keyemet has planted many forests in the country. They already number many millions of trees, but a forest such as this has not yet been planted. The Jerusalem Forest is unlike the rest of the forests in the country, in that it is in Jerusalem. We know what the value of this forest is for us and we know what this forest needs to be if it is to be called by the name of Jerusalem.
>
> This forest will surround the city from its western approaches. It will improve and beautify its slopes and will bring splendor to the city.[20]

---

[18] Henry Kendall, *Jerusalem the City Plan 1948: Preservation and Development during the British Mandate 1918–1948* (London: His Majesty's Stationery Office, 1948); Arthur Kutcher, *The New Jerusalem: Planning and Politics* (London: Thames and Hudson, 1973), p. 50. For a discussion of London's green belt see M. J. Ferguson and R. J. C. Munton, "Informal Recreation Sites in London's Green Belt," *Area* 11, no. 3 (1979): 196-205. Louis Mumford points out that green belts were also part of the American landscape as the concept of garden communities called "green-belt towns" was briefly implemented by the U.S. Suburban Resettlement Bureau in the 1930s. Mumford, *The Culture of Cities* (New York: Harcourt Brace Jovanovich, 1970).

[19] I. A. Abbady, ed., "The Jewish National Fund and the New Jerusalem," in *Jerusalem Economy* (Jerusalem: Jerusalem Chamber of Commerce, 1950) [Hebrew].

[20] Weitz, *Forest and Afforestation in Israel*, pp. 369–370.

The second president of Israel, Yitzhak Ben-Zvi, made comments that promoted the idea of making the area bloom, which, as I indicated in the introduction, was a key theme in Zionist redemption ideology. Ben-Zvi commented that

> it is a great privilege . . . to be partners to the planting of the Jerusalem Forest. For more than seventy generations Jerusalem has been ruined and its surroundings barren with no shade and without a covering of grass. There were in this land large and powerful countries. There were the conquerors of Jerusalem the Romans and Byzantines, generations of Arabs settled here, of Mamlukes, of Crusaders. Four hundred years the Turks ruled here, more than thirty years the land was a British Mandate—a group varied from A to Z, but none of them took care of Jerusalem, to make the city and its surroundings grow, to beautify it with grass and trees. It will be a sign that since the ruin of Jerusalem and the ruin of the nation she [Jerusalem] has been waiting for the return of her sons [who will] surround Jerusalem with trees . . . and the city will rejoice and be revived.[21]

The plan called for the belt to run from Mount Herzl (site of the military and national cemeteries, with Herzl's tomb) in the southwest, through an arc that would pass north through Givat Shaul and Lifta and up to Sanhedria.[22] The land on which the belt was to grow contained 4,000 dunams that were possessed by the Land Development Authority, subordinate to the Treasury. The classification of the land, according to Weitz, was that of state land, though that of the village of Lifta must have been expropriated or it would have been under the care of the Custodian for Abandoned Property.

The land was made available to the JNF for planting under the terms of a lease issued by the Treasury. The lease stipulated that the land be afforested within a five-year period. It would then be leased for a symbolic fee to the JNF for an additional forty-nine years, with the land that remained unplanted reverting back to governmental control. Extensions were received for some of the land, and by 1966 the belt covered 3,500 dunams and contained 1,244,000 trees. Together with the six forests on the Jerusalem outskirts mentioned above, there were in this greater Jerusalem Forest a total of 12,060 dunams totaling 3.5 million trees.

Other afforestation projects in Jerusalem during this period are of interest. The earliest, also undertaken in 1956, was the planting of security groves within the city. As noted, areas of Jewish Jerusalem were vulnerable to sniper fire from the Jordanian side, and it was considered necessary to block the vision of the Jordanians, who were in some places located only a few hundred yards away from Jewish homes. For this purpose, 22,000 eucalyptus trees were planted, most of them in the area of the Mandelbaum Gate, the official crossing point between the two sides of the city. Not long after, however,

---

[21] Ibid., pp. 370–371.

[22] Givat Shaul is the site of Deir Yassin, as discussed above. Lifta was until 1948 the Arab village immediately adjacent to the city's entrance from the direction of Tel Aviv.

they were cut down, and the land used for housing immigrants in buildings designed to minimize exposure to the danger. The second project of interest is one that was never realized. In 1957, 450 dunams were prepared for planting next to the Armon HaNatziv neighborhood, adjacent to the United Nations headquarters in the city. The Jordanians protested this planting, however, and when the UN made clear their opposition, the work was halted.

Afforestation as Consolidated in the Hands of the JNF

In 1952, the government established the Afforestation Council, a coordinating body between the Forestry Division in the Ministry of Agriculture and the Forestry Division of the JNF. This body did not succeed in eliminating the overlap that occurred in the execution of tasks, despite the clear delineation of responsibilities that existed on paper. The problem became rather obvious during the planting of the green belt in Jerusalem, when government crews were working on lands falling within the area of the JNF mandate. As is the case in bureaucratic matters, the overlap generated friction rather than cooperation. Weitz, as head of the Afforestation Council, was in a strong position to forward the interests of the JNF in such issues.

In 1959, an agreement was reached whereby the Ministry of Agriculture would eliminate its Forestry Division, and, subsequently, forestry management was passed to the hands of the JNF.[23] In essence, this was the absorption of a smaller unit by a larger one. In the years between the creation of the state and the unification of the two divisions (or the elimination of one of them, depending on the point of view), the government had planted forests and other trees on 30,000 dunams of land. In that same period, the JNF had planted on 114,000 dunams.

In 1960, several additional significant legislative measures were introduced, these being the Basic Land Law of Israel, the Land Law of Israel, and the Law of the Israel Lands Authority. As part of this legislation, a covenant was signed between the JNF and the government. It entailed the creation of the ILA to manage ownership of all public lands in Israel. A second body created was the Land Development Authority (LDA), which was responsible for carrying out all the tasks of preparation and maintenance of these lands, whether for construction, preservation, or afforestation. The JNF is the principal body in the LDA.

While technically separate, these two bodies are in fact interlocking. A council existing alongside the ILA is composed of seven members appointed

---

[23] Except however on lands supervised by the Nature Reserve Authority, which is under the control of the Ministry of Agriculture. There is a long and deep-seated conflict between the JNF, which generally advocates afforesting as much land as possible, and the Nature Reserve Authority, which often argues for the maintenance of open lands free of planted forests. The law ratifying the arrangement described above was passed in 1964.

by the government and six by the JNF. Similarly, a council existing alongside the LDA is composed of seven members of the JNF and six appointed by the government.

The consolidation did not slow the pace of afforestation, but rather the opposite occurred. It is difficult to say to what degree the reorganization was responsible for the increase in the amount planted over the next ten years. During that period, with responsibility solely in the hands of the JNF, 237,000 dunams were planted, totaling 48,000,000 trees.[24]

It is clear from these figures that while Ben-Gurion's call for the afforestation of 500,000 dunams per year had not been met, the scope of planting had nonetheless increased dramatically, and attained considerable significance in the landscape. At the end of the first two decades of statehood, a total of 90,033,000 trees—over 70,000,000 of them quick-growing evergreens—had been planted throughout the country.[25]

A Shift in the Role of JNF Planting

As settlement and the development of the nation's infrastructure stabilized, the variety of needs for afforestation decreased. The massive influx of immigrants had been housed in cities, development towns, and agricultural communities, and thus the settlement role of afforestation fell by the wayside. So too did the need to provide employment and agricultural training for new immigrants. In fact, following the 1967 War and the influx of cheap Palestinian labor, the work of afforestation increasingly came to be done by Arab hands.[26]

As the amount of land covered by the forests grew, the location and purpose of planting became more selective. Ecological factors—prevention of soil erosion, improvement of hydrologic infiltration, and the stabilization of sand dunes—continued to be important, but the most pressing needs had been met early on. In light of this, the JNF was able to apply itself to afforestation intended to improve "the quality of life." This primarily meant provid-

---

[24] Weitz, *Forest and Afforestation in Israel*, p. 303.

[25] Of course not all the seedlings survive, the acceptable survival rate not falling below 50 percent and rarely rising above 85 percent. There is also a process of thinning some years after the planting in order to prevent harmful density. So, too, do trees fall victim to pests, fires, and grazing. Trees are also cut down to make way for construction and other purposes. The estimate, and it is only that, of the number of trees left standing at the end of this period is 61,615,000; see Weitz, *Forest and Afforestation in Israel*, p. 607.

[26] Eventually the JNF came to lament this fact which, though economically logical, was in sharp contradiction to the Zionist principles that the JNF continues to espouse. At the end of the 1980s the JNF issued an invitation to recently demobilized soldiers, a sector prone to high unemployment, to take part in the afforestation effort. This call was met with a moderate response. Of the eleven work crews operating in the Jerusalem area in 1990, nine were composed of Palestinians and two of demobilized soldiers.

ing forests for recreation and landscape purposes. One area of serious ecological challenge remained, that being the Negev Desert, where the JNF initiated and continues to carry out pioneering work in arid-zone afforestation, generally with great success.

Besides the mammoth task of afforestation in the desert, the JNF increasingly focused on projects in and around the country's urban population concentrations. As these centers grew, the need for the benefits that the forest provides became more pressing, and, in addition, a new role developed in the attempt to control pollution and improve air quality. A primary location of the evolving application of afforestation was in the Jerusalem area, where the JNF began to implement what was conceived of as planting for the creation of an urban park. In many respects, Jerusalem was a test case and a showcase for afforestation in urban areas. However, in light of Jerusalem's political component, urban afforestation in Jerusalem remains unique and problematic.

Forests in the West Bank, 1948–67

The forests in the West Bank had "received some protection and care between 1920 and 1947 but were devastated during the internecine turmoil of 1947–48," and in the 1950s were "in a sadly damaged and depleted condition."[27] Jordanian afforestation efforts, begun formally in 1943, tended to concentrate in the East Bank even after 1948, though efforts were made to preserve what forest and vegetation survived in the West Bank. Some of what remained may, in fact, have been in acceptable shape. Yet

> while attempts [were] being made to extend these areas, despite the best efforts of the Jordanian foresters, many of whom were in the Palestine Forest Service of Mandate times, the plantations have been exposed to considerable pressures for fuel and to heavy grazing use. Many of the natural forests have been completely cleared, or have only occasional grazed-down remnants remaining on barren slopes. Goat grazing has checked regeneration and recoppicing of established growth, and the refugees have lopped trees to excess and grubbed up low vegetation.[28]

As a result, forestland in the West Bank, rather than expanding, contracted during the period of Jordanian rule.[29] The limited scope of governmental afforestation, and its concentration in Jordan proper, is apparent from mapping of the two areas, which reveals that forest planting was carried out

---

[27] H. F. Mooney, "Southwestern Asia," in *World Geography of Forest Resources*, edited by Stephan Haden-Guest et al. (New York: Ronald Press Co., 1956), p. 436.

[28] J. V. Thirgood, *Man and the Mediterranean Forest* (London: Academic Press, 1981), p. 119.

[29] Private-sector afforestation was carried out and is still evident in the Hebron area, where large landowners were encouraged to plant forests in order to improve the soil quality of hilly areas. This work was promoted through low-interest (Jordanian) government loans, and the repayment of these loans ceased with the results of the 1967 War. One estimate places the amount of afforestation in the Hebron district carried out in this manner at roughly 20,000 dunams. Interview with Fuad Dudin, October 15, 1992.

only in the northern part of the West Bank, and even there, in no great measure.[30]

In the Jerusalem area, afforestation was limited to the area near the current settlement of Ma'aleh Adumim. Part of the work was adjacent to a forest planted by the Mandate's foresters, and the Jordanian extension still exists on the site. Though these two forests are not significant in terms of size, they occupy high ground, and stand out in contrast to the seeming barrenness of the surrounding desert. To the east of this stand, along the road to Jericho and the Jordan Valley, the Jordanians planted an additional forest, stretching for nearly a kilometer and covering a steep slope. Of that forest, however, not a single tree survived at the end of Jordanian rule, the forest having fallen to the variety of natural and human-made threats described above. Under Israeli rule, West Bank afforestation efforts have of course played a minor role compared to that in Israel, and by 1987 only 225,000 dunams supported forests in the West Bank, again, primarily in the north.[31] Thus

> today, despite the major afforestation efforts of the past fifty years, large areas of the Palestinian uplands, formerly covered either with trees or with more or less dense *maquis* and *garrigue*, still carry only sparse vegetation, with goat grazing, soil erosion, fires and past lopping and grubbing responsible for the despoliation of the original cover. In the lowlands and valleys, large-scale agricultural clearances and past intensive grazing resulted in an almost complete destruction of tree growth, except where this has been restored or protected in the Jewish settlements. Exceptions are at the isolated sites of tombs and cemeteries, and occasionally near villages.[32]

---

[30] See the United Nations Food and Agriculture Organization Mediterranean Development Project's *Jordan Country Report* (Rome, 1967), presented by Oddvar Aresvik, *The Agricultural Development of Jordan* (New York: Praeger Publishers, Praeger Special Studies in International Economics and Development, 1976), p. 177.

[31] David Kahan, *Agriculture and Water Resources in the West Bank and Gaza (1967–1987)* (Jerusalem: West Bank Data Project and *Jerusalem Post*, 1987), p. 18. A Palestinian figure puts the amount of "forests and woodland cover" at roughly 250,000 dunams as of 1992. Adnan Shuqeir, "The Role of Forests and Nature Reserves in the West Bank in Advancing Internal Tourism," *Shu'un Tanmawiyyeh* 2, no. 2 (Spring 1992), p. 23 [Arabic].

[32] Thirgood, *Man and the Mediterranean Forest*, pp. 120–121.

5

Jerusalem Divided, Jerusalem United

With the reunification of the city[1] in 1967, Jerusalem underwent massive changes in physical, economic, political, and social spheres, which have affected both the Israeli and the Palestinian populations. Beyond the impact on the inhabitants of the city itself, the reunification, and the dismantling of the Green Line, have changed the orientation of the two communities toward the city and its surroundings.

The Centrality of the City

As with the broader subject of land issues discussed in chapter 2, it is important to examine the attachment to Jerusalem professed by both sides in the conflict, as this helps to explain the significance and logic of issues and tactics in the struggle for control of the city. The issue of Jerusalem as a spiritual or political entity, which is of supreme importance to Israelis and Palestinians, relates, in fact, to a combination of the sacred and the profane. Since discussions began during the period of the Mandate concerning the internationalization of Jerusalem, on the one hand, and its division, on the other, the

---

[1] My use of the phrase "reunification of the city" relates first and foremost to a physical reality. To some, however, even qualified use of the phrase is problematic. Kerr states that "on general social and political ground, the argument on behalf of a united city is a highly specious one. The euphoric talk about 'reunification' as an inherent virtue, with its conjuring up of images of Arabs and Jews falling into one another's arms, amounts to no more than silly mysticism, unless it be a calculated manipulation of ignorance; it overlooks the elementary cleavages of identity and allegiance between the two populations." Malcom H. Kerr, "The Changing Political Status of Jerusalem," in *The Transformation of Palestine: Essays on the Origin and Development of the Arab-Israeli Conflict*, edited by Ibrahim Abu-Lughod (Evanston: Northwestern University Press, 1971), p. 370. The elementary cleavages are well noted in this research, but so too are the factors, both physical and human, which create an urban entity that is united in many ways, despite the fundamental and persistent divisions.

boundaries of the city have taken on increasing significance. The delimitation of Jerusalem is currently a subject of intense scrutiny, and yet the *concept* of Jerusalem does not necessarily relate to any of the lines previously drawn, or to those which are part of the ongoing discussion concerning the city's political control.

The concept of Jerusalem is a prime factor in Jewish and Zionist attachment to the Land of Israel, and the actions carried out there are for the realization of spiritual, cultural, and political goals. These are intertwined, such that

> Jews and other people from afar migrated to Jerusalem not because of its mundane attractions, but because of its spiritual appeal. Without that appeal and its specific national implications for Jews, modern Zionism and the establishment of the State of Israel would have been unthinkable. In particular, without it the Jewish population of Jerusalem could not have grown and developed as it actually did over the last 150 years.[2]

Jerusalem in Jewish Tradition

Jerusalem is the only city that has served as the recognized spiritual and political center for the Jewish people.[3] From the time of King David the psalm has exhorted, "Let my right hand lose its cunning, let my tongue cleave to the roof of my mouth, if I do not place Jerusalem above my chief joy."[4] Though political control of the city passed out of Jewish hands for 1,878 years, Jerusalem was never replaced as the focus of religious and national aspiration. The current political attachment to the city is rooted in Jerusalem's early history as the nation's capital, a status first held by the city in the year 1000 B.C.E. Indeed the very term "Zionism" stems from one of Jerusalem's alternate names, Zion, the name of the hill in the city on which King David is traditionally believed to be buried. In the biblical period there was a correlation between religion and politics such as is found in Islam; thus the political importance of the city is interwoven with religious significance. At the same time, however, the city functions as a modern capital irrespective of religious issues, and is treated as such by all Jews, regardless of their religious beliefs.

Jerusalem in Muslim Tradition

The basis of Islam's attachment to Jerusalem stems from the Qur'anic sura called "The Night Journey," which states, "Glory be to Him who made

---

2 U. O. Schmelz, *Modern Jerusalem's Demographic Evolution* (Jerusalem: Institute of Contemporary Jewry, Hebrew University of Jerusalem, and Jerusalem Institute for Israel Studies, 1987), p. 7.

3 Throughout the years of exile other cities served as temporary centers of Jewish life and learning. Initially these were in the Fertile Crescent, notably Babylonia and Israel, but later they were found in other continents. None of these, however, was equal in status to Jerusalem, which served as the constant standard of comparison.

4 Psalm 137.

His servants go by night from the Sacred Temple [of Mecca] to the farther Temple [of Jerusalem] whose surroundings We have blessed."[5] Though Jerusalem is not mentioned by name, the interpretation is that it is to the Temple Mount in Jerusalem that Mohammed came, and from there that he ascended to the heavens.[6] On the spot of his ascension the Dome of the Rock was constructed, and close to it stands the al Aqsa mosque, Islam's third holiest site.

In addition to the holiness that the city gained through Mohammed's miraculous journey, Muslims revere the Christian and Jewish holy sites as well,[7] at least in theory. In early Islamic times, pilgrims who were unable to make the trip to Mecca could come instead to other holy places, and Jerusalem hosted annual assemblies at the time of the Hajj.[8] Over the years Jerusalem has been attributed with a number of virtues of religious significance. Many of these would be termed local folklore by the orthodox, but whatever their origin and doctrinal purity, they are significant to Palestinians. Among these are the beliefs that those living in Jerusalem are spiritually pure, that they will live healthy lives, and that they have an assured place in heaven. These beliefs contribute to the status of Jerusalem and Jerusalemites in Palestinian life.

The Declaration of Unity and Jerusalem's Legal Status

From the inception of Jerusalem's partition in 1948, Israel had not been content with the status of the city, both in terms of its physical division and in terms of the denial of access to Jewish holy and historical sites under Jordanian control. Thus, during the period of the divided city, the legal definition of Jerusalem's boundaries, at least as far as Israel was concerned, remained somewhat fluid. The Basic Law of Jerusalem does not contain a description of the location of the city's boundaries. In fact, it refers to a "complete and united" Jerusalem, though this, too, is not defined.

In a proclamation issued by the defense minister (Ben-Gurion, who fulfilled this task in addition to serving as prime minister), the Jerusalem for which laws were being established was described as containing "the majority

---

[5] The Qur'an, sura 17, "The Night Journey." The sura doesn't specifically mention Jerusalem, though Muslim belief holds that this is the intention of the text. A polemical point made by Israel in the discussion of Jerusalem's importance to the respective religious communities is that Jerusalem is never mentioned by name in the Qur'an, whereas it appears hundreds of times in the Bible in reference to spiritual, political, and mundane matters.

[6] The Temple Mount is the site of Israel's first and second great temples, and the rock from which Mohammed is said to have ascended is held in Jewish tradition to be the stone upon which Abraham was prepared to sacrifice Isaac. It is reputed by Jews that on this same stone stood the Holy Ark in Israel's temples.

[7] Nels Johnson, *Islam and the Politics of Meaning in Palestinian Nationalism* (London: Kegan Paul International, 1982), p. 9.

[8] S. D. Goitein, *Studies in Islamic History and Institutions* (Leiden: E. J. Brill, 1968), p. 137.

of Jerusalem the city [i.e., including the sectors of the city under Jordanian control], part of its surroundings and the western approaches," all of which were depicted on a map. The map that fixed the boundaries was subject to change, however, on the authority of the minister of defense, and a new map would then be the determining item in the legal boundary of the municipality. This order allowed the Minister of Defense to change the boundaries of Jerusalem as he saw fit.[9]

In June 1967, the process of broadening a municipality—any Israeli municipality—was simplified, becoming subject only to a declaration on the part of the minister of the interior. It was this process which was employed (along with regulations for the inclusion of land within the sovereign territory of the state) to expand the Jerusalem municipality to its new size.[10] This was not, however, the final legislation relating to the status of the city.

The Drawing of the New Municipal Boundary

The expansion of the municipal boundaries of the city was designed to achieve a number of goals, all of which were intended to serve the strengthening of the Jewish presence in the city and the maintenance of Israeli control over the united capital. The placement of the new boundary line "was determined according to a strategic-demographic policy and not according to pure planning considerations. The interest of this policy was to include within the city ridges and sites which provided strategic control of the city and the roads leading to it, along with large additional territories containing a minimum Arab population."[11] The northern extension of the municipality was made to include the Atarot airfield, and the corridor leading to it was kept narrow in order to exclude a number of Palestinian villages from the area of annexation.[12]

---

[9] Justice Haim Cohen (High Court of Israel), "The Status of Jerusalem in the Law of the State of Israel," in *Twenty Years in Jerusalem 1967–1987*, edited by Yehoshua Prawer and Ora Ahimeir (Israel: Ministry of Defence and Jerusalem Institute for Israel Studies, 1988), p. 247 [Hebrew].

[10] In 1992 Jerusalem was again enlarged, this time by the addition of roughly 15,000 dunams, almost all of them west of the city. This move was made in order to provide a reserve for immediate and future growth, along the lines of the recommendations of Israel Kimche et al., *Greater Jerusalem Region: Alternative Municipal Frameworks* (Jerusalem: Jerusalem Institute for Israel Studies, 1990) [Hebrew].

[11] David Kroyanker, "The Face of the City," in *Twenty Years in Jerusalem 1967–1987*, edited by Yehoshua Prawer and Ora Ahimeir (Israel: Ministry of Defence and Jerusalem Institute for Israel Studies, 1988), p. 12 [Hebrew]. Had the expansion included only Jordanian municipal Jerusalem, the Jewish population in the new boundary would have been 81 percent. With the inclusion of the broader territory, however, the Jewish population of 267,800 constituted 73.5 percent of the city. Schmelz, p. 64.

[12] The Jordanian Jerusalem municipality had discussed the annexation of a 500-meter-wide strip, running north to the Kalandia airfield, as it was then called. Also discussed during the period of Jordanian rule was the annexation of a larger area to the north of the municipality.

The desire to ensure the unity of the city led to a plethora of plans, some of which were quite extreme. One that was universally rejected was Ben-Gurion's suggestion to tear down the wall of the Old City so that there would be no barrier between the new Jerusalem and the old, which corresponded to portions of the sectors controlled prior to 1967 by Israel and Jordan respectively. Municipal action to erase the distinction between the sectors began immediately after the conclusion of hostilities. One of the first acts was the unification of the city's waterworks, and other infrastructural linkage soon followed. Along the former dividing line thousands of land mines were dismantled, military posts were torn down, and kilometers of fence and barbed wire were removed, so that of the partition itself, little was still visible. More important, however, in terms of strategic planning priorities, was control of the enlarged municipal periphery. In pursuit of this goal, there were differences of opinion and conflicting interests between the bodies engaged in policy development and implementation.

> The municipality strove to preserve the compact character of the city and prevent the dispersion of its historical center. As opposed to this, the Ministry of Construction and Housing, which was responsible for the implementation of most of the government's planning decisions in the physical plane, strove to speed up the process of the creation of new neighborhoods. The ILA, which is the largest land owner in the city, and also plays an important role in the execution of government policy, requested more than once to build in the territories [i.e., the West Bank]."[13]

The question of core versus periphery was decided in favor of the construction of new Jewish neighborhoods, both within the expanded municipality—on land previously outside Israeli control—and beyond the municipal boundary, on land legally within the West Bank.[14] This was something of a compromise, in that it relieved pressure on the city core, while removing some of the new neighborhoods to areas beyond the existing built-up area, leaving a band of open space between them.[15] However, despite the stated importance of solidifying Jewish control of the eastern side of the city,[16] the

---

Neither of these was implemented, however. Daniel Rubenstein, "The Jerusalem Municipality under the Ottomans, British, and Jordanians," in *Jerusalem Perspectives*, edited by Peter Schneider and Geoffrey Wigoder (London: Rainbow Group, 1976), p. 93.

[13] Kroyanker, p. 13.

[14] While physically located in the West Bank, Jewish settlements there are not subject to the same legal system as Palestinian communities. This will be explained more fully below.

[15] A different interpretation of roles has been proposed, albeit with the same basic idea: "The Ministry of Housing, in order to preserve Jerusalem's historic core, is removing pressure from it by building its housing estates at a respectful distance, in Jerusalem's surrounding hills. The Municipality, with its love for the landscape, proposed a compact city with a dense core, so as to prevent the surrounding hills from being despoiled." Arthur Kutcher, *The New Jerusalem: Planning and Politics* (London: Thames and Hudson, 1973), p. 91.

[16] Jerusalem is spoken of in terms of "east," or Arab, and "west," or Jewish. Neither of these terms is entirely accurate, yet for the sake of convenience they will not be modified here. Dis-

effort to implement the policy did not begin for some time after the legal unification.

"Creating Facts" through Neighborhood Construction

The redrawing of the municipal boundary added 70,000 dunams to the
territory within the city. This was, of course, an area vastly larger than the extent of Jordanian municipal Jerusalem. Thus, in addition to including official
Jordanian Jerusalem, the expanded city included Palestinian villages and
open spaces, some of which had been classified as state land during the Jordanian regime. Also classified as state property were government and military
installations in the city and its environs.

Of the 70,000 dunams, many were private land owned by Palestinians,
either in the city, in its immediate urban neighborhoods, or in the villages.
For the most part, the land in the city has been left in the hands of its 1967
owners.[17] Nonetheless, 21,000 dunams of land were expropriated in 1967,
most of it outside the Jordanian municipal area. The intention was to construct new Jewish neighborhoods on this land, or put it to some other use, as
described in the new *Jerusalem Master Plan*,[18] which was completed in 1968.
The plan called for the implementation of what was envisaged as a three-
phase policy. First, construction was to be undertaken which would bind the
city across the no-man's-land that had previously divided it. Second, broad-
ranging construction would encircle the city from the immediate periphery.
Finally, a number of outlying settlements would be built in order to provide
control over a broader Jerusalem region.[19]

Ben-Gurion, by then in retirement, called for the immediate implementation of the first two phases of this plan (his feeling about the third
phase, inseparable from the larger issue of the future of the territories, was
more complicated). His extreme suggestion, relating to the first phase of the
policy, involved destruction rather than construction, as indicated above. He
was vehement, however, about the second phase, calling as early as June 1967
for the immediate population of the eastern side of the city with large numbers of Israelis. This was proposed in order to ensure the unity of the city—in
the physical sense—and Israeli control over it and the surrounding territory.
It was thought to be imperative that there be a Jewish population on the eastern side of the city, thus negating the possibility of a redivision along previ-

---

cussion of the "east" or "East Jerusalem" should be understood to include the sections to the immediate north and south of the Jordanian municipality in the years 1948 to1967.

[17] This does not refer to the Arab neighborhoods and villages that came under Israeli rule in
1948 and in which Jews found residence, or in which new dwellings were constructed.

[18] Hashimoni, Schwied, and Hashimoni, *Jerusalem Master Plan 1968* (Jerusalem: Municipality
of Jerusalem, 1972).

[19] Kroyanker, p. 15.

ous lines. Despite his urging, and that of others, the government dragged its feet, and in the first two years of Israeli rule in reunited Jerusalem little was done to consolidate effectively Israeli control of the land included in the new municipality.

Initially the government attempted to purchase land for the construction of Jewish housing, but this effort met with little success. For ideological as well as practical reasons, it was nearly impossible to provide, through purchase, sufficient land for the scope of building anticipated. An ILA survey indicated that only a few thousand dunams of land on the Jordanian side were owned by the state.[20] Often, this land was in locations incompatible with Israeli building needs. It was thus necessary to expropriate land, the majority of which was held by Arab owners.

The expropriation of land continued in early 1968, and in the first order a total of 3,300 dunams, not all of them held by Arabs, was taken.[21] Among the areas included in the expropriation order were the former no-man's-lands and the enclave of the Hebrew University and Hadassah Hospital on Mount Scopus.[22] Part of the area, however, was *miri* or *mewat* land that had no recent connection to Jewish ownership or use. Temporary housing was quickly established on expropriated land near the university, in the form of a small student housing complex.

In April of that same year, 760 dunams were expropriated in the area adjacent to the villages of A-Ram and Hizma for the construction of the Neve Ya'akov neighborhood, the northernmost Jewish residential sector within the expanded municipality. (The Atarot airfield, and the industrial area later constructed near it, form the northern end of the municipal territory.) The establishment of Neve Ya'akov was also a symbolic statement, in that it carried the name of a Jewish settlement that had been established nearby in 1927 on land purchased from Arab owners, and had existed there until its evacuation, with the loss of this sector to the Jordanians, in 1948. In addition to the symbolism of returning to this site, the location was also intended to create a presence that was part of the municipality, yet far from the core of Jewish residence. In keeping with Zionist ideology and experience, control of territory was fully and finally established only through settlement.

---

[20] Meron Benvenisti, *Opposite the Closed Wall: Jerusalem Divided and Jerusalem United* (Jerusalem: Weidenfeld and Nicolson, 1973), p. 289 [Hebrew].

[21] Ibid.

[22] The Hebrew University and the adjacent hospital remained under Israeli control during the period of Jordanian rule despite their location in East Jerusalem. Use of the facilities was not possible, however, as the Jordanians allowed, under UN supervision, only the maintenance of a skeleton crew for the upkeep and guarding of the buildings. An alternate campus, Givat Ram, served the university between 1948 and 1967. The move back to Mount Scopus in the wake of 1967 was highly symbolic for Israel.

The most significant of the expropriation orders came in 1970, totaling 12,300 dunams. The timing of the expropriation and the location of the sites taken were in direct response to pressure on the status of Israeli rule in East Jerusalem. Specifically, the order came as the government's answer to part of the U.S. diplomatic initiative labeled the "Rodgers Plan," after then Secretary of State William Rodgers. The Rodgers Plan came in the wake of unrest in Jerusalem which was part of the ongoing conflict between Palestinians and Israelis. It called, in part, for Jordanian participation in the administration of Jerusalem, a suggestion completely unacceptable to Israel.

The 1970 expropriation enabled the creation of the significant satellite neighborhoods of Jerusalem: Gilo, East Talpiot, Ramot, and the aforementioned Neve Ya'akov, the planned area of which was increased at this time, as was the number of residents slated for the more proximate new neighborhoods. Gilo, located on the land of the village of Sharafat (among others) anchored the city from the south, and, with its expansion over the years, formed a wedge between Jerusalem and Beit Jalla/Bethlehem. The East Talpiot neighborhood in southeast Jerusalem fell between the Arab villages of Sur Baher, Arab e-Sawachra, and Jabel Mukaber.

The Ramot neighborhood was constructed in the northwest on the land of the villages of Shu'afat, Beit Hanina, and Beit Iksa (fig. 1). Part of the area eventually included in the Ramot neighborhood was already afforested by the JNF in the immediate wake of the 1967 War, and the construction necessitated the partial clearing of that forest. Also developed during this period were the neighborhoods of French Hill and Ramat Eshkol, at the base of the northern municipal corridor. These were intended to create a continuous belt of Jewish neighborhoods, linking the pre-1967 Jewish areas and providing a corridor to the new ones. This was considered essential in light of the isolation of Mount Scopus prior to the war in 1948, a circumstance that also contributed to the fall of Neve Ya'akov.

Again, it should be noted that the land taken was not entirely in the hands of private owners, nor was all of it Arab-owned; by expropriating some Jewish-owned areas, the government was able to offset somewhat the ill will generated by its expropriation of lands owned by Arabs.[23]

In fact, the number of Jewish families forced to relocate by the expropriation was more than fifteen times greater than the number of Arab families compelled to move.[24] At the same time, Mayor Kollek's claim that

---

[23] Kroyanker, pp. 16–18. According to a former Jordanian land official responsible for the area, the land of Neve Ya'akov (and other Jewish-owned land in the West Bank) had been protected from Palestinian squatters in the hope that Palestinian land in Israel would be similarly protected. Interview with Suliman Ayoub, January 16, 1990.

[24] In either case the number was not great, being 350 and 20 families respectively. Benvenisti, *Opposite the Closed Wall*, p. 296.

housing construction occupied "no wooded land or land that was employed for agriculture" is false.[25] Evidence to the contrary can easily be found by examining the 1967 land-use map prepared for the municipality's 1968 *Jerusalem Master Plan*.[26]

Of course the issue of numbers was only one component of the larger picture, as was the type of land taken for construction. The expropriation of Jewish land did little to appease the Arabs, or, for that matter, the "international community," which had expressed its opposition to the expropriations, and in fact to the original expansion of the municipal boundary. The expression of Arab fury was limited for the most part to verbal denunciations of the Israeli acts. The former Arab mayor of the city, Ruhi el-Hatib, advocated physically blocking the bulldozers that came to clear the land, but the members of the (Palestinian) National Guidance Council refused to take steps beyond the issuance of written and verbal protests.

Despite the moderate response of the Palestinians, many Israelis were not convinced that the neighborhoods being constructed would be secure, either in the physical or political sense. Given the compact nature of Jewish Jerusalem prior to 1967, and its orientation to the west, the new areas seemed very far away from familiar territory. In order to encourage Israelis to move to these new neighborhoods it was necessary to offer special terms on prices and mortgages.[27]

Consolidating the Hold

Jerusalem can be thought of as comprising a number of more or less concentric belts. With the unification of the city, Israel began to fill in the northern gap in the circle containing the Jewish neighborhoods that formed, until then, the outer periphery of the Israeli municipality. The next belt out was composed of the neighborhoods mentioned above, Gilo, East Talpiot, Ramot, and Neve Ya'akov. Additional settlements were constructed in the West Bank to form still another belt around the city. These included Ma'aleh Adumim to the east, the Givon block to the northwest, and Efrat in the south. Smaller settlements such as Adam, Kedar, Betar, and Har Adar were sprinkled throughout this belt over the years. Each neighborhood or settlement was located in a strategic site, usually on hills dominating the main roads and

---

[25] Teddy Kollek, "Present Problems and Future Perspectives" in *Jerusalem Perspectives*, edited by Peter Schneider and Geoffrey Wigoder (London: Rainbow Group, 1976).

[26] Hashimoni, Schwied, and Hashimoni, *Jerusalem Master Plan 1968*.

[27] The advantageous terms in home purchasing are (as of June 1992) still offered by the government to those willing to live in the West Bank and Gaza, as well as in a number of Jerusalem neighborhoods, particularly Pisgat Ze'ev. It is here that the municipality has combined with the Ministry of Housing to make a major effort to draw new residents to the city, and prevent economic flight to subsidized settlements beyond the Green Line.

approaches to and from the city. An additional function of the Israeli construction was "to prevent the spread of Arab building."[28]

The primary developmental effort, however, was dedicated to the expansion of the middle belt, composed of the new neighborhoods hugging the municipal periphery. When first undertaken, these neighborhoods were small, lacked services, and were considered remote from the city center. They were perceived to be as distant as suburbs, yet without amenities that would compensate for the distance.[29] Neve Ya'akov is seven kilometers from the city center, Ramot is approximately five kilometers out, and Gilo is a relatively close four kilometers, though it is separated from Jewish neighborhoods by the Arab village of Beit Tzafafa. From Gilo most of the city is visible, thus reducing the sensation of isolation that—at least initially—dominated Ramot and Neve Ya'akov.

The growth of each of the neighborhoods has been dramatic, and for the most part it continues today at a healthy pace. Gilo currently contains some ten thousand housing units, while Ramot, East Talpiot and Neve Ya'akov also have reached several thousand units. Each one of these neighborhoods is expanding, with further growth planned for the future. In light of the housing shortage in Jerusalem, and the high price of housing stock in the older neighborhoods, there is little risk that the increase will prove superfluous.[30]

While there are definite deficiencies in each of these areas, the quality of the infrastructure developed in them in many ways surpasses that found in Jerusalem's older neighborhoods. In part, of course, this is due to the difference in age, and advances in technology and material in the intervening years. An additional factor, however, has been the disproportionate budget devoted to these projects. The commitment on the part of the government to invest significant resources in the development of the neighborhoods has allowed the creation of an infrastructure that precedes the growth of the population. This, too, is an outcome of the political nature of developing the city, as indicated below.[31]

---

[28] Kroyanker, p. 29.

[29] This is less true of East Talpiot, which, unlike the other neighborhoods mentioned, is nearly contiguous with pre-1967 Jewish neighborhoods. As a result, its actual and psychological distance is not as significant.

[30] It is interesting to note, however, that while Jerusalem's share of new immigrants was 50 percent throughout the 1980s, fewer than 15 percent of the Russian immigrants of 1989–90 have chosen to settle in the capital. The municipality and the Housing Ministry are trying to rectify this situation, primarily through methods mentioned in note 26, above.

[31] At the same time mention should be made of the problems involved in rapid neighborhood development in the newest areas of Jerusalem, particularly the area of Pisgat Ze'ev East. Infrastructure and basic services were still not provided long after new-home buyers were to have moved into the area. Under Arik Sharon the Housing Ministry contracted for building on as

The most recent focus of growth in Jerusalem, however, has been the neighborhood of Pisgat Ze'ev, located between Neve Ya'akov and French Hill. The neighborhood's function is to help fill in the area between these two earlier neighborhoods, thus contributing to a continuous area of Jewish residence on the eastern side of Jerusalem's northern strip.

Initially the orientation of the Pisgat Ze'ev neighborhood was west-east, running from near the main Ramallah road eastward in the direction of the village of Hizma, which is outside the municipal line. In recent years, however, Pisgat Ze'ev has been expanding rapidly to the south, in part on expropriated land. It is this neighborhood which is closing in on King Hussein's palace, as discussed below.

While the expansion to the south helps to continue the area of Jewish residence, it is unlikely that the link can ever be complete. Between French Hill and Pisgat Ze'ev there is a Palestinian refugee camp, Shu'afat.[32] For political reasons the camp cannot be moved, and because it is a focal point of political violence, the land surrounding it is of dubious worth in Israeli planning schemes.[33]

Jerusalem's Arab Sector under Jordanian Rule

With the cessation of hostilities in 1948, Jordan gained control of East Jerusalem and the approaches to the city from all directions but the west. The inclusion of the Palestinians of the West Bank and Jerusalem in the Hashemite Kingdom, along with many refugees from inside the Green Line, threatened the social and demographic character of the state. The Emir Abdullah,

---

much land as possible, in the shortest time possible, with consumer and quality issues sacrificed on the alter of politically motivated construction.

[32] This camp, within the municipal boundary, is the only refugee camp within Israel. It was created in 1965 by the Jordanians, who transferred its residents from the Jewish Quarter of the Old City, where they had squatted since the Jews were driven out in 1948. Municipal plans to rehabilitate the camp have been resisted for political reasons by both the United Nations and the PLO, as well as by camp residents themselves who are suspicious of Israel's intentions. Recently proposals have been made to construct housing for the Arab community on lands close to the camp. This plan too has aroused controversy and suspicion. As for the continuous strip of settlement, under the auspices of Ariel Sharon, former housing minister and thus responsible for the ILA, there had been discussion of building from Pisgat Ze'ev to the east, then turning south to link with Ma'aleh Adumim. Owing to opposition to construction in the West Bank at that time, the scheme was not carried out. Also in question are plans to fill in the space between Pisgat Ze'ev and Hizma with temporary housing for immigrants. As work began to prepare this area, residents of Pisgat Ze'ev protested, objecting to expansion that would lead to a common border with the village of Hizma. In light of this opposition, the plans to settle the intermediate zone have been frozen.

[33] Since these lines were written the expansion of Pisgat Ze'ev to the south and east has continued unabated, and has even accelerated. Thus, the distance between Pisgat Ze'ev and the Shu'afat camp has become minimal, and it is now possible to see a future linkage between the Pisgat Ze'ev and Tzameret HaBirah neighborhoods, bracketing the camp and providing the continual Jewish residential strip sought by the government.

and later his grandson Hussein,[34] sought to counter the addition of a large number of Palestinians in ways that had direct impact on Jerusalem and its population.

> Jordanian rule over Jerusalem and over the whole of the Western bank, started off with mistrust and heavy suspicions on the part of the Palestinians, who were convinced that Abdullah was ready to betray them and that he had not used his full military capacity in the defence of the Arab parts of Palestine.[35] Ever since then, all of the authorities' steps were watched with suspicion and criticism, and everything was looked upon as intentional and deliberate discrimination, whether or not there was ground for these accusations.
>
> The Jerusalemites' claims concentrated on the economic situation. Jerusalem's economic situation was precarious, owing to the war of 1948. In the days of the Mandate, the economic basis of the city was founded on the presence of the staff of the central government. . . . Since Amman was the capital, there was no way of preventing the transfer of the central government offices there and so Jerusalem was emptied of the chief offices that had been located there.[36]

The transfer of government offices from Jerusalem to Amman was more than just an economic issue. For the Jerusalemites, and indeed for Palestinian society, it was insulting to have Jerusalem subordinate to Amman. Compounding the insult was the tangible injury that accompanied Jordanian rule, both economic as suggested above, and in terms of personal liberties and political expression.

In light of the inclination of the king to strengthen the Hashemite identity and weaken Palestinian nationalist sentiment, the East Bank (that is, Jordan proper) was given priority over the West Bank throughout this period. This meant that support for development was lacking in Jerusalem, which came to rely primarily on the tourist industry, as opposed to the governmental, service, and market roles it had held before the city's partition.

Owing to these issues, and others, there was a measure of opposition among Palestinians to Jordanian rule and policy.[37] What political culture was

---

[34] Abdullah, emir of Jordan, was assassinated on the Temple Mount in Jerusalem in 1951. His killers were Palestinians. Among the suggested motivations for the murder are the emir's supposed negotiations with Israel, and the establishment of Jordanian rather than Palestinian rule in the West Bank. In 1952 Hussein, Abdullah's grandson, replaced his father, who was unfit to rule. Palestinians in the area of Hashemite rule outnumbered non-Palestinians at that time by nearly two to one.

[35] On this point see Avi Shlaim, *Collusion across the Jordan: King Abdullah, The Zionist Movement, and the Partition of Palestine* (Oxford: Clarendon Press, 1988). Shlaim's conclusions support some of the Palestinian charges.

[36] Naim Sofer, "The Political Status of Jerusalem in the Hashemite Kingdom of Jordan, 1948–1967," *Middle Eastern Studies* 12, no. 1 (1976): 79.

[37] Jordan was ruthless in putting down efforts of protest, and strictly limited political organization; thus it is difficult to gauge the true depth of Palestinian opposition. While today many political and economic links continue between Palestinians and Jordan, Jordanian rule in Jerusalem is not missed.

was able to develop under Jordanian rule, however, did find its focus among the Jerusalem social and intellectual elite. "It was among them that antagonism arose towards the undemocratic ways of the government, towards the limitations on the freedom of expression and of organization, and towards the concentration of government in the hands of the Transjordanians, whom they considered to be their inferiors."[38]

The opposition was not limited to the elite, however, and East Jerusalem was rocked by riots on a number of occasions in the 1950s and early 1960s. The bloodshed in these events further embittered the Palestinians, and gave emphasis to their aspirations concerning the city. One of these was that Jerusalem be made the capital of the Hashemite Kingdom, and, barring that, be recognized as a "secondary capital," or at least as the "spiritual center."

One catalyst for the Palestinian demand that the authorities in Amman upgrade the status of Jerusalem was the transfer in 1953 of the Israeli Foreign Ministry to the Jewish-controlled portion of the city. In being presented as a response to the move of that ministry from Tel Aviv, "the demand [to bring such bodies to Jerusalem] was camouflaged as an anti-Israel step and not as a Palestinian demand, directed against the Jordanian rulers."[39]

Most of the Palestinian hopes for the city were not met. After more than ten years of Jordanian rule, however, some of the slogans concerning Jerusalem's spiritual and political roles were adopted by the government. "This acceptance came about as a result of outside pressures that threatened the standing of Jordan on the West Bank. In fact, these proclamations were not accompanied by any action."[40] Symbolic of the Jordanian period in Jerusalem is the sight of King Hussein's western palace, located on a hilltop in Beit Hanina, which prior to 1967 was not in municipal Jerusalem. Plans were repeatedly presented for the inclusion of this and other areas within an expanded municipal boundary, but throughout the period of Jordanian rule no substantive action was taken.[41] Begun in 1963, Hussein's palace was never completed, and its skeleton is today guarded by Israeli troops to prevent it from falling prey to Palestinian vandals.[42]

---

[38] Sofer, p. 81. In fact, the first and third of these complaints are linked, and were the primary cause of Palestinian discontent during this period. The pie was divided in favor of the Jordanians, and within Palestinian society Jerusalemites had previously been accustomed to a proportionately exaggerated share of status and power.

[39] Ibid., p. 85. Because of conditions during the 1948 War a number of Israeli governmental bodies had been moved to or established in Tel Aviv. Their location there, however, was always considered temporary. The one exception was the headquarters of the army and the Defense Ministry, which, for security reasons, remain in Tel Aviv.

[40] Ibid., p. 86.

[41] Rubenstein, p. 93.

[42] Also symbolic is that in recent years the Jewish neighborhood of Pisgat Ze'ev has steadily encroached on the palace, which used to stand in relative isolation. Today the neighborhood is

Jerusalem's Arab Sector under Israeli Rule

Changes in the physical elements of Jerusalem's Arab sector in the wake of the 1967 War have also been heavily influenced by political factors. An immediate distinction was made between "Jerusalem Arabs" and "West Bank Palestinians" with the expansion of the municipal boundary. Those Arab residents of expanded Jerusalem who were present at the time of the census, conducted after the city boundaries were changed, were given an option in regard to citizenship. Those who wanted Israeli citizenship could accept it, at the cost of forfeiture of their Jordanian citizenship.[43]

While few Palestinians accepted this offer, and of the few who did, many later renounced it, the status of Jerusalem Palestinians was, nonetheless, changed by the state.[44] While not considered citizens of Israel, on the basis of their refusal of the offer, they have voting rights in Jerusalem municipal elections and are legally permanent residents of the state. As such, they are subject to a number of rights and obligations that do not pertain to West Bank or Gaza Palestinians. Two visible factors distinguish Jerusalemites from those in the territories: on the one hand, Jerusalemites carry the blue identification cards of Israel, while those of the territories carry orange cards. This is increasingly significant, as a blue card allows unrestricted access to the area within the Green Line, while those with orange cards are, during periods of particular tension, prevented from crossing that line, and are also occasionally prohibited from entering Jerusalem.

On the other hand, a disadvantage to being a Jerusalem resident is that vehicles owned by those living in the territories bear blue license plates, while Jerusalemites and Israelis have yellow license plates. Cars with yellow plates are targets of violence in the West Bank and Gaza, particularly since the outbreak of the Intifada. More than one Palestinian has been killed as a result of violence directed at an "Israeli" vehicle. The practical outcome is that Palestinians who have cars registered in Jerusalem are deprived of secure travel in the West Bank and Gaza. While Israelis share this handicap, the Palestinians are more hindered by it, in that the lack of access to these areas is a

---

closing in on it from different directions and expanding up the hill on which it sits. Palestinians are thought to be interested in vandalizing the structure as an expression of the anti-Hashemite sentiment felt by many in the nationalist camp.

[43] West Bank Palestinians had been made Jordanian citizens with the annexation of the West Bank by Jordan in 1950. Though that annexation was recognized only by Britain and Pakistan, the extension of citizenship was accepted by the Palestinians and not contested abroad. In addition to forfeiture of Jordanian citizenship, acceptance of Israeli citizenship carried with it the risk of classification in the Palestinian community as a traitor. An additional issue was that a Jordanian passport allowed travel in the Arab world, while an Israeli passport bearer was denied entry into Arab countries, with the exception today of Egypt and sometimes Morocco.

[44] Approximately 1,500 Palestinian residents of Jerusalem currently hold Israeli citizenship, roughly 1 percent of the Palestinian population of the city. Ha'Aretz, July 9, 1992.

proportionately more significant deprivation than for Israelis, whose common milieu is within the Green Line.

Palestinians living in Jerusalem are linked with Israeli bureaucracy in a number of ways. The most advantageous aspect of the linkage is that they are entitled to the benefits of the Israeli medical and national insurance system, which includes old-age, unemployment, and welfare payments.[45] On the negative side, Jerusalem residents are subject to strict taxation on everything from income to television sets, to the same degree as the Israeli population.[46] West Bankers and Gaza residents are taxed only sporadically, and prior to the Intifada, enforcement was quite lax. Given the steep rate of taxation in Israel, the advantages of the bureaucracy listed above are sometimes offset and even outweighed by this burden.

Despite this, Jerusalem residence is considered desirable by Palestinians, and the benefits of the system are zealously guarded.[47] One such benefit is that Jerusalemites are protected to some measure from the effects of the Intifada. Others are that students in the Jerusalem municipality have been largely spared the extended school closures common in the West Bank, and curfews in the Palestinian neighborhoods and villages within the municipal boundary have been used much more sparingly than in the territories. For a variety of reasons, there have also been far fewer casualties proportionately in Jerusalem than elsewhere.[48]

Though the advantages to living in the city are considerable, many Palestinians who wish to do so are unable to. The right to reside in the city is officially restricted to the 65,857 Palestinians who were present during the first

---

[45] Thus if the property of a Jerusalem Palestinian is damaged by an act of the Intifada, or of an antistate terrorist nature, the owner will—in theory—be compensated by the state for the damage. If a resident is injured or killed in an attack, medical bills and a pension will be provided by the state. Currently a number of Knesset members are attempting to extend the same privileges to Palestinians affected by Jewish terrorist acts. None of these conditions apply to non-Jewish residents of the territories.

[46] To the same degree, that is, in terms of the rate of taxation. However tax collection is currently being used as a form of collective punishment in East Jerusalem. Thus, when Jerusalem neighborhoods and villages are put under curfew in the wake of Intifada disturbances, the tax collectors descend on the area with a harsh campaign of fines and confiscations. Tax delinquency has long been an issue in these same areas.

[47] National Insurance officials complain that those leaving Jerusalem fail to report their change of address in order to maintain the benefits they receive. They also claim that deaths are frequently unreported so that pensions will continue. The expense for burial in the case of deaths that are reported, however, is covered by the national insurance.

[48] Owing to its location within the Green Line, Jerusalem is for the most part under the authority of the Israeli police rather than the army, though there is some overlap. The orders and tactics for dealing with acts of the Intifada within the city are designed to minimize the number of serious injuries. With the change in police department personnel following violence on the Temple Mount in October 1990, a new "aggressive" policy, employing more frequent curfews, is being implemented.

Israeli census following the expansion in 1967, and their offspring.[49] In part this limitation is justified by the government on the basis of the services that residence confers, as described above. In fact, the primary motivation for restricting free access to the city for Palestinians is the desire to maintain a Jewish majority in the city, which in 1967 stood at 73 percent versus 27 percent Arab.[50] As indicated, part of this effort involves the preservation of land for Jewish building, with the accompanying restriction on Arab growth.

The tremendous growth in the Palestinian community, both within and outside the municipality, has led to problems of density and a lack of adequate housing. A primary consequence of this has been the rapid increase in the population and size of the towns and villages in the West Bank which are close to the city, as well as unofficial growth within the municipal boundaries.[51] For the most part, this process has not benefited from any form of local or regional planning. Indeed, through the 1970s and 1980s much of the official involvement in Arab development came in the form of hindrance rather than assistance.[52]

In the absence of formal planning and supervision, Palestinians constructed homes, without obtaining permits, in places most convenient to them.[53] In the outer neighborhoods and villages, this meant at the periphery of the residential core, that is, on the edge of agricultural land, and alongside roadways. Such growth particularly cluttered the strip along the road from Jerusalem to Ramallah, as well as along the road from Jerusalem to Jericho. Expansion was significant in all but a few of the villages in the region, generally spreading in the direction of the city.[54]

---

[49] Appeals for Palestinians to rejoin their families in Jerusalem are often granted on the basis of family reunification if their residence was in the city prior to the war.

[50] Ori Stendal, "Changes in the Arab Population," in *Twenty Years in Jerusalem 1967–1987*, edited by Yehoshua Prawer and Ora Ahimeir (Israel: Ministry of Defence and the Jerusalem Institute for Israel Studies, 1988), p. 112 [Hebrew]. See also Schmelz; and the *Statistical Yearbook of Jerusalem* (Jerusalem: Jerusalem Institute for Israel Studies and the Municipality of Jerusalem, 1992.)

[51] Adding to the Palestinian population of Jerusalem is unauthorized in-migration from the West Bank. There are no firm numbers for the size of this migration, and estimates range from 10,000 to as high as 80,000 Palestinians. Similarly, there is a range of estimates for the number of legal Palestinian Jerusalemites who have had to leave the city for the surrounding area in order to find adequate housing.

[52] Shaul Ephraim Cohen, "West Bank Village Planning," March 1992, Manuscript.

[53] The issue of construction permits has been discussed elsewhere. It is somewhat easier in Jerusalem than in the West Bank to get a building permit, though the process is difficult in either case. Shaul Ephraim Cohen, "Political Factors in the Determination of Jerusalem's Territorial Framework," in *Politics and Society in Jerusalem*, edited by Ifrach Zilberman (Jerusalem: Jerusalem Institute for Israel Studies, in press).

[54] The few cases in which villages grew at a slower pace are related to one of two factors. For some the village is located such that access to the city is particularly difficult. For others, such

While housing expanded at the expense of agricultural land, another factor contributed to a decline in the importance of farming in the Palestinian villages within and around Jerusalem. The access to wage employment in Jerusalem and other areas within the Green Line drew huge numbers of Palestinian youth away from their traditional occupation in agriculture. This pattern had existed in the Jerusalem area prior to 1967 as well, but, owing to the limited opportunities afforded by the economic situation in Jordanian Jerusalem, with much less impact. The increased opportunities and greater wages earned in the Israeli marketplace stimulated in turn the building of housing in the Palestinian sector. Because of both the greater income and the societal changes that came in the wake of 1967, Palestinian housing style itself changed.

Rather than add additional rooms or units onto an existing family structure composed around an enclosed courtyard, Palestinians increasingly built independent, detached, single-family housing. This change contributed to the expansion beyond the traditional village core. That this came at the expense of agricultural land was deemed less significant in light of the decreased importance of agriculture in family subsistence, a result again of the wage income earned primarily across the Green Line.

Another factor allowing and encouraging the shift to single-family housing was the assistance offered to those building by outside sources who wished to encourage the Palestinians to remain in the area, rather than go abroad.[55] In this respect, Palestinian building is no less political than Israeli construction. Indeed, in some cases, dwellings are constructed in order to take advantage of the financial aid and to maintain possession of the land, even though the family is not yet in need of the living space. Such buildings, usually with the frame completed but the interior as yet unfinished, can be seen on the Jerusalem periphery and throughout the West Bank.

The Decrease in Jerusalem's Open Spaces

The construction described in the above sections contributed to a decrease in the open areas in and around Jerusalem. In addition to creating a shortage of future building sites, it also decreases the availability of open and recreational spaces. The seriousness of this problem is better appreciated in

---

a high percentage of the young men have left the village for work abroad that there is little change or even some decrease in the population. A study conducted of changes in the Jerusalem region (though not including the area within the Jerusalem municipal boundary) showed that the built-up area increased by 119 percent in the years 1967–84. Israel Kimche et al., *Arab Settlement in the Metropolitan Region of Jerusalem* (Jerusalem: Jerusalem Institute for Israel Studies, no. 16, 1986), p. 65 [Hebrew].

[55] This funding, furnished by or at least channeled through the PLO and Jordan, ranged between $17,000 and $25,000. It was given with terms for repayment, but often these were forgiven.

the light of traditional concern for Jerusalem's lack of open area, a problem addressed as early as the Mandate period.[56]

The British implemented a policy that for the most part has been followed to this day, at least in those areas under Israeli control, of attempting to preserve open spaces in close proximity to residential areas. The British design was to construct housing on the upper portion of slopes and along the crests of Jerusalem's hills and ridges, while the valleys, wadis, and lower portions of the slopes would be preserved as open public areas.[57] Despite this,

> according to generally recognized international standards, Jerusalem has less than half of the parkland and open space required for a city of her population. The amount of open space in Jerusalem which has actually been made into parkland is extremely small, representing about one tenth of her needs. Although the city is growing rapidly, no coordinated policy to expand her parkland correspondingly has been developed.[58]

Because of the lack of land in the city itself, much of the expansion or formalization of open space is taking place on the outskirts of the city. In that location it fulfills a multifunctional task. In terms of the political context of this open land, the planting of trees in a belt around the municipal periphery plays a central role. "The importance of this belt is the boundary demarcation of the city and the prevention of the spill-over of the peripheral neighborhoods to the center, and the opposite."[59] In fact, the creation of a green belt around the extended municipal periphery was contained in the city's municipal master plan of 1968, which called for "a clearly defined edge, surrounded by a green belt of open space" for the purposes listed above, along with a variety of recreational and other functions.[60] One function of the green belt was clearly to assist in the domination of unused land, some of which was to remain as open space, but much of which was destined for future Israeli construction needs.

---

[56] Henry Kendall, *Jerusalem the City Plan 1948: Preservation and Development during the British Mandate 1918–1948* (London: His Majesty's Stationery Office, 1948).

[57] Kroyanker, p. 59.

[58] Kutcher, p. 94.

[59] Kroyanker, p. 59.

[60] Kutcher, p. 54.

6

Land Law, Policy, and Practice in the West Bank

In addition to the differences between the West Bankers and Jerusalemites as a result of the citizenship factor discussed in chapter 5, there are a host of ramifications for land issues stemming from the legal status of the West Bank, as opposed to that of Israel. In order to comprehend the way in which landownership, possession, and control are carried out, we need to understand the legal system pertaining to the West Bank.

In light of its presence as a belligerent occupant in the West Bank, Israel cannot apply its law to the citizens of the occupied territories.[1] Indeed the

---

[1] The Palestinians, that is, who hold Jordanian citizenship. Officially Israel does not view itself as a belligerent occupier, in that it views the territories as "disputed" and not "occupied." Nor does it view Jordan as the sovereign of the area. Thus many elements of international law that would apply were Israel the temporary ruler of the territory are not acknowledged as relevant. Nonetheless, the Israeli judicial system has chosen to be guided by the Hague Conventions for occupied lands which read in part, "The occupying state shall be regarded only as administrator and usufructuary of public buildings, real estate, forests and agricultural estates belonging to the hostile state and situated in the occupied territory" (Hague Convention, article 55). A common legal interpretation holds that "not merely does the occupant have a right to take possession of government property and enjoy its usufruct, but it has a duty so to do in order to safeguard the property, as provided in article 55." Israel National Section of the Commission of International Jurists, *The Rule of Law in the Areas Administered by Israel* (Tel Aviv: 1981), pp. 43–44.

An exception to this is the application of Israeli law to Jewish settlers in the territories, who remain full citizens of Israel despite their residence beyond the Green Line. For information on the juridical status of the West Bank according to Israel and others, see Allan Gerson, *Israel, the West Bank, and International Law* (London: Frank Cass, 1978); Israel National Section of the International Commission of Jurists, *Rule of Law*; Moshe Drori, "The Israeli Settlements in Judea and Samaria: Some Legal Aspects," in *Judea, Samaria, and Gaza: Views on the Present and Future*, edited by Daniel E. Elazar (Washington: American Enterprise Institute for Public Policy Research, 1982).

most recent internationally recognized sovereign law in the West Bank is that of the Ottoman Empire. The British Mandatory authorities amended Ottoman law in accordance with the needs of the local population, for whose welfare they were responsible. Jordan's annexation of the West Bank made the situation somewhat more complicated. While to some extent Jordanian law was applied to the West Bank, the Ottoman and British regulations remained largely intact, and the spirit of the land law was for the most part unaffected. And, as has been noted, only Britain and Pakistan recognized the Jordanian annexation of the West Bank; thus the status and legality of Jordanian legislation for the area are debatable.

Israel, as an occupying power, is for its part, enjoined to restore order, maintain the welfare of the indigenous population, and uphold the law, affecting the status quo only as necessary until the occupation is concluded and the area handed back to the previous ruler.[2] Thus Israel creates new regulations in the form of military edicts, ostensibly for the welfare of the local population, although it would be difficult to interpret them as being designed to facilitate handing back the area. An important difference from the Jordanians, who claimed sovereignty over the area, is that Israel is also afforded (as were the British during the Mandate) broad power to enact legislation deemed necessary for its security interests, *as determined by Israel.*

The most significant feature of Israel's rule in the West Bank is that, as successor to the Jordanians, Israel is the custodian of all property belonging to the previous government.[3] It should be recalled that, under the Ottoman land system, this could be interpreted as giving Israel control of nearly all the land in the West Bank, with the exception of *mulk* and *waqf* lands. Though Israeli policy in this matter has evolved over the years, it now holds that all land categorized as *matruka* or *miri* for which claimants lack sufficient proof of possession, again, as determined by Israel, will be considered state land.[4] The ramifications of this policy are enormous.

Land Registration under the Jordanians

During the period of Jordanian rule, land regulation in the West Bank was a much more relaxed affair than during both the preceding and subse-

---

[2] Drori, p. 49.

[3] Those who contend that Israel is not occupier, but sovereign, see the Israeli government not as custodian, but rather as owner of this land.

[4] "Although, according to the Ottoman Land Code, there was no category of public or state land, the British Mandate government introduced this category through the 1922 Order-in-Council. Article 2 of the Order-in-Council defined 'public lands' as 'all lands in Palestine which are subject to the control of the government of Palestine by virtue of Treaty, Convention, Agreement or Succession and all lands which are or shall be acquired for the public service or otherwise." Cited in Raja Shehadeh, "Some Legal Aspects of Israeli Land Policy in the Occupied Territories," *Arab Studies Quarterly* 7, nos. 2–3 (1985): 45.

quent periods. To begin with, *miri* land was considered by the Jordanian government to be no different than *mulk*, which is to say that most of the land worked in the West Bank, for which taxes were paid, was akin to private land.[5] In addition, the process of registering land in the official books was simpler than during either the Ottoman or British period. Beginning in the north, land surveying was conducted in the West Bank by the Jordanians under the auspices of the "Settlement of Disputes over Land and Water Law." By 1967 much of the hill area north of Jerusalem had been surveyed and registered, while south of that line almost none of the land had been surveyed or registered in the landholding books (*Tabu*). The total registered was about one-third of the land in the West Bank.[6]

Even those areas that were surveyed remained in a state of documentary disorder, at least by Western standards. In large part, this was because the Jordanian officials were familiar with the villages, and owing to the resulting informality, their system of registration rarely included careful mapping or field inspection. Rather, the official would meet with the village mukhtar and gather from him the pertinent information. This was usually inexact at best, and to those not from the village or unfamiliar with its lands, often entirely obscure.[7] In general the claims presented would be verbal, that is, the mukhtar would report who owned what, and where. For the Jerusalem area, much of the existing documentation was destroyed in a fire in 1948; thus the weight of verbal claims was even greater. Only in the case of dispute was documentation required. Barring that, however, the confirmation of the mukhtar was deemed sufficient.[8]

Once the land claim had been filed, the information was sent to Amman. From there, five copies of the registration were issued. One went to newspapers in the town or city nearest the village, one went to the village mukhtar, one was posted in the village mosque, and two remained with the government in Amman. If no objections were forthcoming within one month, the land was entered in the books as owned by the individual who had filed the claim.[9] A map was included along with this registration, but generally it was in crude form, usually merely the product of the official's visit with the mukhtar. The mukhtar was the conduit for all transactions

---

[5] See Jordanian law 41, "Law to Transfer Land from Miri to Mulk," *Official Gazette*, February 16, 1953, and law 49, "Law Concerning the Use of Real Property," *Official Gazette*, March 1, 1953.

[6] Shehadeh, p. 43.

[7] Interview with Suliman Ayoub, Jordanian land official for Jerusalem and northern West Bank, January 16, 1990.

[8] In the case of dispute, documents were often of little assistance, owing to the lack of clarity discussed above. Thus, evidence was often gathered and decisions made based on the testimony of village neighbors as to the ownership and location of disputed plots.

[9] Interview with Reuven Halima, Israeli land official for East Jerusalem, January 22, 1990.

with the government, and in many cases copies of the map and registration never reached the individual owners.

The Jordanian period was thus marked by an attempt to organize land-holding, but in a style that was almost casual in its nature. That is not to suggest that a bureaucracy did not exist, or that little energy was expended in the pursuance of land matters. The attitude of the Jordanians was, however, that if taxes were paid and disputes settled, there were no problems. Aspects such as underreporting of holdings, confusion in terms of locations and divisions, transfers of ownership, and determination of land categories—with all that these implied—simply were not major issues. Though the Jordanian land law stated that "any right in any land or water which is not proven by any claimant shall be registered in the name of the treasury,"[10] this article was rarely applied. Thus, much of the land of the West Bank remained unregistered, and as a result, largely undisputed.[11]

Changes in the West Bank Land Regime under Israeli Rule

Though declaration of an area as state land has been the primary Israeli method of preventing Palestinian use, a number of other significant tools exist for this purpose. Not all the methods are relevant to this study, but I shall describe a number of types of restrictions and seizures that occur in the research area. Their relevance is due to the variety of legal measures with which the Palestinians have to contend, the range of tools available to the state, and the types of land reclassification that, at times, lead to afforestation by the JNF.

In the immediate aftermath of the 1967 War, the Israeli army made an effort to secure any documentation relating to the Jordanian administration of West Bank affairs. Land documents were collected from mosques and other places, and the remaining files of the land settlement offices were taken, though a great deal of material had been hurriedly transferred to Jordan. In December 1968, an Israeli military regulation essentially eliminated the land registration process, which, in any case, had been frozen since the termination of Jordanian rule.[12] As a result, nearly two-thirds of the land in the West

---

[10] Shehadeh, p. 46, citing "Settlement of Disputes over Land and Water," article 8(3).

[11] Undisputed at least in terms of government involvement. Jordan, like most states, had a mechanism for expropriating land for public purposes, and this serves as the legal basis for Israeli expropriations of this kind. During the Jordanian period land was expropriated primarily for public works projects and military needs. Currently most of the Palestinians in the area of this research rarely express the same degree of opposition to the Jordanian expropriations as to the Israeli actions. Disputes among villagers were common and vigorous, however. Many of these were solved within the context of the family or the village, and thus did not entail a governmental role and, at times, even prevented it.

[12] Israel Defense Force, Military Order 291, "Order Concerning Settlement of Disputes over Land and Water."

Bank remained in a state of limbo, not registered in the landholding books of the Jordanians.

Some of this land was documented in British tax registers, and some in Ottoman land books, though the problems of location and inexactitude existed in these documents as well. An additional factor complicating land issues was that, during the 1967 War, a wave of refugees left the West Bank for Jordan. Their land was therefore placed under the supervision of the Custodian for Abandoned Property, an office similar to the office of that name within Israel, which in the West Bank is a department of the ILA.

With many landowners absent, the problem of proving ownership became even more difficult, in that some refugees had taken documents with them when they fled. Others had taken with them personal knowledge, and were no longer available for testimony. This became particularly important when the Israeli government decided to increase its efforts to identify as much land as possible for inclusion in the category of state land. To this end, a survey was conducted of land registration in the West Bank. The survey indicated that "the majority of land in the West Bank was not registered and fell into the categories of *miri*, *matruka*, and *mewat* lands. In 1980, the government decided to consider all unregistered lands falling into one of these categories to be State land."[13]

In fact, according to the Ottoman Land Code, all these categories were, in one form or another, the property of the state. As has been related, however, *miri* land had increasingly been treated by the administrations prior to Israeli rule as basically indistinguishable from *mulk*, or private land. Further, the villagers had become accustomed to using the *mewat* and some of the *matruka* land in the village environs without government opposition, so they considered it their own. The underlying Palestinian attitude concerning all land in the West Bank is that it belongs to Palestinians, either individually or in corporate.

Since 1977 (the inauguration of the Begin government), the official attitude of the Israeli government concerning landownership in the West Bank has been quite different from that of the Palestinians. According to the government's view, all land is state land unless it can be proven otherwise, and the burden of proof is wholly on the civilian claimant. The burden of proof in these cases is quite rigid and demanding. In the case of an appeal of a declaration of state land, the appellant is compelled to use a lawyer, provide maps and documents, and secure the cooperation of his neighbors and mukhtar. The first two of these are cost-prohibitive for most villagers, even if they are feasible in other respects, which is rarely the case. The survey maps demanded by the authorities can themselves cost more than the annual income

[13] Shehadeh, p. 50.

of a Palestinian farmer. Palestinian lawyers, who prefer not to take on land cases, also charge high fees.[14]

In cases wherein the documentation supports the claim of ownership but is not in the form of a *Tabu* deed, or is in some way insufficient to confirm the claim, a further test imposed by the government is continuous cultivation of the land in the period of ten years prior to the filing of the claim. Of course in the agricultural conditions described above, particularly in relation to rainfall, it is quite common that in any ten-year period there would be years in which the land was not worked. It is also common in agriculture to let the land lie fallow on a periodic basis, and this enters into the question of "continuous cultivation" with varying outcomes. For the clarification of this issue, the government employs aerial photographs and commercial records. The Palestinians can produce receipts for their crops, if any exist, and, as with the issue of ownership and boundaries, the testimony of neighbors.

The factor of cooperation of neighbors and the mukhtar is, at times, problematic. The signature of a neighbor can be secured only if there is agreement over the boundaries of the land in question. Given the vague nature of such delineations, this is often not a simple matter. It also presumes the presence of the neighbors in question, and frequently this is not the case. And, as I indicated in the introduction, land is a particularly sensitive issue in the West Bank, one that often creates a spirit that is anything but cooperative. When there is a dispute between neighbors, or between a villager and his mukhtar, signatures can be hard to come by.[15] On the other hand, when signatures are presented, accusations of forgery and counterfeit are commonly exchanged by both the authorities and the villagers, depending on which way the case is going.

Other Forms of Land Alienation

A number of restrictions in the area of Jerusalem (and elsewhere in the territories) limit Palestinian land use, while not changing its ownership. Those that are related to security issues prevent construction in or entrance to specific areas. The first of these gives the military command the right to prohibit any new construction within a two-hundred-meter strip bracketing

---

[14] Palestinian lawyers prefer to avoid taking land cases because of the length of time they demand, the difficulty in preparation, and the low chance of success. Legal aid groups take up some of the cases, but many are left without representation because of inability to provide the fee. Even when the case involves a number of individuals who can share expenses, many cannot come up with the necessary sum, or, perceiving it as a lost cause, prefer to save their money. Interviews with Mona Rashmawi, former director of Al-Haq, Law in the Service of Man, August 6, 1990; interview with Abdallah Hassan el-Halabi, January 10, 1990.

[15] It is not necessary to discuss the function and nature of the mukhtar in Palestinian villages, but it should be noted that oftentimes the mukhtar is hostile to some or all of his villagers. This can be for reasons related to or independent of the Israeli administration.

main roads, with lesser restrictions along the margins of smaller roads. Given the Palestinian propensity to build along roadways, rather than expand onto agricultural land, this restriction seriously affects land use. Construction can also be prohibited on the land adjacent to military installations and Israeli settlements. As settlements grow, so too do the restricted areas around them.

Another restriction on land use comes from the declaration of military training zones, in which the army is not responsible for damage to property which it causes. The villages on the eastern side of Jerusalem have had such zones declared on the portions of their land which are farthest to the east. At the discretion of the military, an additional form of closure can also be applied to specific areas. In this form, an area can be declared closed for security reasons, and entrance to and exit from the area allowed only by written permission from the military command. Benvenisti and Khayat suggest that this move is sometimes the "first step towards . . . seizure and the establishment of Jewish settlements."[16]

In addition to closing areas, a step that itself does not affect ownership, the army can requisition areas that it deems necessary for military purposes. Unlike the previously mentioned measures, military requisition is accompanied by an offer of payment for land use and compensation for damage caused to the land. More than any other form of compensation (for outright expropriation, for example), Palestinians are inclined to accept and even seek compensation for damage to their land. When villagers fear that an area is going to be requisitioned, they try to plant it—usually only perfunctorily—in order to gain entitlement to compensation for loss of crops. They also vigorously press claims for damage done to trees on their property.[17]

Also restricting land use in this area is the declaration of nature reserves. While declaration of an area as a nature reserve does not negate ownership rights, there are severe limitations on land use and construction within the reserve, and the reserve status is entered in the land registry, thus affecting its value in future sale. The creation of nature reserves and their location are seemingly not only matters of wildlife preservation.

> The declarations of nature reserve areas, covering 250,000 dunams by 1983, and in the final stage, 340,000 dunams, are part of a program of "land seizure." According to [*Master Plan and Development Plan for Settlement in Samaria and Judea*], "afforestation, grazing areas and parks" are part of a "program for land seizure prepared by a decision of the Ministerial Committee for Settlement. . . .

---

[16] Meron Benvenisti and Shlomo Khayat, *The West Bank and Gaza Atlas* (Jerusalem: West Bank Data Base Project, 1988), p. 62.

[17] "High Court: Permissible for the Army to Take Land Temporarily from Residents of the Territories," *Ha'Aretz*, February 10, 1990. Following an appeal by a Bethlehem landowner, the court directed the army to take care not to damage trees on property that it had requisitioned and to pay the owner compensation for the period of time for which the orchard would be off-limits, as well as for any damage caused to the trees.

According to the Plan, "in addition to the benefit of seizing land other benefits can be accrued, such as monetary profits, improvement of the quality of life
and the environment, etc."[18]

Two other factors should be discussed in relation to land issues as they
are played out in Jerusalem's West Bank periphery. One of these is outright
expropriation, and the other is private or governmental purchase or lease.
The first of these is carried out according to the outline of Jordanian expropriation procedures, though in an abbreviated fashion that provides less time
and opportunity for review, and less governmental supervision. In theory,
expropriations are to be carried out for the benefit of the public. In fact, the
most significant of the expropriations are for the extension of the infrastructure supporting Jewish settlements. In such cases, as within the municipality,
Palestinians almost always decline the compensation offered by the government.[19]

As to the purchase or lease of land in the West Bank, this was officially
the sole right of the government and the JNF until 1973, at which time contractors were given the opportunity to purchase land for construction within
settlement areas approved by the government "through the conduit of the Israel Lands Authority."[20] The purchase by public agencies did not proceed at a
particularly fast pace, but a clear concentration of land purchased can be found
in the Jerusalem area.[21] Accompanying the agency purchases, however, were
a large number of illegal land purchases by nongovernmental parties. Private
purchase of land has been accompanied by significant public scandal, an indication that the matter is substantially prone to the same type of manipulations that marked land transfers in this area in the past. The problems that
come to light often involve the use of Palestinian middle men or other tools
for disguising the religion (Jewish) of the purchaser. There are also many
cases (including those described in chapters 9 and 10) in which the vendor is
not recognized in the village as having rights to part or all of the land in question.[22]

---

[18] Meron Benvenisti, *The West Bank Data Project: A Survey of Israel's Policies* (Washington:
American Enterprise Institute for Public Policy Research, 1984). The plan cited is from the
World Zionist Organization and the Ministry of Agriculture, 1983.

[19] In fact, Palestinians are generally opposed to expropriation no matter who the benefactor is,
and there is often difficulty in attaining land for the construction of infrastructural elements in
Palestinian areas. There are of course exceptions, one of which will be related in chapter 9.

[20] Gerson, p. 148.

[21] "By 1973 the Israel Lands Administration had, by its own account, succeeded in purchasing
over 30,000 dunams in the West Bank and about 18,000 dunams in Jerusalem." Ibid., p. 141.

[22] Many other methods exist for facilitating the sale of land in questionable circumstances,
some of which work "within the system." One of these involves a fictional dispute between two
parties, neither of which has any real claim to the land in question. Cases are known wherein a
decision concerning the allocation of the land is reached by the court, and the land is subsequently transferred to a third party, the original sponsor of both of the contending claimants.

The scope of the outcome of these methods of alienating land from Palestinian hands—both officially and unofficially—is disputed. But, despite contrasting figures, the total is agreed to be significant. According to Benvenisti, the amount of government (or state) land in the West Bank registered during the period of Jordanian rule came to 527,000 dunams, with an additional 160,000 dunams viewable in this same category. The result of the policy shift that came with the tenure of the Begin government, which put the burden of proof on the Palestinians, was that an additional 1.5 million dunams became eligible for declaration as state land. Not all of this total has been formally declared state land however, and

> once sufficient land for unlimited Jewish settlement was assured, the pace of declaration [of state land] slowed considerably. A survey of the Civil Administration (1985) showed that *300,000 dunams (out of a total 2.15 million dunams) located and mapped as potential "state land" cannot be "declared" due to "illegal Arab cultivation" or for other reasons.*[23]

When the other forms of restriction and alienation are included, the amount of land affected goes far beyond the 2.15 million dunams mentioned above. While these figures apply to the West Bank as a whole, a number of important factors relate specifically to the Jerusalem region. First, where priority is given to settlement or security efforts by the government, the search for eligible land and the process of declaring it state land continue with intensity. One of the primary areas in which this is the case is the Jerusalem periphery, particularly to the east of the city, as well as between the northern Jewish neighborhoods.

Second, there is a recognition that "illegal Arab cultivation" can hinder or prevent the declaration of state land. The manner in which Arab cultivation achieves this can be either practical or legal, and owing to the protection that Ottoman laws afford to those working the land, one often leads to the other. It should be recalled that much of the West Bank, including Jerusalem's eastern periphery, appears to be stony, barren ground. Even minimal agricultural activity is visible in such a landscape, and serves to demonstrate attachment to the land.

Where competition for control of the land is especially important, such activity can draw the attention of the Israeli authorities, and precipitate or sharpen a localized conflict. In less contested areas, however, or for a variety of other reasons, the existence of Palestinian activity on the land can serve as a deterrent to the initiation of Israeli projects. The primary reason for this is that the expense and time consumed in contesting the landownership is sometimes judged to be greater than the benefit afforded by a particular location, especially if there is untouched land nearby.

---

[23] Benvenisti and Khayat, *West Bank and Gaza Atlas,* p. 61, emphasis added.

A secondary reason, though one gaining significance of late, is the risk involved in initiating projects on contested lands. The degree of sabotage of various kinds is naturally greater when the land in question is either proximate to Palestinian activity or, for whatever reason, particularly subject to competition.

The Official Appeal Processes

While I have mentioned the burden of proof placed on Palestinians, I have not yet described the mechanism of appeal. And though it has been pointed out that many Palestinians cannot or will not avail themselves of this avenue of recourse, it nonetheless is an aspect of the procedure which is of crucial importance from the Israeli perspective. Furthermore, it is an essential tool in the determination of many of the basic principles contributing to land issues and the relationship between the two contestants. Finally, for those who do choose this option, the outcome is, of course, of primary significance.

In light of Israel's status as an occupying power, local West Bank courts are not empowered to rule on the actions of the military, or those of its direct adjunct, the Civil Administration. To provide a mechanism to replace the functioning of these local courts vis à vis the West Bank government, a number of review boards have been established. These boards are an element of that same government, however, and thus all appeals to the boards are channeled though the Civil Administration. Even issues such as intracommunal land disputes among Palestinians which involve registration are directed to the review boards, and are not brought before indigenous courts.[24]

The review board itself is in many ways quite distinct from a common court of law. The board is composed of three members, generally Israelis who are doing their annual army reserve duty. Only one of the members must be a jurist in his regular occupation. The rules of evidence and procedure are also different from those of an Israeli court, and it is often difficult for attorneys representing Palestinians to adapt to or prepare for the procedures employed.[25]

The decisions of the review board are expressed only as nonbinding recommendations, and in lieu of their being adopted, the original action remains in force.[26] Among Palestinians there is a broad perception that this provision, together with the low rate of approval for appeals filed, confirms

---

[24] During the Intifada a number of West Bank communities have created or reactivated *sulha* committees, traditional peacemaking forums. Land disputes and other problems are sometimes brought before such unofficial forums for resolution.

[25] Usamah Halabi et al., *Land Alienation in the West Bank: A Legal Spatial Analysis* (Jerusalem: West Bank Data Project, 1985), pp. 68–69.

[26] Israel Defense Force, "Order on Review Boards (Judea and Samaria)," no. 172, 1967.

the suspicion that the review boards are simply a device that allows the administration to carry out its policies while maintaining a posture of sound juridical supervision. Those charges are answered, in part, by the fact that there is a further level of appeal beyond the review board.

In a situation almost unique in the history of military occupation, the residents of the West Bank have access to the highest court of the occupying power. The Israeli High Court has ruled that in its authority over the organs of state, specifically the military, it has the power to review the actions, orders, and in some cases intentions of the military government (and subsequently the Civil Administration) in the territories, and consider them against the standard of the Hague Convention.

In the spirit of that convention, the court has maintained the principle that "privately owned land seized by the authorities could, even if justified by security considerations, only be 'requisitioned' (not 'confiscated or expropriated') on a temporary basis and in exchange for rental payments."[27] This principle opened the way for appeals based upon the claim that government actions in land issues (and other matters) were incompatible with the Hague Convention. Further, adherence to the Hague Convention applied a number of strictures that shaped the discussion, if not the execution, of Israeli practices in the West Bank.

The court decision with the best known impact on Israeli-Palestinian land disputes, at least in terms of Jewish settlement, was issued in the Elon Moreh case.[28] In this case, the details of which are discussed specifically by Lustick and dealt with in many other forums, the court held that the selection of the location of the Elon Moreh settlement had political rather than military motivation, and thus the use of the privately owned Palestinian land was not permissible. This had a significant impact on the settlement ambitions of the government through its determination that

—No land, whether public or private, can be permanently confiscated. Land may only be "requisitioned" on a temporary basis.
—No settlement, whether established on private or public land, can be considered permanent.
—If requisitioned land is privately owned, title remains in the hands of the owner, and rental payments are to be made while the land is in use.
—If requisitioned land is publicly owned, the "rules of usufruct" apply to the occupying power's use of the land. At minimum this means that its possession cannot be permanently alienated, nor its basic character transformed.

---

[27] Ian Lustick, "Israel and the West Bank after Elon Moreh: The Mechanics of De Facto Annexation," *Middle East Journal* 35 (1981): 559.

[28] Officially known as *Dwikat et al. v. The Government of Israel, High Court of Justice,* 3900/79, but commonly referred to as the Elon Moreh case after the settlement, the establishment of which was the subject of the dispute.

—Settlements on privately owned land in the occupied territories are legal
only if their establishment and the land requisitions involved are "really
necessary for the army of occupation."[29]

While there is no doubt that these criteria restrict the government in
its pursuit of land in the West Bank,[30] given the amount of land affected by
such declarations and restrictions, it is clear that the government has found
ways to fulfill many of its needs and ambitions. From the perspective of individual Palestinians, national feeling may be significant, but the fate of their
own land is a much more immediate and compelling issue. As will be shown
in the following chapters, the appeals process has, in fact, little to offer to most
landowners. Nonetheless, there is repeated approach to the appeal mechanism in the hope of maintaining a hold on the land.

In the area of the Green Belt, there have been a number of cases appealed to the review boards and to the high court. The results have been
mixed. Most, but not all, of the cases have been decided in favor of the government. Even in cases where the government has won, however, the application of that decision has not always followed the anticipated course.
Nonetheless, the Palestinian perception is that the system is unreservedly
and unalterably in pursuit of their land. There is little hope and less faith in
the judicial and supervisory bodies. In fact, there is only slight awareness of
how these bodies operate, and, given the widespread belief that they are only
part of a game, there is scant motivation or intention to understand how to
use this avenue more effectively. Palestinian professionals, on the other
hand, both legal and agricultural, are gaining expertise in these matters, and
are learning to contend with them within the Israeli frame of reference.

The Land Conflict as a Cultural Issue

The basic difficulty in classifying an area as state land is that conflicting
standards of evaluation are applied by the parties involved. Israel imposes a
Western legalistic tradition, demanding forms of proof which are common in
many countries, including Israel, and are acceptable within a tradition of rig-
orous application of land regulation. The Palestinian villagers, however, are

---

[29] Lustick, p. 562, citing an affidavit submitted by Elon Moreh settlers to the High Court of
Justice, *Piskei Din*, 1980, 390/79/vol. 34(I), Jerusalem, pp. 21–22.

[30] In his autobiography Ariel Sharon, who has twice had control of the ILA, first as minister
of agriculture and then as minister of housing, writes that in searching for state land in the
West Bank he and his assistant counted wheat stalks and sheep droppings, "to be sure that we
were not claiming the remnants of a squatter's farm" and "in order to determine if herders had
perhaps been using some particular place in a regular habitual way." From evidence readily
available in a casual examination of many areas declared as state land, it is clear that either
Sharon has trouble recognizing and counting the indicators he has chosen for gauging Palestinian land use, or that his statement is somewhat disingenuous. Ariel Sharon with David
Chanoff, *Warrior: The Autobiography of Ariel Sharon* (New York, Simon and Schuster, 1989),
p. 360.

unfamiliar with this approach, and are at a loss when faced with the demands of the Israeli system. When confronted with the need for specific documentation, and the evaluation of a hostile judiciary armed with aerial photographs, archival material, and seemingly unlimited resources, the Palestinians retreat to their basic claim: the land is Palestine, belonging to Palestinians, and no measure of proof in the possession of or regulation passed by the Jews is legitimate.

On each side there are elements that deviate from this basic approach, both in practical and political ways. On the Israeli side, there has always been a measure of opposition to an ongoing presence in the West Bank and Gaza Strip. The elections of 1992 brought this position representation in the government, albeit through the offices of a junior coalition party. The new Labor-led government has slashed settlement-building in the West Bank, and with it the pursuit of additional lands. The ultimate impact of this change remains to be seen, but in the meantime it has done little to affect the political discourse concerning the future of the West Bank.

Because of the political, and even more so the academic, focus on land practices in the West Bank, there has developed an open discussion of these issues. They have been systematically studied and reported on by the West Bank Data Project and others, including the daily media. Much of this discussion carries a political tone, or is in keeping with a particular agenda, and since the election, government actions under the Likud have been subjected to particular scrutiny. Nonetheless, prior to Israeli rule, and during it, little information has been available concerning the impact of government policies on small landowners. A symptom of this has been the chronic vulnerability of this group to those, private and public, who have incompatible interests in land practices and ambitions. As a result, there has been almost no awareness of methods for attaining and protecting individual land rights. The information presented by Israelis, much of which can be mustered *only* by Israelis,[31] represents for the first time a body of information, analysis, and criticism concerning government land practices.[32]

---

[31] Israeli institutions, both governmental and quasi-governmental, guard their information very closely. Beyond the customary freeze on government documents (thirty years for national government papers, twenty-five years for those of the Jerusalem municipality), there is commonly a reluctance and often an unwillingness to talk to outsiders. Not infrequently this policy of silence applies to Israelis as well, and thus even simple questions often go unanswered. It is all the more difficult for Palestinians to get specific information from land agencies and the Civil Administration.

[32] The number of Palestinian groups tracking developments in the territories is burgeoning. These groups are limited, however, by the restrictions they face in access to information and institutions. Therefore much of their material is second-hand or lacking hard documentation. Its tenor is also often stridently partisan, and, according to the characterization of Palestinians, the products are frequently political rather than academic. Nonetheless, some of the groups are gaining sophistication and making a real contribution to the study of these issues.

The nature of Palestinian actions that deviate from the basic position of opposition to Israeli land acquisition is traditional in form and motivation. While it is conceivable that some Palestinians may assist Israel for ideological reasons, the overwhelming motivation for Palestinian participation in land transfers is financial. This ranges from the need to sell land in order to provide food and shelter, to profit-taking by large landowners, as well as the manipulations by middle men and swindlers.[33] At times, Palestinian employees of the Civil Administration also assist those offices engaged in the search for state land.[34] This is, however, only a minor part of the effort to dominate land use, and most of the work is carried out by a variety of agencies working both individually and in concert.

Interagency Linkage and Priorities

The different Israeli land-control agencies in the Jerusalem area operate according to their own needs and priorities, and each of them is affected by its relationship to the partner institutions. The municipality depends on the ILA for the granting of land on which to place housing or recreational areas, on the Housing Ministry for authorizing, funding, and contracting for the construction of housing, and on the JNF for carrying out the planting, maintenance, and supervision of the forests.

The ILA is purely a bureaucratic body, though one with tremendous influence in Israel. It is often the ILA that determines the pace, scope, and direction of the growth of communities in Israel, be they small villages or larger cities. As executor of land, however, the ILA is compelled to preserve its single asset, and to do this it depends in part on the JNF, and, when problems arise, on the court system. Land is viewed as a scarce resource in Israel, and therefore unbuilt areas are considered a reserve for the future. Thus, the ILA distributes land in a miserly fashion. At the same time, however, much of the funding available to the ILA (a percentage of which is passed on to the JNF) comes from the sale of land. The ILA must, therefore, work in coordination with the JNF and the Housing Ministry to manage this resource.[35]

---

[33] For details on how some of these patterns were present prior to and during the British Mandate, see Kenneth W. Stein, *The Land Question in Palestine, 1917–1939* (Chapel Hill: University of North Carolina Press, 1984).

[34] Shehadah, p. 49. This is no doubt less common in the wake of Intifada pressures that have caused many Palestinians to quit their jobs working for the Civil Administration, and discouraged many of those who remain from participating in activities that would provoke the population into retaliatory acts.

[35] As indicated in the introduction, the ILA has recently been transferred from the Agriculture Ministry to the Ministry of Housing. Under the previous system, agriculture was given priority in land-use considerations, and thus very little land was available for the expansion of housing beyond the borders of existing communities. The transfer of the ILA came in response to the pressures caused by the massive and rapid Soviet immigration, which left the country with an immediate shortage of some 100,000 housing units. As a result of the need to build quickly and in

The Housing Ministry coordinates with the municipality and the ILA as related above, and relies upon the JNF for the execution of many of its tasks. Primary among them are the preparation of land for construction (carried out by the JNF's land development division) and the preservation of land for future ministry projects by way of afforestation. The Housing Ministry also relies on the JNF and the ILA to locate, research, and secure land for new construction. The principal issue involved in these tasks continues to be clarification of landownership, as well as the preservation of state land in the face of incursion.

Despite the cooperation and coordination of the above-mentioned agencies, each tends to operate in pursuit of its own interests. Within these agencies, between departments and between levels, there are conflicting views, goals, and priorities. For a number of reasons it is most important to understand the role of the JNF in the control of land in and around Jerusalem. The focus on the JNF stems from its critical position in the planning and execution of many of the land policies, and its dominant role in the creation of the Green Belt. Further, more than any other agency, the JNF comes into contact with Palestinian landholders in the mutual contest for control of specific plots of land. Thus, while a host of bodies have direct and indirect participation in the creation of the Green Belt, it is the JNF that provides the key to the understanding of events on the Israeli side of the conflict, and the use of planting as a tool in the competition for the land.

---

and in quantity, the ILA relaxed its hold on the land, easing the way for the Housing Ministry, to which it was subordinate. This constituted a revolution in Israeli land policy, the consequences of which are not yet clear, but which will no doubt be significant. This is especially so in light of the declared policy of former Housing Minister Sharon to use construction as a political tool, both within and beyond the Green Line.

7

Jerusalem's Green Belt

The notion that the green belt could be a continuous, uninterrupted strip of forest encircling the city is not one held by the agencies associated with its creation. Rather, the green belt is composed of a large number of afforested sites, differing in size and function, which fall more or less within a ring around the municipality (fig. 2). The total of these sites is estimated to encompass approximately 35,000 dunams, upon which 11 million trees have been planted. The location, purpose, and character of many of the sites is determined according to a master plan for the green belt drawn up by the private landscape architecture firm of Aronson, Ltd., as commissioned by the JNF. The Aronson plan, which loosely guides the planting of the green belt, reflects the needs and goals of the different groups that sponsor the afforestation, according to their own specific interests. The afforestation itself, however, as well as the care, supervision, and guarding of the trees, is the domain of the JNF.

The aim of the Aronson proposal was the "creation of a multiyear plan that will document areas for afforestation and recreation around the built-up area of Jerusalem while giving an answer to the following problems: the widely varied landscape of the Jerusalem surroundings, the need for forest as a central recreation area for the residents of Jerusalem *and the problem of possessing government land.*"[1] The report suggested that the immediate motivations for the project were the "growth of the construction in the new neighborhoods on the periphery of Jerusalem and the necessity of fixing ownership on government land," and that to this end, 4,000 dunams should be

---

[1] Shlomo Aronson, "Master Plan for Jerusalem: Intermediate Report no. 2," September 7, 1982, p. 2 [Hebrew]. Emphasis added.

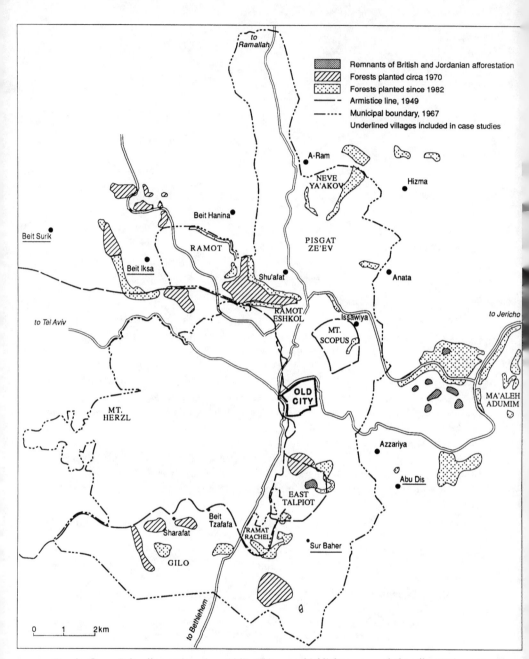

Fig. 2. Green Belt afforestation since 1967. This map highlights many of the afforestation projects carried out since the reunification of Jerusalem.

planted annually in the Jerusalem area.[2] For the first time, the plan described an overall concept of afforestation for the city and its surroundings as a whole, in keeping with the style of the plans that had been developed and implemented in West Jerusalem before 1967.

The Locating of Afforestation Sites

The discrete sites that comprise the green belt were chosen on the basis of their individual merit in terms of the problems listed above. The sites range in size from fifteen to over a thousand dunams within a given project, and are either isolated or linked into larger blocks of forest. Aronson lists about a hundred such sites, and for each describes the local conditions of soil, vegetation, and ownership, the function of afforestation in that location, and the recommended type and scope of work to be carried out. Since the afforestation on the western side of the city was largely completed prior to the inception of the Aronson plan (and in fact prior to 1967), the proposal concerns that portion of the region accessible only in the wake of the 1967 War.

Within this area there are afforestation sites adjacent to or within the municipal boundary, along with some that are a number of kilometers away, closer to the outer ring of encircling communities described in chapter 5. Afforestation is also concentrated along major routes that radiate out from the city, and in areas between the municipality and the ring of settlement. As a result, forests now exist, and continue to be planted, between the villages that ring the city. At times the forests are distant from any fixed habitation, but in general they are immediately proximate to areas of either Jewish or Arab residence.[3]

The Recreational Function

The Aronson plan generated afforestation projects that fall into two main categories, according to principal function: those that were recreational or landscape in nature, and those that were intended to preserve the land for other use (and, at the same time, prevent use by Palestinians), or had some other political or strategic function. As for the first of these categories, the bulk of recreational or landscape afforestation came either within or in close proximity to the municipal boundary, or around the perimeter of the outlying settlements. While such forests could also have a political function (as in the case discussed in the following chapter), the nonpolitical task of the forest is obvious, and the presence of paths and parks gives evidence of their use.

---

[2] Ibid., p. 2.

[3] Because of the policy of constructing on hilltops and ridges and leaving the slopes and valleys green, there is at times an open space between "proximate" usages, especially when the slopes are too steep for either planting or building. This space can be as much as several hundred meters.

For the most part, it is the landscape/recreation function of the green belt that is presented to the public as its purpose and character. Thus the discussion of the green belt as a whole differs significantly from the (internal) treatment of its component parts. Nonetheless, the political character of land redemption through afforestation penetrates even the description of forests as recreational areas. A poem published in a JNF booklet about the organization's activities describes "a forest that increases and grows as a green wall around Jerusalem / Forests that have a political value, that are a symbol and a decree and a sign."[4] The Aronson plan, and the institutions associated with the planting are certainly cognizant of the multifunctional potential of the forest sites, as indicated by the list of goals cited in the plan. The Ministry of Agriculture, for example, recommends afforestation on unused agricultural land in order to "prove possession of these lands, and at the same time to create a recreational element."[5]

Political Planting in the Green Belt

As indicated, many of the individual afforestation sites are selected on the basis of some political or strategic function, whether it be immediate, or with an eye toward future use. The preservation of land for future use by the government, generally for the Jewish community, is clearly a priority of the ILA and the Ministry of Housing, among others. The relative importance of the various goals of planting is revealed in the documents that deal with these matters. In summarizing the planting around Jerusalem, for instance, an ILA document requests a "general authorization that all the planting in the framework of Jerusalem (which is not via the Grazing and Afforestation Committee) is intended *first of all for the preservation of land* and for the creation of a green belt."[6]

This same priority holds, and is even greater, for lands that are beyond the Green Line. Since the West Bank is under the bureaucratic authority of the Civil Administration, the ILA and Housing Ministry must coordinate their actions with this body for that portion of the green belt outside the municipal boundary. For the purpose of preserving state land, the ILA receives direct contributions from the Civil Administration, which it then channels to

---

[4] Haim Hefer, "Green Land," in *Tale of Acts: The Keren Keyemet L'Yisrael* (Jerusalem: Keren Keyemet L'Yisrael, 1988), p. 6 [Hebrew].

[5] Ministry of Agriculture, Office of the Director-General, "Summary of the Discussion on Unused Lands in Moshavim," April 27, 1989. *Yediot KaKaL*, no. 86 (July 1989) [Hebrew] lists areas within Israel and beyond the Green Line that are being planted with trees in order to preserve land that had previously been used for agriculture.

[6] State of Israel, ILA, District Manager's Office, "Summation on Planting around Jerusalem [1988]," August 17, 1987. Emphasis added. The Grazing and Afforestation Committee is composed of representatives from the associated bodies, and determines among other things the scope and location of some of the afforestation. Its role in relation to the green belt, however, is minimal, as it does not deal with municipal land, or with that beyond the Green Line.

the JNF for afforestation.[7] A JNF memo discusses the manner in which the land is protected:

> The purpose of taking possession of areas is to protect state land from being bitten off by individuals. There are a number of methods for taking and protecting areas—grazing, afforestation, and land improvement. The method that the JNF is responsible for is taking areas by way of . . . [afforestation] and land improvement. The activities of sustaining the forest in its first years include active guarding of the area. The regular presence in the area of the work crew prevents the surrounding [sic] from entering the area and this is the greatest advantage of this system.[8]

The Issue of Private Land

Along with the emphasis on the realization and protection of rights on public or state land, there is an effort to avoid activity on private land, land that can be proven to be in Palestinian ownership. The desire to avoid costly litigation, unnecessary provocation, and increased attacks on the trees is reflected throughout the agencies involved. Statements to this effect are explicit. The Civil Administration, nominal benefactor of the local population, stresses the point, saying that "only on registered land [in the state's name] or in areas recently declared state land" will planting be allowed, and that such work should not go beyond the area included in the map of declaration.[9]

Within the Green Line, the municipality too began from the premise that only public lands should be planted on, though it did instruct that the legality of planting on private land be investigated.[10] The conclusion was that barring expropriation of private land for public purposes, private land was off-limits for such planting. As a result, the JNF found that in light of "the difficulty in registering public areas with precision sometimes open areas are forfeited."[11] Planting on land that was not declared as state land could even result in the intervention of the Civil Administration, which was authorized to order a cessation of such activities.[12]

---

[7] State of Israel, ILA, District Manager's Office, document no. 2574A, "Planting for the Purpose of Preserving and Realizing State Land in the Area of Judea and Samaria," December 31, 1985.

[8] JNF, "Taking Possession of Areas: Approach and Planning Discussion Proposal," appendix A, Summary of Discussion from September 29, 1982, Judea and Samaria File. A number of points in this document are unclear. The reference to the "surrounding" is taken to mean the West Bank residents. A reference in the body of the document to "grazing" as a function of the JNF is surely a mistake, because afforestation is the activity intended.

[9] State of Israel, Ministry of Defense, Division of Settlement and Infrastructure, Department of Planning and Infrastructure, 1015, October 10, 1985.

[10] Municipality of Jerusalem, Department of City Planning, "Summary of Meeting on the Subject of Tree Planting of May 16, 1982."

[11] JNF, 3307/701, October 1, 1986, p. 2.

[12] JNF, S/3-289, December 14, 1987. See also chapter 9 for an example of this.

Indeed, the importance of staying within the boundaries of areas where planting was permitted was emphasized from the highest levels of administration to the lowest workers in the field: "An order was given to the workers on the site, that any appeal to us with any proof of private ownership on the site will cause our removal from the area of private ownership—to wit planting will only be in the area *which is not privately owned*."[13] This principle was sufficiently firm that the JNF could not even engage the assistance of security forces in protecting work crews if the legal status of the land was not in keeping with the statutes relevant to planting.[14]

At times, the consideration was even broader than the exact legal status of the land in question. This is illustrated by the planning for afforestation near the railroad tracks adjacent to the village of Battir, which is in the West Bank.[15] Concerning an area from which trees were to be uprooted, the JNF stated that

> the land is indeed within the Green Line of the state and owned by it, but on the other hand according to agreements in the past with Jordan the area has been worked [agriculturally] for many years. From the bottom of the area there are terraces of rain-fed agriculture and many olive and grape orchards, and there is no doubt that they will have to be uprooted. This situation creates ownership problems of a legal character, and these must be solved before an order is received allowing the use of the land for security purposes.[16]

Periodic observations—sometimes in the form of complaint—were made by the staffs of the related agencies as to the inability to extend the scope of planting (and other activities) on the basis of lack of available state land, or other ownership problems. Their contention was that there no longer was any opportunity for significant planting to the east of Jerusalem.[17]

Dunam by Dunam: The Competition for Land

Despite the respect for private land, and in keeping with the perception that the amount of available land has decreased significantly, there is intense and increasing competition for control of unused land.[18] Thus, not infre-

---

[13] JNF, 3300/709, October 19, 1987. Emphasis in original.

[14] Israel Police, Jerusalem District Headquarters, Office of Patrol and Operations, TzM/01, July 27, 1986.

[15] During the Intifada the trains between Jerusalem and Tel Aviv were frequently attacked near the village of Battir. The attackers took advantage of the orchards close to the tracks to gain cover, and thus requests were made by railroad and security authorities to uproot the trees nearest the tracks. The area is very close to the Green Line, with the tracks falling within Israeli territory.

[16] JNF, 3307/71, June 1, 1989.

[17] Interview with Tzvi Avni, September 13, 1990. Interview with Nina Amir, JNF forest planner, January 14, 1990.

[18] Included in this category are areas of intermittent grazing.

quently, land that is privately owned or subject to claim of private ownership is involved in a dispute over planting. More than this, land that may not be owned by those using it is planted by both Israelis and Palestinians. The spread of land usage is incremental, and boundaries are often vague; thus the incursion onto land affiliated with "the other" is initially hard to discern.

Frequently, however, the expansion is deliberate and planned. Since both sides appreciate that the amount of land available for expansion is shrinking, the competition is often quite sharp, and the tactics conform to whatever works best. The field workers of the JNF continually observe the increase in Palestinian presence on the land in various forms of use, and respond with proposals for planting land either adjacent to or unrelated to their original mandate. In order to facilitate the continuation and extension of planting, the JNF sometimes asks the Civil Administration to declare particular areas as state land, if they do not yet have that status.[19]

So too the Palestinians, observing the spread of the JNF forests, try to put land into use in order to prevent its alienation. At times this results in intertwined patterns of planting, as each side strives to block the expansion of the other. Both sides describe this piece-by-piece competition as a "war."[20] In light of this attitude, one of the highest priorities for planting is in areas wherein there is an issue of incursions. This matter is a consideration in the Aronson plan, as well as in proposals that stem from developments observed in the field.

Planting to Take Possession of Land

As detailed in the previous chapter, since 1980, the government of Israel has considered all land in the territories to be state land, if not proven otherwise. One of the ways of removing any confusion regarding the status of a particular plot of land, and of protecting its status from future challenge, is to put it into continual use. Afforestation plays a principal role in the effort to take possession of, establish, realize, and hold what the government considers to be state land.

At times it is the JNF that requests or initiates the process of declaration of state land, but, much more frequently, it is the associated agencies that request that the JNF plant a given area in order to assert the right of possession. Occasionally the planting commences prior to the registration of the plot as state land, especially if there is a possibility that Palestinians could establish a counter claim in lieu of immediate action.[21] In some cases, however, the area planted is not intended for any particular use, and the planting is, in essence,

---

[19] JNF, S/3-289, December 14, 1987; Request to Department of Coordination, Judea and Samaria, Ministry of Defense.

[20] Field survey with G. Sopher, area supervisor for central East Jerusalem, November 8, 1989.

[21] JNF, 3300/141, March 9, 1987.

essence, to preserve it as unused land. One of the agencies sponsoring such planting is the Custodian for Abandoned Property, under the auspices of the Defense Ministry in the West Bank.[22] In theory, actions directed by this agency would constitute the protection of the land for its Palestinian owners, with intermediate use in some way intended for the welfare of the general population.

More commonly, an area slated for future Israeli use is found, planned, and planted, with the planting used to confirm the status of state land. To this end, there are specific budgetary allocations, contributed by the participating agencies, with the exception of the municipality.[23] When Palestinian activity exists on the land in question, the plots that "are not planted or possessed," that is, utilized in some way, are planted by the JNF.[24] In these cases, the tendency of the JNF to plant quick-growing trees (such as pine, cypress, and eucalyptus) is reinforced by the desire to establish a visible presence as soon as possible, as well as to delineate the area as being off-limits. The trees then serve as a "screen" showing that "up until here, that is your territory; here someone has worked and is taking care and is planting" and it is forbidden to go farther.[25]

The Tzofim, Anata, and Ramot Forests

One of the largest open areas remaining in the immediate vicinity of Jerusalem lies between the villages that are east of the Hebrew University's Mount Scopus campus (Har HaTzofim, in Hebrew). Within this area are found the villages of Issawiya, Anata, and the adjacent Shu'afat refugee camp, Za'im (an extension of the A-Tur neighborhood of Jerusalem), and on its fringes, Hizma in the north, Azzariya and Abu Dis in the south. Of the villages, Issawiya and parts of Anata and Azzariya are within the municipal boundary; Hizma and Abu Dis begin adjacent to it but fall within the West Bank, as does the greater part of Anata.

It is on the land of some of these villages that the town of Ma'aleh Adumim—the largest Jewish settlement in the territories—was erected.[26] An

---

[22] JNF, 563/Judea and Samaria, June 8, 1988.

[23] JNF, 3300/499, August 10, 1986. Money can be transferred, however, from a project with municipal cooperation to one that is outside the area of interest to Jerusalem. In such a case, the municipality is indirectly contributing to afforestation elsewhere, for the purpose of possessing land related to some other governmental body. JNF 598/Judea and Samaria, August 20, 1984. In this case, budget resources were transferred from the Tzofim Forest, east of Jerusalem, to an afforestation project near the settlement of Shiloh.

[24] JNF, 3300/unnumbered, Hill Region General File, February 19, 1988.

[25] Interview with Nina Amir, January 14, 1990.

[26] The case of Ma'aleh Adumim will be discussed further in chapter 10. Part of this land was purchased, part taken as state land. There is disagreement among the villages as to which one owned the land in question prior to 1967.

important goal of planting in the green belt has been to secure land in the proximity of Ma'aleh Adumim and land between it and Jerusalem. The Tzofim Forest has thus been extended from near the campus to the south and east, in the direction of Ma'aleh Adumim. The area is bisected by a new road leading to Jericho, constructed in order to bypass the villages of Azzariya and Abu Dis, along the old road leading to the east.[27]

The forest, in large part, is being planted to follow this road, and to continue along the original Jericho road to the east, both on the slope of Ma'aleh Adumim and on the opposite slope. The area includes the remnants of forests planted during the Mandate and Jordanian periods. Some of the current afforestation is in locations where the Jordanians planted, but which, following the failure of those trees, have remained barren. The surviving forests are insignificant in terms of size, occupying only a few hilltops. In terms of landscape, however, this sets them apart from Israeli planted forests, which tend not to occupy high ground. Thus as one looks to the east from Jerusalem today, many of the trees standing out in the landscape are those planted by the British and the Jordanians.

Within the area in which the Tzofim Forest is being planted, there are a number of bedouin communities, none of which exceeds more than a few families. Some of these live near villages in fixed sites, while others maintain at least minimal mobility.[28] Most of these groups have been affected by the afforestation efforts through the interdiction of grazing, which has seriously disrupted traditional practices.

Since for the most part the bedouin lack adequate documentation to support their land claims, they are particularly vulnerable to encroachment. Within the general Tzofim Forest area, there are bedouin who are being limited and edged out despite the fact that government claims to their land have been only partially established. In contrast, JNF workers who are on familiar terms with the bedouin attempt to avoid moving those families who have remained in fixed spots since afforestation in the area began. The groups are, however, sometimes surrounded by the growing forest.[29]

Much of the land being afforested in this area is already scheduled for alternative use in the near future. A significant portion of it is intended for

---

[27] This route is of tremendous strategic importance, as it serves as the main corridor from the central part of the country to the Jordan Valley and Israel's longest land border. It is also the principal route from Jerusalem to the northern and southern interior, an alternative to taking the hill route through densely populated areas of the West Bank. Thus, in addition to its function of bypassing Arab villages, the road serves as an improved transportation artery.

[28] This does not include the bedouin units that have established themselves in villages of their own, as discussed above.

[29] Field survey with G. Sopher, November 8, 1989. While the site of the bedouins' dwelling may not be directly affected by the afforestation, the gradual constriction of their grazing area will force a further change in either the method or the location of their livelihood.

the expansion of residential Ma'aleh Adumim and the construction of an accompanying industrial development. Construction west of Ma'aleh Adumim
has already begun, and plans call for the addition of a thousand housing units
in this area.[30] Another section of the area is planned as the new cemetery for
Jerusalem. The JNF had hoped that the exposed bedrock of the cemetery
grounds would effectively prevent this usage, and that the trees planted—
four hundred dunams—would remain as a forest. To their regret, fill-burial is
now being called for, and thus the trees will likely be cut down.[31]

To the north of the Tzofim Forest, there is a section of forest unique in
the green belt in terms of its ownership. The Anata Forest, located north of
Anata Down (i.e., the original village core, which is located in the West
Bank), is on land owned by the Muslim *Waqf* of Jerusalem.[32] The land was
first planted in 1969 and 1970, and then totaled four hundred dunams.[33] It is
unclear under what framework this forest was sponsored, though the work
was carried out by the JNF, apparently at the request of the *Waqf* itself.[34]

A long lapse ensued in the expansion of this forest, and work was resumed only in 1984. At that time, an additional fifty dunams were planted adjacent to the existing forest, and the following year maintenance work was
carried out on the mature trees.[35] Following that work, however, the forest
was abandoned in the wake of a disagreement between the JNF and the *Waqf*.
Another section of the area was slated for afforestation in the planting season
of 1986–87. Prior to planting, however, the JNF insisted that the *Waqf* fence
off the area and provide a guard to protect against damage to the trees.[36]

According to the JNF, the *Waqf* was not only failing to take the steps
necessary to protect the area, but as the legal owner, it was choosing not to

---

[30] *Ha'Aretz*, January 28, 1991. Whether this construction constitutes an extension of Ma'aleh
Adumim or is the initiation of a new settlement is subject to political interpretation. Currently
certain forms of U.S. funding for housing construction are being linked to a freeze on settlement
building in the territories. The government claims that what is being built on this site is merely
a new neighborhood of Ma'aleh Adumim. Another large section, running to the north of Ma'a-
leh Adumim up to the settlement of Adam, is under discussion for future housing construction.

[31] Interview with Tzvi Avni, September 13, 1990. Leftist groups in Israel have objected to the
idea of burial beyond the Green Line, and threaten to take the issue to the high court. As a result, the matter is being reexamined, and the cemetery may be located elsewhere.

[32] The *Waqf* is the administrative body responsible for the management and maintenance of
religious sites and affairs, including all land having *waqf* status, as described above.

[33] JNF, Judea and Samaria/643, August 30, 1984, p. 4.

[34] This according to Avni, who was not involved with the planting, as it long preceded his
tenure. Other suggestions hold that the JNF planted without coordination with any Palestinians, and at a later stage the *Waqf* successfully asserted its rights to the land.

[35] JNF, unnumbered, Jerusalem Forest file, "Summary of Afforestation Plan 84/85 after Survey
of August 15, 1984."

[36] JNF, Judea and Samaria/587, September 8, 1985.

pursue or prosecute those who had or would damage the forest.[37] In part, it is the limited standing held by the JNF in forests planted on land not owned by the state, and the problems thus caused, which strengthened the policy of planting only on public lands.

The Ramot Forest, in north Jerusalem, serves as one of the city's largest park areas. The forest runs east-west, and divides among the Jewish neighborhoods Givat HaMivtar, Ramat Eshkol, and Ramot, and the Palestinian neighborhoods of Shu'afat and Beit Hanina. The forest also straddles a new road to the Ramot neighborhood, and limits the approach of Palestinian agriculture to the edge of this road.

Much of the northern portion of the Ramot Forest is located on what is called the Shu'afat Ridge. Most of the land there belonged to Palestinians from the surrounding neighborhoods and villages, but part of the area was expropriated in the 1970s for the construction of a sports complex. After many years of delay, the planned sports complex was moved to another location, leaving the Shu'afat Ridge without a planned municipal function. Currently a neighborhood for Jerusalem's expanding ultraorthodox Jewish community is being constructed on the site. When this change in plans was made public, the former owners of the land appealed to the High Court, contending that the change in use made the original expropriation invalid. The court denied their appeal, and the land, including part of the Ramot Forest, was thus converted to residential use.

Other Sites of Significance in the Green Belt

Of the locations chosen for planting according to the Aronson plan and its amendments, a sizable number are identified on the basis of their strategic worth, whether in the context of the attempt to control state land, as outlined above, or for other reasons. Some of these are purely military in nature, such as the desire to control the land adjacent to Jerusalem's Atarot airfield[38] and the heights around the city. Others have combined functions, such as the planting along the approaches to the city from the south and the north. The planting next to the road leading to Bethlehem in the south, for instance, serves as a memorial to a pilot whose plane was shot down over the site in the 1967 War. The olives planted there are officially called a park, bearing the name "the Hill of the Plane."[39] The planting alongside two main northern routes serves to bracket a military base.[40]

---

[37] Interview with Tzvi Avni, September 13, 1990.

[38] The description for the A-Ram planting in the Aronson plan reads, "The area is outside the municipal domain of Jerusalem and is within Samaria. Because of its proximity to the airfield it has land and strategic importance." Aronson, "Master Plan," area 70, August 1982.

[39] This area is part of the green belt, and is a continuation of the agricultural and open area of the village of Beit Tzafafa. Plans have been implemented for the creation of a caravan site—temporary housing for new immigrants and others—on 170 dunams of land covering the Hill of

Other locations have a combined security and settlement role, and there is an effort to plant specifically the areas around Jewish neighborhoods and settlements.[41] One of the major obstacles to the execution of this task, however, is the drastically increased pressure for the construction of housing, such that the density of areas is being increased far beyond that planned and approved, and the building is being carried out on all available land.

As a result, housing spreads to the limit of the designated area, whether it be a neighborhood or a settlement, thus encroaching on the space that had been slated for the planting of a green area. In the wake of such developments, the adjacent green areas for some neighborhoods, Neve Ya'akov and Pisgat Ze'ev for instance, are actually some distance from the last row of housing, at the bottom of a steep slope. These wadi bottoms thus provide little in terms of recreation and landscape improvement, as they are often visible only from the ridge above them. What the planting does accomplish, however, is the prevention of use of the wadi floor for agriculture. The preservation of the wadi bottom as an open space serves to insure a buffer between Jewish and Arab communities. Many such activities—the planting of wadi bottoms, residential fringes, and the broader open spaces—create friction, and sometimes meet with active or passive opposition.

Planting to Prevent Incursion

According to a JNF field supervisor, the goal of preserving state land is a difficult, often frustrating process, in which "I bother them [the Palestinians], they bother me. I plant, they tear up. They plant, I tear up. They come with goats [to eat the seedlings], tear up trees, do what they can. Trees which are not protected are damaged."[42] In fact, there are two forms of incursion dealt with by the JNF—that which precedes planting and jeopardizes Israeli control of land, and that which comes after planting, as an attack on the trees and the status that they represent.

The first of these essentially comprises the extension of Palestinian land use to new areas, or the continuation of Palestinian land use in areas that have been declared at some point to be state or closed land, for one of the reasons listed in chapter 6. In such cases, the express purpose of the planting by the JNF is to "sever the connection" to the land of those whose use is con-

---

Hill of the Plane. After a period of five years the temporary homes are to be replaced by permanent structures, housing upward of 5,000 people.

[40] Part of this planting is in fact within the base. The two routes in question are the Ramallah Road (or Derech Shechem in Hebrew nomenclature), and the new road linking Neve Ya'akov, Pisgat Ze'ev, and the French Hill neighborhoods, constructed to eliminate the need to travel through the Arab neighborhoods of Beit Hanina and Shu'afat.

[41] JNF, Judea and Samaria/643, August 30, 1984.

[42] Interview with G. Sopher, November 8, 1989.

sidered unauthorized.[43] One of the areas in which this applies within the Green Line is on land that was inaccessible to West Bank villages as a result of the armistice agreement with Jordan in 1949. Such land was taken over by the custodian of abandoned property or declared state land in the years following that first war. In the wake of the 1967 War, villagers resumed or began to use the land within the Green Line, something the ILA seeks to prevent through afforestation (fig. 3).[44] A Ministry of Agriculture plan to convert unused agricultural land to forest calls for priority to be given to "areas in danger of incursion by the flocks of minorities."[45] Land slated for future industrial construction is also protected in this manner.[46]

On land that has been used by the bedouin, who generally have no formal rights to the area they traverse, planting is sometimes carried out after their physical removal from the land in question.[47] In other cases, planting is located in such a way as to limit or prevent the traditional patterns of bedouin grazing so that the eventual abandonment of their traditional use of the territory is assured.[48]

Deliberate Damage to Planted Trees

As indicated above, each side considers the struggle for land to be a war of sorts, and in that war, trees are used as tools, almost as if they were weapons. As a result of what they represent symbolically, and the rights that they convey practically, trees are subject to different forms of damage and attack. Some of this is the by-product of other activities, primarily the grazing of goats.[49] While there are many accusations that shepherds deliberately bring their flocks to contested locations wherein trees have been recently planted, it is likely that some of the damage caused thereby is independent of political motivation.

More obvious in its destructive intent is the uprooting of newly planted trees. The seedlings planted by the JNF are only some ten centimeters

---

[43] JNF, 3300/unnumbered, Hill Area General File, February 19, 1988.

[44] JNF, 3300/710, July 24, 1989. The opposite, uprooting of trees on village land within the Green Line, also occurs (see below).

[45] Ministry of Agriculture, Office of the Director-General, "Summary of the Discussion on Unused Lands in Moshavim," April 27, 1989.

[46] JNF, 3300/104, April 30, 1989.

[47] Civil Administration, Division of Infrastructure and Deployment, Mitzpeh Yericho, 1090–15, June 14, 1983; and JNF MPK/125/NS, Judea and Samaria, February 18, 1983. "No formal rights" is intended only in the sense of possession of documents that give clear title to the land.

[48] Interview with G. Sopher, November 8, 1989.

[49] Goats and sheep do not exhibit a preference for eating pine species, and this is a minor consideration in the choice of tree type when planting. Despite this, pines are still vulnerable to flocks, in that many of the young seedlings that are not eaten are trampled underfoot.

Fig. 3. Green Line afforestation. This forest dominates the Green Line and no-man's-land near the Har Adar settlement and the orchards of Beit Surik.

in height at the time of transplanting, and thus it requires no great effort to uproot what has been used to cover dunams of land. Acts of this kind are not frequent, but nor are they rare. The phenomenon is not limited to the territories either, and is particularly familiar in areas of land conflict in the Galilee. For instance, five thousand recently planted eucalyptus saplings were uprooted in the course of one night on land that was subject to a dispute between the JNF and the village of Kfar Kanna.[50] At times mature trees are cut down or damaged in such a way that they perish as well.

Arson in the Forests

Most of the arson associated with trees planted by the JNF, as well as that affecting natural forests, occurs within the Green Line. The bulk of the arson that occurs beyond the Green Line, however, is within the area of the green belt. The deliberate burning of the country's forests, fields, and to an even greater degree, open areas (termed, generally, grazing areas) has struck a particularly sensitive nerve in Israel. As noted above, such acts, characterized as "nationalistically motivated," are specifically called for in the leaflets of the Intifada. In fact, arson of this sort long predates this period,[51] but the dimensions of the damage and the frequency of attacks grew dramatically during the period of the Intifada.

The proliferation of the arson, and the anger it aroused among Israelis, led to a response that literally threatened to fight fire with fire. Many of the attacks were carried out in the forests and fields that are close to the Green Line.[52] The perpetrators of these acts were often from villages near to the areas burned. A leaflet distributed in Arab villages across the Green Line by Israeli farmers said, in part:

> Dear neighbours, you have betrayed our trust. An evil hand is burning our trees. Co-existence here has become unbearable. I call upon you to restore peace immediately. It is clear to us that the saboteurs are sent by perpetrators from outside [i.e., the PLO] who spend large sums of money. You must expel them from your villages before we take our own measures.[53]

The measures taken, not specifically in this case or area, included the burning of Palestinian fields and orchards, as well as other acts that will be described below. What is significant about the above leaflet is that its sponsors

---

[50] *Jerusalem Post,* May 5, 1989.

[51] The JNF believes that these acts are officially encouraged and even directed by PLO sources outside Israel and the territories, on the basis of documents taken by Israel from PLO headquarters in Beirut during the war in Lebanon in 1982. Arson in the background of the national conflict, spontaneous or organized, predates even the declaration of statehood in 1948.

[52] The primary factor dictating the concentration of arson in forests near the Green Line is convenience, that is, the ability to approach and withdraw with great ease.

[53] *Jerusalem Post,* June 20, 1989. The leaflet is signed by the head of the Beit She'an Regional Council.

were members of kibbutzim, traditionally a moderate sector of the Israeli population. In fact, many of the sponsors belonged to a political party that leads the Israeli camp in calling for the creation of a Palestinian state alongside Israel.

That the harsh response to the acts of arson came from broad sectors of the Israeli population is understandable in light of the symbolic significance of the forests to the people, and the extent of the damage caused. It was assumed that the fires were intended directly against the Israeli people, and that the arsonists "felt that on this subject we are sensitive. This is our soft underbelly. We're not prepared to have them touch our trees. More than anything else. The people [felt] that they were hurting us more than throwing stones on the cars and all that. The burning of forests had a much more painful effect."[54]

In the first year of the Intifada a rough count of 1,207 acts of arson consumed some 1.2 million trees.[55] Many of the fires at a particular site were set in a number of different spots in order to increase the area burned, and specific forests were torched repeatedly. The area affected included approximately 10,000 dunams of planted forest, while the scope of the open areas burned approached 140,000 dunams, some ten times the area burned the previous year.[56] The means and techniques for fighting fires could not handle the number and size of the blazes, and this contributed to the impact of the arson. Further hindering the efforts to protect the forest were the booby-traps laid by the arsonists for those who came to fight the fires, including both crude and sophisticated land mines placed on forest access roads.

The Response

In addition to the fury that came in response to the arson, there was a more organized and constructive reaction, coordinated for the most part by the JNF, and supported fully by the government. The campaign, begun after the first summer of Intifada arsons, had as its cornerstone the goal of broadening the scope of new planting beyond that which had been planned for the coming planting season. Making the increased planting possible was a widespread drive to collect money, through donations, both in Israel and abroad. The name of the campaign was "A Tree for a Tree," based on the biblical injunction "an eye for an eye." In this case, however, the intention was to plant ten trees in place of every one burned by nationalistically motivated arson.

---

[54] Interview with Mordechai Ru'ach, January 22, 1990.

[55] *Kol Ha'Iyr*, April 28, 1989.

[56] *Yediot KaKaL*, no. 86 (July 1989): 3. Interview with Mordechai Ru'ach, January 22, 1990. The JNF plays a major role in fighting forest fires, with the assistance of the Nature Authority, local fire fighters, the military, and others. Exact figures on forest fires, including investigations of the causes, are kept by the JNF.

The rhetoric of the campaign was quite political, as evidenced in the statement by Israeli President Chaim Herzog that "through this project all who love the land, both Jews and Arabs, answer the land's enemies and destroyers, whose despicable actions prove them unworthy of this goodly country."[57] In the information distributed concerning the campaign, tree planting was presented as an activity beneficial to both Arabs and Jews, and a common goal. Thus, the arson was termed "an evil plot to encourage hatred and burn the bridges between Jews and Arabs in Israel."[58]

The tactic of planting in response to destruction paralleled the action in the wake of the destruction in 1913 of the tree planted outside Jerusalem by Theodore Herzl, when some two hundred trees were planted. And, as occurred following forest burning during the Arab Revolt of 1936–39, funds collected for the JNF through donations increased dramatically when the scope of the damage was publicized. In all these cases, the area planted subsequent to the acts was significantly greater than the area afforested prior to them.

As a result of experience gained and the funding that began to flow, by the second year of the Intifada the authorities were better prepared for what was called the "fire season," both in terms of fire fighting and fire prevention. The improved fire fighting effort was based on acquisition of additional equipment and increases in staff. Fire prevention was enhanced through extensive supervision of the forests, including a significant volunteer effort. In light of the preparation for the expected attacks, arson was reduced in the second year in terms of damage by nearly 50 percent, despite an increase in attempts to torch forests and open areas. The fight against forest arson was supervised by an interministerial committee (Defense, Police, Interior, and Agriculture) created specifically to deal with "nationalistically motivated arson."

Arson in the Jerusalem Area

Because of the heavy concentration of forests in the Jerusalem Corridor, and its proximity to the West Bank on several sides, that area has borne the brunt of arson in the center portion of the country. Up to 80 percent of the arson in this sector has occurred in corridor forests, some of which have been torched repeatedly. Despite preventative efforts, including observation points and mobile guards, perpetrators are rarely caught. According to the JNF, the arsonists have observed the habits of the forestry workers and have determined the most efficient times to light fires, in terms of both reaction time for extinguishing crews, and the efforts made to catch the arsonists.[59] Whether directed from the outside or not, the arsonists have gained a degree of sophistication.

---

[57] JNF Publications and Audio-Visual Aids Department, "A Tree for a Tree," 1988.

[58] Ibid.

[59] Interview with M. Ovadia, JNF area supervisor for northern Jerusalem, December 12, 1989.

Persistence, however, more than sophistication, has taken its toll on the forests of the Jerusalem area. Primary targets of arsonists have been the forests in the corridor, as indicated above, and those on Jerusalem's northern tier. One forest that is subject to arson several times a month during the dry season is that near the West Bank village of Battir, discussed earlier in this chapter. Within the municipality, the Ramot Forest has been the target of repeated fires, usually set by residents of the adjacent Beit Hanina or Shu'afat villages (since 1967 the Shu'afat village and New Beit Hanina have been within the municipal boundary. Old Beit Hanina, some kilometers away, is in the West Bank). Though none of the forests related to the green belt has been destroyed in its entirety, accumulated damage is upward of four thousand dunams. With some eighty fires in Jerusalem forests per season, the issue of arson has become a serious problem for the JNF, and a consideration for those bodies commissioning forests in order to establish land claims.[60]

Interference with Palestinian Planting

Acts that limit, hinder, or damage Palestinian planting fall into two categories: those that are sanctioned by the government, and those that are carried out by private citizens. The latter are relatively limited in scope, though their impact cannot be measured by numbers alone. For example, fires in the fields and orchards of the West Bank village of Anabta—three in one week—convinced Palestinians that a revenge campaign by Jewish settlers was in the offing.[61] More frightening to the Palestinians was the spraying of herbicide on vineyards adjacent to Jewish settlements in the Hebron region. Such acts, though sporadic, created serious anxiety among Palestinian farmers.

Of much greater impact, however, are the restrictions on planting and the uprooting of trees which are carried out by the authorities. The primary restriction on planting occurs through the general limitations on land use described in chapter 6. Additionally, the planting of new trees is theoretically regulated by the government. According to Palestinian claims, the Civil Ad-

---

[60] When guards are required to protect a forest the cost is shared between the sponsoring agencies. The Jerusalem district has the highest expense in this regard of all areas of the country. Many of the individual forests are supervised by full-time guards, generally Arabs from the surrounding area. JNF, Judea and Samaria/643, August 30, 1984, and interview with A. Zahavi, interim director, Jerusalem District, JNF, November 1, 1989. An interesting outcome of the arson has been the reintroduction of grazing in Israel's forests. Until recently black goats were prohibited from forest areas because of the damage that they tend to cause to the trees. With the upsurge of arson, however, it was found efficient to have goats graze the underbrush that is critical to the spread of forest fires. As a result, Arab-owned goat herds are now trucked from the Negev desert to forage in the forests in the spring, with a decline in fire damage as the outcome.

[61] According to press reports, Jewish settlers prevented fire fighters from putting out the blaze. *Jerusalem Post*, May 19, 1989.

ministration "prevents the planting of fruit trees and vegetables in the West
Bank without a special permit from the authorities."[62] Their claim is based on
a military order that reads in part, "No one may plant, transplant or sow fruit
trees in an orchard, except after receiving a written permit from the certified
authority, and [only] in accordance with the conditions determined by it."[63]
The penalty for planting without permission was fixed at one year in jail, a
fine, or both. The fine applied would continue to accrue with each day that
the offending plantation was not destroyed.

In fact, this order was rarely enforced. One of its stipulations was that
within ninety days of its publication, "anyone who controls, holds, or owns
an orchard, must notify the certified authority of this in the manner that it
determines." Such reports were not made, and for the most part planting continued in the West Bank without the application for or granting of permits.
The order placed Palestinian planting in limbo, however, pending application
of the stipulation carried therein.[64] Stricter enforcement was applied to the
operation of commercial nurseries,[65] and in general the functioning of Palestinian agriculture is heavily regulated, interfered with, and limited.[66]

The Uprooting of Trees

Like the deliberate burning of trees, the uprooting or cutting down of
trees also falls into two categories, official and unofficial. Examples of each
will be provided in the following chapters, but the overall phenomenon requires a bit of background information. Trees can be uprooted when land has
been expropriated by the government. In such a case, landowners are entitled
to transplant the trees on their property. Generally, Palestinians refuse to
move their trees, rejecting the legitimacy of the expropriation. When this
happens, the trees are cut down or removed forcibly.[67]

Midiya

So, too, trees may be removed from land that is declared state land,
whether it be in the West Bank or within the Green Line. Two cases have

---

[62] *Ha'Aretz*, October 29, 1989, based on a press conference held by Dr. Ahmed Tibi, head of the
Arab Academic Group for Development Research and Studies.

[63] Military Order 1015, "Order Concerning the Supervision of Fruits and Vegetables, Judea and
Samaria," 1982.

[64] The Arabic press in East Jerusalem carries periodic reports of trees uprooted when a permit
was lacking.

[65] Nurseries are regulated under Military Order 1002, "Order Concerning Amendment of the
Law of Nurseries, Judea and Samaria," 1982.

[66] See for example *Bitter Harvest: Israeli Sanctions against Palestinian Agriculture during the
Uprising, December 1987–March 1989* (Jerusalem: Jerusalem Media and Communication Centre,
1989).

[67] See for example *Yerushalaim*, November 28, 1989.

drawn particular attention. The first occurred in the village of Al-Midiya, drawing primarily the attention of the Palestinians; the second, Katannah, is infamous among Israelis as well. Midiya, a village southwest of Jerusalem, claims ownership rights to land reported by the ILA to be state land. In 1986, the ILA initiated the uprooting of trees that, according to it, were illegally planted on state land. A curfew was imposed on the village, and some 3,300 trees were uprooted. According to the authorities, the trees removed were all younger than five years in age, proof of their recent planting.[68]

The villagers claim that only 25 percent of the trees were of this age, and that the rest ranged from six to over forty years old, with a clear majority over eleven years old.[69] In that Midiya is primarily an agricultural village, the loss of these trees was a serious economic blow, particularly to the twenty-two owners of the trees affected. Forest trees were subsequently planted on part of this land to prevent a renewal of agricultural use by the villagers.

Compounding the issue, the villagers accused the JNF of bringing many of the mature trees into Israel for replanting.[70] They indicate the locations where the trees can currently be found, and provide photographs to substantiate their claims. Though the villagers held protests at the prime minister's residence, made appeals to the Ministry of Agriculture, arranged visits to the village, and raised the issue in the Knesset, nothing was done to mitigate the situation, and the matter quickly faded from public view.

Katannah

The case of Katannah is perhaps the most widely known incident in Israel of the uprooting of trees. Katannah lies to the northwest of Jerusalem, and in the wake of the war in 1948 much of its land remained on the Israeli side of the Green Line, and was thus taken over by the government. On the land in question there was a large number of olive trees, and these were sold to a nearby kibbutz. For a number of years following the 1967 War, the villagers made no approach to the trees, but gradually they resumed harvesting from them, generally under cover of darkness.[71]

The harvest by the villagers first alerted the kibbutz, and through it, Israeli authorities, that the village was renewing its use of the land. According

---

[68] *Jerusalem Post,* June 30, 1986.

[69] Nure Al 'Uqbi and Jamal Talab, *Olive Trees under Occupation* (Jerusalem: Arab Studies Society, 1987).

[70] According to Israeli law, olive trees are a protected species, and their destruction is allowed only by special permit from a committee that oversees their protection. Thus trees that need to be removed are, in all cases possible, to be transplanted rather than destroyed. The JNF is bound by this regulation, and when it departs from it, is subject to legal action. See the case of Zichron Ya'akov, as reported in *Ha'Aretz,* February 21, 1991.

[71] *Chicago Tribune,* May 20, 1988.

to a JNF official, "the government decided to take . . . 'drastic action' after it realized that, under an Ottoman law, failure to use the land could let the trees slip back into the villagers' hands."[72] In the course of the action taken, again at the initiative of the ILA, some three thousand trees were uprooted. Many of them were replanted at different sites within Israel.

Since that time, there have been parallel campaigns to gain compensation for the people of Katannah, one by the villagers and their representatives, the other by Israelis enraged by the uprootings. To date, neither has yielded anything of significance. For Arabs, Katannah has become the byword for Israeli destruction of Palestinian trees. In this case, as in others, some trees have been replanted by villagers and sympathizers—both Jewish and Arab. For the most part, however, the disruption of village agriculture remains.[73]

Uprooting for Security Reasons

The uprooting of trees in greatest number is carried out by the army, and is done on the basis of security needs. An example of this, along the railroad tracks near the village of Battir, was provided above. For the most part, tree uprooting in the West Bank occurs along roadways, on the premise that the trees (generally orchards) provide a hiding place for attacks on road traffic.

With the proliferation of such attacks during the Intifada, the number of trees uprooted has risen. In most cases, there is little argument as to whether the attack took place or not, but it is also true that, in most cases, the owner of the orchard from which the attack took place is uninvolved in the act itself. Despite this, owners are not entitled to compensation for trees lost.

According to Palestinian sources, in the first year of the Intifada 23,440 trees were uprooted by the army. The army, while admitting that they do not keep accurate statistics, suggested that between 1,000 and 2,000 trees were uprooted during this period.[74] By the third year of the Intifada, Palestinians were suggesting that 100,000 trees had been uprooted by the army.[75] Whatever the exact number may be, Palestinians suggest that

> if the intention of the IDF is to deter demonstrations and stone-throwing, then interviews conducted with the villagers suggest that they should rethink their

---

[72] Ibid.

[73] Similarly, illegally planted olives were uprooted in the Nebi Samuel area north of Jerusalem's Ramot neighborhood. The uprooting was carried out by the Nature Reserve Authority at the behest of the ILA. Jewish and Arab activists sought to replant the area, but were prevented by the authorities from doing so. *Jerusalem Post*, January 26, 1986.

[74] *Ha'Aretz*, March 29, 1989.

[75] The Palestine Human Rights Information Centre claims that 100,000 trees were uprooted or destroyed in the first year of the Intifada, but does not substantiate this estimate. A much more conservative figure of 19,000 trees—at least—destroyed during the period December 1987 through March 1989 is offered by an alternative Palestinian source, the Jerusalem Media and Communication Centre in *Bitter Harvest*.

strategy. For the Palestinians their trees represent a powerful symbol of their ties to the land. When trees are uprooted by the army the result is invariably to mobilise a spirit of collective solidarity within the community. Often volunteers will replant the land with new seedlings.[76]

Summary

The destruction of trees by either side, whatever its scope may be, pales in significance when compared to the extent of planting activities. For both Palestinians and Israelis, the planting of trees is multifunctional.

For the Palestinians, the planting serves as an agro-economic activity, and as a landholding tactic. Indeed, the planting of olive trees is currently more effective in terms of politics than economics, as the olive market is glutted and worsening. For those villages within the green belt, agriculture is seen in most cases as supplemental to income earned by wage labor in Jerusalem or elsewhere in Israel. Of these villages, most, but not all, have in recent years engaged in protecting their land from alienation. Those that attempt to preserve the land do so through planting activities and legal procedures.

There are also villages within the green belt which do little to protect their land from alienation. The reasons for this are difficult to confirm because of the gap between rhetoric and action concerning land issues. Seemingly, the factors contributing to inaction fall into three main categories. The first of these is the absence of young men to carry out agricultural activities, because of either migration or employment in more lucrative positions. The second factor is the conservative nature of the villagers, who are suspicious of innovations that could be effective in land protection, and even more suspicious of outside Palestinians, that is, those with professional training, who advocate such measures. A third reason is that many Palestinians take a fatalistic approach, believing that if Israel wants to take their land, there is nothing that they can do to prevent it. The great majority of Palestinians, however, advocate the protection of land from alienation, at least in theory, if not in practice.

Israeli planting in this area not only is multifunctional, but also fulfills different purposes for the respective agencies involved. For the JNF, afforestation is carried out to provide recreational sites, to create a landscape in keeping with Zionist ideology, and, through its role as subcontractor, to provide the JNF with income. The municipality and the Housing Ministry share the first two of these purposes, and also have an interest in acquiring and protecting land for future development, as does the ILA. While these are also practical purposes, they clearly have political motivations and implications.

---

[76] *Bitter Harvest*, p. 17.

The Village Cases

The following chapters detail elements of afforestation in the green belt as they relate to four Palestinian villages, and the activities of the villagers in response to the JNF planting activities. Three of the villages are outside the Jerusalem boundary, though in fact the municipality is involved in afforestation in the area of all but one of the four cases.

The factors contributing to the land conflict facing these villages involve many of the issues raised in this and previous chapters. The afforestation discussed hereafter affects both public and private land, takes place on both sides of the Green Line, is carried out on behalf of a variety of Israeli agencies and is met in return by Palestinian planting, and, in each location, is also accompanied by the mutual destruction of planted trees. Though the amount of land and trees involved in the disputes in these villages is small compared to the totality of the green belt, and minute in relation to the situation throughout Israel and the territories, the following cases reveal much of the character of the conflict in terms of its mechanics, its participants, and its consequences.

8

The Village of Sur Baher

In December 1985 a memo was sent to the JNF by the Jerusalem district manager of the ILA concerning the afforestation of the land in a valley adjacent to the Arab village of Sur Baher. The memo stated that the planting to be carried out was within the framework of creating a green belt around Jerusalem. Noted in the memo, however, was that the land in question had been expropriated in 1970 for the purpose of construction of housing, and there was no mention in the order of afforestation or a green belt. This discrepancy led to a case decided by the Israeli High Court of Justice which was to become important to the future extension of the green belt. Opposition by the villagers to the afforestation was intense and came despite the stated intention of the municipality, together with the ILA, to construct housing for young couples from the village on part of the expropriated land.

The original expropriation of 2,240 dunams of village land was made in 1970, and was designated for the construction of the Jewish neighborhood of East Talpiot, just across the valley from Sur Baher. Each year between 1970 and 1985 the construction of East Talpiot covered more of the expropriated area, but no work or afforestation was carried out in the valley immediately adjacent to the village. Plans existed, however, for continued development of the remaining open land, and as a result it was felt by the ILA that "it is not possible today to plant a real forest, rather more of a thin forest *whose principal purpose is the guarding of the area*, not the planting of a real forest, and that [only] until the determination of various uses for the land in question."[1]

---

[1] State of Israel, ILA, Jerusalem District, 7472, December 16, 1985, memo to the JNF, "Afforestation of the Sur Baher Area." Emphasis added.

The plan for afforestation evoked strong protests from the villagers, who contended that such a use was not within the mandate of the expropriation order. They thus demanded a return of the expropriated land to their ownership, indicating that their traditional use of that land, that is, agriculture, was in keeping with the purposes of the green belt. Some of the Jewish neighbors from the surrounding community were also offended by the intention to convert an area of olive trees worked by the villagers to one occupied by forest trees, ostensibly designed to provide a green area. As a result of the involvement of these Israelis, the case of Sur Baher received a good deal of attention, and followed an unusual course. Thus, the conflict over afforestation in Sur Baher reveals a wide range of characteristics common to disputes of this type, as well as some elements unique to this case, and it therefore deserves detailed examination.

The History and Location of the Village

Not many sources exist that shed light on the history of Sur Baher, in part for the same reasons that contribute to the lack of pertinent literature on villagers in general. In fact, the residents of Sur Baher themselves know relatively little about the early history of their village, though they are currently attempting to research the topic. Perhaps the earliest sources for information on the village are the Ottoman *daftars*, or books relating to the taxation of the area in which the village is found. Hutteroth and Abdulfattah present the figures for Sur Baher as taken from the *Daftar-i Mufassal*, compiled in 1596–97 C.E. The statistics of this *daftar* were taken from the Ottoman census of the region, the last to be conducted during the period of Ottoman rule. These numbers, therefore, were the only ones available to Ottoman officials until the mid-nineteenth century.

The numbers indicate that the village was governed under a *za'ama* system, akin to that discussed in chapter 2. The village was ascribed the number 318 in the registry for the Jerusalem region. It lists twenty-nine family heads, all of them Muslim.[2] The common calculation for population size during that period is five times the number of family heads, yielding for Sur Baher a population of roughly 145 in the year 1596 C.E.[3]

The taxation taken from a variety of crop types is also listed, giving a rough indication of the agriculture as it was then. Tax was taken at one-third the value of the harvest, with nine portions of the revenue thus generated

---

[2] The names of the original family heads are found in the original *daftar*, but they are not provided by Hutteroth and Abdulfattah, who list hundreds of villages in this work.

[3] Wolf-Dieter Hutteroth and Kamal Abdulfattah, *Historical Geography of Palestine, Transjordan, and Southern Syria in the Late Sixteenth Century* (Erlangen: Selbstverlag der Frankischen Geographischen Gesellschaft in Kommission bei Palm & Enke, 1977), p. 36, n. 1. This calculation accounts for unmarried men, that is, those potentially outside a family framework, but no such men are indicated in the *daftar* for this village.

going to the local ruler (of the area, rather than of the village), while fifteen portions went to the *Waqf*, or Muslim religious authority. The list indicates that Sur Baher was involved in the cultivation of wheat and barley (3,000 and 2,800 Ottoman *aqja* taken respectively), olives and a combined category of vineyards and fruit trees[4] (5,618 *aqja* taken for each), and finally a combined category of goats and beehives (1,300 *aqja* taken).

The total "of all taxes, tithe and toll for the official revenue holder, not including the share of the waqf" came to 12,983 *aqja*.[5] In relation to the total taken from the other villages falling within the current green belt, Sur Baher ranks third in size, with the largest being Abu Dis at 15,000 *aqja* and the smallest being Beit Surik at 2,000 *aqja*.[6] Those villages in the green belt mentioned in the *daftar* are Azzariya, Sharafat, Issawiya, Shu'afat, Beit Hanina, Anata, Um Tuba, and Beit Tzafafa.[7] A map of all those villages mentioned in the *daftars* of the sixteenth century also indicates a significant number that can no longer be found in the Jerusalem region.[8]

Today the village of Sur Baher is within the municipal boundary, though prior to 1967 it had been outside Jordanian municipal Jerusalem. Until recently the village was primarily agricultural, and claimed approximately 8,000 dunams of land southeast of the city. Now many of the villagers are employed in Jerusalem proper, a drive of only ten minutes from Sur Baher. The village is currently surrounded to the north by the neighborhood of East Talpiot, to the west by the kibbutz Ramat Rachel, which sits on land purchased from the village,[9] to the south by the village of Um Tuba, and to the east by open lands.

Between Sur Baher and East Talpiot there is a valley, the lands of which form the center of the dispute (see fig. 4). To the west there is an open area between the village and the kibbutz, part of which was also expropriated, and over which the villagers wanted renewed control. It was in this open space that the Green Line separated Jordan from Israel until 1967. At the west-

---

[4] It is impossible to know which of these, if not both, were cultivated in the village, as both are possible given the location. The same is true of the category of goats and beehives.

[5] Hutteroth and Abdulfattah, p. 120.

[6] Ibid., pp. 119 and 117.

[7] The lack of mention is according to Hutteroth and Abdulfattah a nearly certain indication that the village did not exist when the survey was taken. Despite the low populations of these villages, their classification indicates that they were considered, from an income-producing perspective, to be in the category of the largest type of agricultural settlement.

[8] Ehud Toledano, "Sanjak Jerusalem in the Sixteenth Century: Village Settlement and Aspects of Demography," in *Chapters in the History of Jerusalem at the Beginning of the Ottoman Period*, edited by Amnon Cohen (Jerusalem: Yad Izhak Ben-Zvi, 1979) [Hebrew].

[9] Yehoshua Ben-Arieh, *A City Reflected in Its Times: New Jerusalem—The Beginnings* (Jerusalem: Yad Izhak Ben-Zvi, 1979), p. 522 [Hebrew].

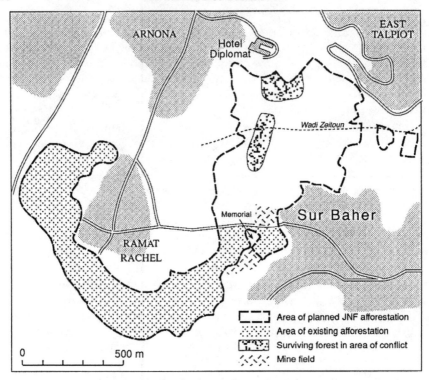

Fig. 4. The planting conflict in Sur Baher

ern edge of the village, the Jordanians constructed an outpost, surrounded it
with mine fields, and constructed a fence to mark the border. A no-man's-
land on both sides of the fence preserved the open area distancing the two
communities. The last houses of Sur Baher were adjacent to the fence, but
they were sparsely distributed this close to the no-man's-land, and significant
open spaces surrounded them. The houses nearest to the Jordanian outpost
were destroyed when the position was conquered by Israel in 1967.

Like all the Palestinian villages in the Jerusalem region, the built-up
area of Sur Baher has expanded significantly since 1967. To the north, it is
contained by the agricultural land in the valley and on the lower slope,
though the newer houses are scattered among the cultivated trees. To the
south, the village has begun to merge with its neighbor Um Tuba, and there
is little land there remaining for expansion. Thus the primary direction of
growth has been to the east. To the west, the growth has been checked by the
remnants of the mine field, an Israeli war memorial on the site of the Jordanian outpost, and the afforestation carried out by the JNF. Without restrictions, however, the natural growth of the village would have been in this

direction, along the road to the city. Of course since 1967 very few building permits have been issued for the western side of the village.[10]

Prior to 1967, relations between the kibbutz and the village were not hostile, even when separated by a border zone.[11] The villagers quietly observed the growth of fruit orchards on the Israeli land adjacent to the border, an area planted on the instruction of Prime Minister David Ben-Gurion, who saw the trees as a symbol and message to the neighbors across the fence. The one incident of note during the 1948–67 interlude occurred when Jordanian soldiers misunderstood the activities of a group of archaeologists visiting a site within the kibbutz grounds. The troops opened fire, and six of the archaeologists were killed. Not long after the shooting, the notables of the village came to the kibbutz to express their regret and effect a *sulha,* or peacemaking. Members of the kibbutz speak of good relations with the villagers during this period, whereas the villagers do not recall any relations to speak of.[12]

Despite the lack of tension between kibbutz and village, the municipality, following the expansion of the city in 1967, did not want them to grow toward each other The presence of the Israeli war memorial, the remaining mine fields, and the fields being worked to the east of the kibbutz helped to contain the spread of the village to the west. The land expropriated in 1970 was on the valley floor—named Wadi Zeitoun, or the Olive Valley. Land was also taken to the west of the built-up area of the village, on the slope and crest, and on land beyond the village groves on the far side of the valley bottom. This land had primarily been used for grazing village flocks and for rain-fed cultivation of grains. British mapping of the area from the 1930s shows the land in question with the Arabic plot names used by the villagers, giving some evidence of village use, though this does not necessarily confirm ownership.

The expropriation in 1970 was based on the authority of a land order issued by the British Mandate in 1943 concerning acquisition of land for public purposes. According to this ordinance, land deemed urgently necessary by the minister of the Treasury was taken by force of law from its owners, who in re-

---

[10] Illegal construction, in both the Jewish and Arab sectors, is punishable by either a fine or demolition, and in a few cases, both. Home demolition is also a punitive measure in the West Bank for security offenses, and thus it is a political issue all around. Most illegal construction goes unreported, and much of what is reported is basically ignored. The city is currently under severe criticism for lack of enforcement of restrictions on construction. In December 1990, two houses in Sur Baher were demolished by the municipality.

[11] One could suppose that the lack of hostility was precisely because the two communities were separated, but this seems not to be the case. Sur Baher has been quite active during the Intifada, and the source of more than a little violence, but there is no record of the violence being directed at the kibbutz, though East Talpiot has been targeted.

[12] Interviews with Y. Katz, historian of Ramat Rachel, October 8, 1988; and Hassan Abu-Asala, December 8, 1990.

turn received compensation agreed at through negotiation. The compensation could be a monetary sum, or it could be in the form of alternate land. The villagers of Sur Baher, like many other Palestinians, refused to negotiate for compensation in order to avoid recognition of the government and its right to carry out the expropriation. Sometimes in such cases a sum of money is deposited in a bank account for the day when the compensation will be accepted.

Because the villagers were not attempting to gain something in return for the land, indeed refused to engage the government in negotiation, issues of ownership and the proof thereof did not arise. The expropriation order itself does not mention the village, but speaks only of land in "south-east Jerusalem."[13] The construction of the East Talpiot neighborhood did not begin on the border of the expropriation closest to the village. Through 1991 the building did continue in that direction however, while remaining within the boundary of the expropriation order.

Planning for the Afforestation of Sur Baher

The separation between the Jewish areas and the village was in keeping with both municipal and national planning policy, though for different reasons. The municipality prefers to have a buffer zone between areas of Jewish and Arab residence, feeling that adjacent or intermingled residence is a recipe for increasing friction.[14] From the national planning perspective, two issues relate to the boundary zone between East Talpiot and Sur Baher. The first is a general policy that every newly constructed area in Israel include in its design an area of green on the periphery of the development. While this is often neglected in the contruction phase, the plans must include the green area in order to get approval from the Ministry of the Interior. The second issue is that in the national planning scheme Jerusalem is designated to be surrounded by a green belt and contain within it open spaces, both as parks and as groves.

In fact, the afforestation scheme drawn up for the southeastern sector of Jerusalem leaves Sur Baher as something of an island, its built-up area enclosed in each direction, except the east, by forest trees.[15] The Aronson plan of 1982 calls for the afforestation of 250 dunams, 150 of them called "east Ramat Rachel," to the south of the Bell Fort [the former Jordanian fort, now a

---

[13] State of Israel, *Digest of Publications* [*Yalkut Pirsumim*], no. 1656 (August 30, 1970): 2808 [Hebrew].

[14] Interview with Sara Kaminker, August 28, 1989.

[15] South of Um Tuba there is a forest under the management of the JNF. Plans were approved in the fall of 1990 for the construction on this land of the Jewish neighborhood Har Homa, a project that will eliminate most but not all of the forest currently there. The JNF is pressing a suit against the government, contesting the expropriation of this land from its ownership. Whatever the decision in that case, construction is likely to replace most of the forest.

war memorial], and 100 dunams on the slope north of the fort. The first part of the plan for this land says that the planting will be on the area "between kibbutz Ramat Rachel and the village of Sur Baher, and after the planting [it] will constitute a part of the green belt around Jerusalem."[16] However, a separate table produced by Aronson indicates that this area, the others adjacent to Sur Baher, and sites throughout the city are for "public construction in the future [with] forest as an intermediate use."[17]

The second section of the plan describes the area as "intended for the construction of homes in the future, as part of East Talpiot." It should be noted that housing that is part of East Talpiot is not the same as that proposed by the municipality and the Housing Ministry for young couples from the village. No mention of that proposal can be found in the Aronson intermediate plan. The report continues, "It is recommended in any case to create in the middle [of the valley] a broad path for pedestrians, afforested in order to create a connection between the different forest sections in the area, and on this the agreement of the Housing Ministry should be received."[18] The description of this section suggests that it is "uncultivated, with relatively deep soil, the remnants of orchards, and north of it the vineyards of the village of Sur Baher." The report recommends planting the land with olives, carob, oak, and nettle trees in the center, with pines and other types along the sides.[19]

The Aronson report spoke of one more area in connection with this afforestation, an archaeological site in East Talpiot which was to be made into an archaeological park. This area is smaller, only fifteen dunams, and no specific tree types are recommended for the planting. The work is listed as part of the afforestation plan for East Talpiot, but in its location it will constitute "a continuation of the garden areas of Sur Baher."[20]

The Dispute Erupts

Afforestation work on the land did not begin until the fall of 1985. At that time the area was entered by the JNF for the purpose of preparing the site for planting. As in other places, this entailed preparing access roads (usually unpaved, as in this case), clearing the area of existing growth through manual weeding and use of herbicides, and opening pits for the planting of seedlings. In this phase of preparation two kilometers of roads were plowed in the open

---

[16] Shlomo Aronson, "Master Plan for Greater Jerusalem: Intermediate Report no. 2," August 1982, section 60 [Hebrew].

[17] Aronson, "Table of Potential Areas for Afforestation in the Municipal Area of Jerusalem," JNF, 3307/unnumbered, May 5, 1982.

[18] Aronson, "Master Plan," section 61.

[19] Ibid., section 61.

[20] Ibid., section 62.

land north and west of the village. Sixty dunams of land were cleared, and a thousand pits opened for the planting of trees.[21]

The appearance of the JNF workers and the commencement of their activities in preparation for planting came as a surprise to the villagers of Sur Baher. Since the expropriation order in 1970, they had watched East Talpiot grow on the slope opposite their own homes. The progression of the neighborhood in their direction was obvious. The area entered by the JNF, however, was not contiguous with the built-up area of East Talpiot. Instead, it was on the land closest to the village, in Wadi Zeitoun and on the slopes, as described above.

In the absence of Israeli use of these lands, the villagers had maintained a degree of agricultural activity on them, evidence of which can be found in the descriptions in the Aronson report of 1982. There, is however, disagreement about the extent of the agriculture being practiced on the land; and the stories, claims, and interpretations of the villagers on the one hand, and the JNF and associated official bodies on the other, differ about this and a number of other points.

The Beginning of Resistance

The villagers protested the afforestation, saying:

> Look what's happening in an area wherein the economic situation is terrible, and instead of encouraging a man to bring his bread forth from the land, or to create his own food, look what they're doing. The land on which we're growing wheat and barley and all kinds of things, and which helps the livelihood of these families, becomes a park or becomes a forest.[22]

Also offensive to the villagers was that the preparations for planting indicated that the trees would come as far as the line of the lowest houses on the slope of the village, and in some cases even between the houses. The original line of expropriation had been adjacent to the built-up area of Sur Baher, and from the work in progress it appeared that JNF trees would soon follow along that line.

The villagers responded in a number of ways. Initially, their reaction was to come out of their homes and challenge the work crews of the JNF, composed for the most part of West Bank Palestinians, a challenge characterized by the JNF as "violent disturbances."[23] When the extent of the planting became clear, the mukhtar and several notables consulted with the villagers and decided to file suit in the Israeli High Court to prevent the planting, and to ask for the return of the land. Their claim was that afforestation was not in

---

[21] JNF, 3300/unnumbered, Avni to Sass, November 11, 1985.

[22] Interview with Hassan Abu Asala, November 9, 1989.

[23] JNF, 3300/1156, December 14, 1986.

keeping with the purposes stated in the expropriation order of 1970, and therefore that the order should be canceled and the land returned.

The high court recognized that afforestation was not explicitly included in the language of the original order, and noted that the purpose of the expropriation was "expressed at that time as 'the construction, development, and population of Jerusalem by way of the establishment of new residential neighborhoods.'"[24] The villagers further claimed that through the fault of the authorities they had been unaware of the extent of the original expropriation, and that this was grounds for canceling the order for the lands that remained between the village and the surrounding Jewish communities.[25] In arguing the case, the villagers claimed that the conversion of agricultural land to a forest was not a reasonable use, and that the authorities were motivated by "exterior considerations" that were irrelevant to the case.[26]

On the December 12, 1985, the high court issued a temporary restraining order prohibiting the JNF from entering the area while the matter was taken under consideration.[27] This order was passed on to the JNF staff by their legal advisor, and in both the court order and the internal memo the land is referred to by both its Israeli parcel nomenclature and by the Arabic customary names for the plots included therein, among them Wadi Zeitoun.[28] The area included in the restraining order covered five hundred dunams, this being more than the area proposed for planting.

A rally organized by the villagers and the activists from the Jewish neighborhoods was held on the site. The protest was unusual in that it was attended by both Arabs and Jews in equal numbers, and in common cause. Attendance was estimated at seven hundred people, and the media and a number of city officials attended as well. The resulting newspaper coverage brought the matter, at least briefly, to the attention of the Israeli public in general, and of Jerusalemites in particular. On December 22—not long after the rally—Teddy Kollek, the mayor of Jerusalem, appealed to the minister of agriculture to cancel the expropriation order for the land that was being worked by the villagers, an appeal that was ultimately not accepted.[29]

---

[24] Decision of the High Court of Justice, Case 704/85, November 18, 1986, p. 2.

[25] State of Israel, High Court of Justice, Case 704/85, December 12, 1985.

[26] Ibid.

[27] Ibid.

[28] JNF, 3300, December 19, 1985. Memo to Forestry Division from Gara Korn, JNF legal advisor.

[29] The rejection was issued on January 28, 1986, with the justification that the development of the area had not been completed and thus the expropriation could not be canceled. The municipality is quick to point out its intervention in this case on behalf of the village. Local activists and city officials suggest that it took extreme community pressure—on the part of Israelis—to motivate the intervention.

Political Planting?

While the case was being processed, changes were occurring on the land. According to the claim of the JNF, the villagers exploited the period of the restraining order to sow seed and plant olive trees on the disputed land in an attempt to "change the status of the area."[30] The JNF therefore appealed to the high court, and an additional order was issued on February 10, 1986, barring the villagers from the same area that had been made off-limits for the JNF and other actors involved in the issue. The JNF maintains that the planting of "tens of olive trees" continued even after the issuing of this order.[31] The version offered by the villagers holds that while the existing trees were maintained, no new trees were planted during this period, and that the olive trees in question were all between the ages of five and ten years old.[32]

In either case, the future of these trees, and of the entire area, awaited the decision of the high court, which was rendered on November 18, 1986, just prior to the JNF planting season for that year. In the intervening period, as part of the court's discussion of the issue, the minister of the treasury indicated that "the afforestation of the area which is the subject of the appeal, in the framework of the inclusive plan for the development of the area of Armon HaNatziv [a name for part of the area adjacent to and including East Talpiot], fits with the purpose of the expropriation and constitutes a part of it."[33]

The High Court's Decision

The judgment of the court was to reject the appeal in all its components. The denial was based on a number of factors relating to the various claims made by the residents of Sur Baher. As to the claim that the villagers had not known of the expropriation order in its fullness, the court found that in essence the villagers revoked that element of the case "when it became clear that all the obligatory procedures of the expropriation were done according to the law."[34] The claim that the purpose of the expropriation order had not included afforestation was rejected as follows:

> In that the entire area was expropriated for public purposes, these purposes included the construction of residences, also the development of the area, which is by nature, roads, public buildings, and areas that will be put to the use of the public for the improvement of the quality of life and the environment in the area. The meaning of 'populating new quarters in the city of Jerusalem' is not narrow in the sense of confining it to the construction of dwellings for the

---

[30] ILA, 4990-6-11130, January 27, 1986.

[31] JNF, 3307/58, Avni to Ziv, Jerusalem District Manager of the ILA, February 9, 1987.

[32] Interview with Hassan Abu Asala, December 15, 1990.

[33] Cited in JNF, 3300/1156, December 14, 1986.

[34] This and other quotations from the court's decision are taken from Decision of the High Court of Justice, Case 704/85, November 18, 1986.

housing of residents, [but means] rather also the development of the entire area
from the standpoint of broader public needs, within the neighborhoods *and in
the immediate surroundings*. It is said, therefore, that the original purpose of
the expropriation indeed included the construction of the neighborhood, but by
the nature of things also included planting and green areas which would be put
at the use of the public.

The planting of a forest on the belt of land between the said residential
neighborhood [East Talpiot and Ramat Rachel] and the community of Sur Baher is part of the development of the area.

Regarding the question of the reasonableness of converting agricultural
land to forestland for the creation of a green belt, the court considered that it
had responded to this question in the statements included above. The court
then went on to relate its decision to the general principle of the use of expropriated lands for open areas adjacent to residential neighborhoods. This part
of the decision would be of great utility to those bodies interested in land use
at the periphery of built-up areas in general, and tree planting in such areas in
particular. The court remarked that

it is even possible to say that it would not be reasonable if the respondents did
not designate alongside such a broad built-up space a "green" area, that is: gardens or parks or groves or a forest, that would be put to public use. Therefore it
cannot be said that the decision discussed herein and the use that was made of
the expropriated land is not reasonable—it certainly cannot be said that the
planting of the forest is the product of a decision made from considerations exterior to the matter.

The considerations which need to direct the planning authorities and the
Minister of the Treasury [the person responsible] who request to expropriate
land in order to put it at the use of the public are, first and foremost, planning
considerations, that is: what is good and desirable from the inclusive view of
populating community locations while preserving values of nature and environmental quality. In the case under discussion, the planning answers these considerations, and it cannot be said that it stems from considerations exterior to
the matter.

The court's decision canceled the restraining orders concerning access
to and use of the land in question, and it further obligated the villagers to pay
the costs of the respondents, to the sum of 3,000 shekels.

The decision was viewed by the JNF and the ILA as a major victory.
More significant than the afforestation of the land adjacent to Sur Baher, the
opinion of the court was interpreted as establishing a principle that would
serve the interests of these institutions throughout Israel.[35] Indicating that
belief was an internal JNF memo summing up the court's decision which was

---

[35] Subsequent decisions of the court have proven this to be the case, and not only in reference to
planting issues, but also in regard to the question of land usage that was not originally anticipated in an expropriation order. See for example the case concerning the Shu'afat Ridge in
north Jerusalem, December 1990, which was noted in chapter 7 in the context of the discussion of
the Ramot Forest.

entitled, in part, "Backing from the High Court for the planting of an urban forest on an expropriated area."[36]

The Evolution from Conflict to Accommodation

With the decision of the high court, the villagers were convinced that their formal efforts had failed, the land was lost, and their trees and fields would be converted to a forest. Sporadic opposition, however, such as blocking JNF access roads and other similar acts of vandalism, continued. In fact, though the legal phase of the case was concluded, the issue of what would be planted, where and by whom, was not yet decided. For the most part, this was due to the intervention of Jewish Israeli residents of the area, and their refusal to accept the logic of the court and the Israeli planting and land institutions. The main premise of "the neighbors" was that a green belt was just as well composed of olive trees as forest trees, and that the villagers should be able to maintain and benefit from their traditional agricultural practices on the land.[37]

Nonetheless, with the cancelation of the restraining orders the JNF resumed its activities, first in preparation of the land, and then in planting it. In part this included the uprooting of "many tens of olive trees which [according to the JNF] were planted by the residents of Sur Baher, at the time when their entrance to the area was forbidden by the order of the High Court." The trees uprooted were "transferred to the residents (except for eighteen which are still being treated and are awaiting planting in the Peace Forest)."[38] When the trees were uprooted, as well as on a number of other occasions, the villagers protested the actions with such vigor that the JNF felt compelled to call upon the local border guard unit to ensure the safety of the workers and enable the completion of the task.

As the planting of forest trees began, the neighbors met with the villagers to discuss what steps could be taken. The villagers, however, had lost faith in the system, and were not receptive to the appeal for action. The local committee of the Jewish Armon HaNatziv neighborhood, with the prompting of a number of indigenous and outside activists, decided to approach the JNF with a compromise plan. Its basic outline was that the expropriation order of 1970 would stand, but that olive rather than forest trees would be planted on the disputed area, and, for a symbolic rental fee, the villagers would have the right to continue to harvest the crop.

---

[36] JNF, 3300/1156, December 14, 1986.

[37] Interview with Hillel Bardin, November 14, 1989.

[38] JNF, 3307/58, February 9, 1987. The villagers claim that the trees had been planted a number of years prior to the dispute, as detailed in note 32 and above. The Jerusalem Peace Forest, located next to the neighborhood of Abu Tor, is the site of the local headquarters for JNF afforestation activities.

Initially this plan was anathema to the JNF because it would necessitate the uprooting of those trees already planted, something akin to apostasy among the ranks of the foresters. Gradually, however, the JNF came to agree to the plan, at least in theory. The proposal from the neighbors entailed the planting of thousands of olive trees along the valley bottom and the lower slope. The JNF was inclined to plant olives only where the pine and cypress trees already planted failed to thrive. While this negotiation was proceeding, relations between the JNF and the village continued to be poor.

Preventing the cooperation between these two groups was a conflict over principle. According to the JNF administrator responsible for carrying out afforestation in the area,

> If the residents of the village had exhibited courage of heart—and it really takes courage of heart . . . we could have come to a written agreement that . . . the area is expropriated and . . . they're prepared to lease . . . the land for temporary use for the planting of olives. We would have preferred the planting of olives more than the forest that we made. Whenever you ask them to sign on a paper that gives some kind of opening for an admission by them that the land isn't connected to them, at that stage they don't respond.[39]

For their part, the villagers, as always, refused to recognize the validity of the expropriation. They therefore continued to be unwilling to sign a paper agreeing to the terms that the JNF sought. Thus each side refused to commit an act that, according to the Ottoman tradition of land law, would or could increase the rights of the opposing side. In addition, the JNF felt that the successful outcome of the legal suit and the planting that, despite opposition, was completed, "constitutes eternal proof that with stubbornness and will on the part of the institutions and their representatives it is possible to protect and realize the possession of state lands."[40] Having successfully defended their principle, the JNF was not inclined to back down. Nonetheless, in April 1987, in the face of continued pressure, the JNF agreed to plant olive trees on the site.

Initial plans for olive tree planting, however, were for only thirty to forty dunams in the area of the bottom of Wadi Zeitoun. The JNF was also insistent that in places where forest tree saplings had earlier been uprooted by the villagers, principally on the slope near the houses, only forest trees would be replanted.[41] This deviated from the understanding of the compromise held by the neighbors and the villagers, who had expected that the area would be planted with olives wherever the soil was appropriate. The neighbors also charged that not only was the JNF failing to plant olive trees wherever possi-

---

39 Interview with Tzvi Avni, January 30, 1990.

40 JNF, 3307/58, February 9, 1987.

41 JNF, 3300/482, July 26, 1987.

ble, but that olive trees were being planted only where the forest trees had failed.[42]

The neighbors, together with the village mukhtar, Khader Dabash, also indicated that

> to the residents of the village and the Jewish neighborhoods it is very impor-
> tant to complete the planting [of olives] with urgency and in a good spirit
> within the current planting season. If the JNF and the municipality lack the re-
> sources to plant more than 1,000 olives this year, we are ready to donate the
> remaining saplings to the JNF, and/or to carry out the planting of them.[43]

Though originally slated for a completion of planting in 1987–88, in the winter of that season the JNF decided that the work would be conducted over a period of three years instead. The motivation for this decision was twofold: first, there were mundane budgetary limitations on the scope of planting, and second, it was thought desirable to observe the way the villagers were responding to the compromise. That is to say, the planting was intended to be on a trial basis, with continuation contingent on the cessation of damage to the forest trees planted by the JNF.

In February of that winter, a survey was conducted of the area in the presence of representatives of both the village and the JNF. Among the topics discussed were the planting by the JNF in accordance with the compromise, the continued uprooting of seedlings on the slope by the villagers, and olive planting carried out by the villagers.

It was concluded by the JNF that olive planting would continue on the valley floor, but that in stony areas (primarily the slope) evergreens would be planted, and that "in every place where seedlings were uprooted planting [of forest trees] would be renewed immediately." The recommendation of the JNF representative was that the olive trees planted by the villagers should be uprooted, while the village representative recommended that that not be done "in order to preserve the quiet and cooperation of the villagers."[44] The response of the ILA to the JNF recommendation held that "after all the concessions and arrangements with the residents of Sur Baher and after the management of the JNF and the mayor went in their favor beyond the original agreements—there is no place to suffer an additional deviation from the agreement and planting by the residents of the place."[45]

---

[42] Letter from Mukhtar Khader Dabash and Hillel Bardin to Mayor Teddy Kollek, JNF Chairman Moshe Rivlin, Minister of Agriculture Arieh Nahemkin, and others; January 22, 1988.

[43] Ibid.

[44] JNF, 3300/33, February 11, 1988.

[45] ILA, 540, February 21, 1988.

The Fading of the Issue

When the planting season of 1987–88 was concluded, a significant area had been planted—part with pine and cypress, part with olive—but much of the land remained bare. On the slope closest to village homes, few of the trees planted by the JNF now remain. On the opposite slope, however, especially to the northwest, the trees are growing taller each year. So too is the grove planted immediately to the west of the village, adjacent to the memorial and along the main road into town. This grove forms a wall, symbolically blocking the spread of the village, and it is only a few meters from the nearest home.

Nearly all of the olive trees planted by the JNF perished within the first year after their planting. The villagers suggest that the seedlings were too small to withstand the dryness of that year, and they believe that the trees planted were of weak stock and likely to perish, and that this was, in fact, intentional. The JNF reports that the year was unusually wet, and that the subsequent abundance of weeds and other growth blocked the sun necessary for the olives to survive.[46]

However that may be, with the conclusion of the planting season, JNF activity on the site effectively ceased. The element of cooperation, both between the villagers and the Jewish neighbors, and between the village and the JNF—such as it was—fell victim to the hostility and mistrust that grew with the outbreak of the Intifada. From time to time a number of forest trees are uprooted, burned, or consumed by herds of goats. Even so, the JNF remains passive in the area, and has no plan to continue planting—olive or pine—on this site.

The status of the land remains officially unchanged. Nonetheless, the JNF states that it is "not preventing the residents of the village [from] approaching the older trees that they come to collect from; we're not acting like masters. We're not looking to create conflict unnecessarily."[47] As a result, the situation has returned to the status quo ante. The villagers continue to work the valley bottom, and to some extent the slope as well. The JNF is rarely seen on the site.

The villagers are hesitant to take the initiative and plant olive trees in those areas designated for that type in the deal worked out with the JNF, fearing that anything they plant on the land involved in the dispute will be uprooted. The neighbors have given up their drive to have the olive planting

---

[46] The rainfall recorded for that season in central Jerusalem was 666.6 millimeters. While it is quite possible that the area in question received less rainfall, 666.6 millimeters is greater than the average annual rainfall for Jerusalem. Shimon Bigelman, ed., *Jerusalem Statistical Yearbook 1988* (Jerusalem: Municipality of Jerusalem and Jerusalem Institute for Israel Studies, 1988).

[47] Interview with Tzvi Avni, January 30, 1990.

completed. In doing so, they abandoned the notion, originally conceived with the village, of a joint planting ceremony by Jewish and Arab children for the creation of an olive grove that was to be a sign of their hope for "justice, dual existence, and good neighborliness."[48]

---

[48] Letter from Dabash and Bardin.

9

Beit Iksa and Beit Surik

Two neighboring green belt villages present radically different responses to the land pressures created through Israeli afforestation, settlement
construction, and neighborhood expansion. Beit Iksa and Beit Surik lie to the
west of Jerusalem's Ramot neighborhood, just north of the pre-1967 corridor
(fig. 5). Because of their location, each of the villages has land on both sides of
the Green Line, and occupies sites considered strategically important in controlling the principal approach to the city. What is striking about Beit Iksa and
Beit Surik is the different way each has reacted to the growing Israeli presence
that, in an attempt to dominate the area, is bracketing their villages.

Beit Iksa, sitting outside the municipality on a hilltop some four hundred meters west of Ramot, has been in a constant retreat from its land since
the upheaval of 1948. Today its resident population is primarily composed of
young children, women, and older men. Agriculture, the primary method of
maintaining land use, is a dying occupation in the village. As a result, the
amount of land worked is inexorably contracting, and the challenge to Israeli
growth is generally feeble or nonexistent. Thus, the ring of Israeli land use is
tightening around the village, eliminating many of the areas of potential village use that still remain.

In contrast, the village of Beit Surik is responding vigorously to the Israeli challenge, albeit with only partial success. Though the village falls just
outside the green belt, villagers from Beit Surik are affected by afforestation in
Beit Iksa and on other sides of their village, and by Israeli neighborhood expansion both within and beyond the Green Line. In response to Israeli
growth, Beit Surik is currently cultivating more land than at any time in the
recollection of the villagers, and seeking to expand even further the amount
of land in use. Significantly, the villagers are monitoring the Israeli moves,

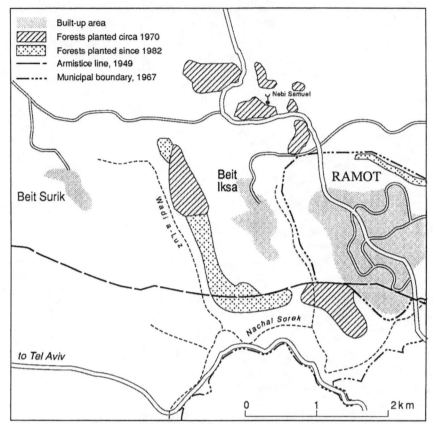

Built-up area
Forests planted circa 1970
Forests planted since 1982
Armistice line, 1949
Municipal boundary, 1967

Nebi Samuel

Beit Iksa

RAMOT

Beit Surik

Wadi a-Luz

Nachal Sorek

to Tel Aviv

0   1   2km

Fig. 5. *Afforestation encircling Beit Iksa. Legal disputes, arson, and uprooting concentrated on the forest area to the west of the village.*

and seeking to devise strategies to anticipate and protect their land from future developments.

It is striking that two neighboring villages, facing essentially the same challenges, respond in such different manners. Beit Iksa suffers from a lack of manpower due to the absence of many residents and their families, now living in Jordan and elsewhere. The remaining work-age male population seeks wage labor in Israel, and thus fails to maintain the land and agricultural tradition. There is a clear perception in Beit Iksa and the surrounding area that this is a village that has, in large part, given up on its land.

Beit Surik has the opposite reputation. Though it has lost significant amounts of land, and is currently facing further alienation, Beit Surik is known and respected in the Palestinian community as a village that cares for its land and works it with dedication. Here, too, there are problems such as a drain of young men to wage labor, but, despite this, an attitude of aggressiveness concerning the maintenance of land tenure is clearly predominant. In Beit Surik there is also less resignation concerning the future of the land than there is in other villages, and, thus, a sense that the status of the land is a matter subject to the actions of both sides in the conflict. This is in contrast with the prevailing attitude in most villages on the West Bank that the government will, ultimately, do what it wants with Palestinian land.

The Beit Iksa Slope

Because Beit Iksa does not work all of its agricultural land, for many years some its fields and groves have been rented to farmers from Beit Surik. One area in which such an arrangement continues is the slope to the west of Beit Iksa, facing Beit Surik across a deep wadi.[1] It is on this slope, running perpendicular to the corridor and straddling the Green Line, that a significant afforestation project is being conducted by the JNF, affecting both villages directly and indirectly (fig. 6). In part, this work is designed to link a number of forests located to the north and to the west of Beit Iksa. A goal that was more immediate and specific to the location of this project was "taking possession of territory and creating a hold on it, as this is a strategic site which is adjacent to the main ascent to Jerusalem."[2] This is in keeping with Israel's desire to expand and dominate the area of access to Jerusalem from the coastal plain. In fact, afforestation of this location had begun as early as 1969, and, today, a mature forest stands on 215 dunams of land. Current efforts are intended to broaden that forest to an additional 1,150 dunams, as approved by the national Grazing and Afforestation Committee in 1984.[3] A JNF memo on the topic outlined the plan and enlisted the assistance of the Civil Administration, which is responsible for the portion of land in the West Bank on which some of the forest is located:

> The JNF is currently conducting broad development and afforestation activities between the neighborhoods of Ramot in Jerusalem and Mevasseret Tzion. In the framework of these activities we are cutting new roads and afforesting the slope of the village Beit Iksa along the Green Line. In order not to create a forest which ends at an artificial line—the Green Line—and in order to take possession of areas that are not in private ownership, we are interested in broadening the planting northward. The intention is in the center of the Beit Iksa slope to get up to the olive orchards which are south of the village, and west up to the existing forest on the slope facing Wadi a-Luz. In the examination which we conducted, we found that almost all the area mentioned is "rocky ground." We would appreciate it if you would act for the declaration of the area as state land in order to allow our activity on it.[4]

---

[1] The wadi is called Wadi a-Luz, and it joins Nachal Sorek.

[2] JNF, 3300/709, October 19, 1987.

[3] Ibid.

[4] JNF, 3300/1146, December 11, 1986.

Fig. 6. The Beit Iksa slope. The forest carves out sharp lines in the landscape. Beit Surik plum trees are in the foreground; the Nebi Samuel mosque is on the ridge.

The examination discussed in the above memo referred to a check of the site, conducted by a variety of forestry and legal authorities, following the complaint by a Beit Iksa resident that preparatory work for afforestation was being carried out on his land. A summary of that check notes that "in the examination carried out by Mrs. Plia Albeck, the Legal Advisor to the Government and JNF representatives, it was determined that the area is appropriate for planting of forest trees by the JNF, *except for areas being worked by the locals*, and that the area is not settled [i.e., it has not undergone the land settlement process]." The findings of the examination are detailed as follows:

A. The area in question is located on a slope that in our impression has never been worked.

B. According to the claim of the local resident, his claim concerns 20 dunams in block 6, parcel 773, "Erech al Hamim."

C. The complainant, who was present, exhibited for us a *melia* [certificate of payment of property tax and compensation fees from Jerusalem].

D. According to the map from 1934 which is in our possession, there is no trace of this name and, more than that, the complainant had no map in his possession to support his claim.[5]

The conclusion reached was that the claim was unsubstantiated because the *melia* did not constitute proof of ownership. It is also noted in the summary that "the cause of the agitation of the residents and their claim of ownership on the land in the area stems from the preparatory activities of the JNF."[6] Though private ownership of the land was denied, it was incorrect to assume that the land was automatically state land. Thus, the Civil Administration alerted the JNF that "in a check that we conducted in the field, the areas requested [by the JNF] are not state land but appear here as areas the ownership of which the state will claim some day."[7] The lack of a prior declaration of state land is what led to the JNF appeal to the Civil Administration cited above.

A formal request for the declaration of state land was made on December 22, 1986, by the head of the Defense Ministry's Settlement Unit. The Civil Administration did not bring matters to a quick resolution, however, and the process of clarification of the land's status continued. Despite this, the JNF pressed ahead with its preparations until the following notice was received from the Civil Administration:

1. On the slope of Beit Iksa there was a request by the JNF to carry out afforestation along the Green Line but you received an answer from the Infrastructure Division of Judea and Samaria [of the Civil Administration] that

---

[5] Civil Administration Ramallah District, KMA 72–37, October 16, 1988.

[6] Ibid.

[7] Civil Administration of Judea and Samaria, Infrastructure Branch, Supervision Division, 1352–452, December 8, 1986.

the area is not *declared* state land [but is] rather areas that the state is interested in owning.

2. On September 7, 1987, the head of the Beit Iksa Council appealed to me and
   complained that you were cutting roads for afforestation on private land of
   the residents of Beit Iksa and that you are preparing the infrastructure for
   afforestation.

3. From an earlier examination by the Coordinator of the Custodian [of Prop-
   erty] Ramallah District it seems that this claim is justified and that the
   JNF has no authorization for carrying out the work from the certified authorities. . . .

4. I request that you order the immediate cessation of work until a check of the
   facts and the authorizations, in the case there are any, but we do not know of
   them.[8]

The JNF was thus instructed to suspend its activities on all land for
which it had not specifically received permission to work. The JNF renewed
its request for a declaration of state land on a parcel of 720 dunams,[9] and an
additional examination of the site was conducted on February 4, 1988, with
the following decision reached:

A. The area . . . is seemingly state land, was held for the most part by the Jordanian authorities, and is currently held in part by the JNF and it is permissible to hold it and to allow the JNF to plant it.

B. The area has not undergone a process of declaration and is not registered as
   state land and therefore if there is any opposition at the time of JNF activity in the area, the work must desist in the portion for which there is opposition, the details of the opponent should be written and the material
   brought to Mrs. Plia Albeck for an additional check in light of the claims.[10]

As it happened, the claims mentioned above did not come to pass, at
least in terms of bureaucratic proceedings. The case discussed earlier, wherein
the evidence concerning a claim of twenty dunams was found unsubstantiated, had an interesting outcome. Having rejected the evidence and concluded that there was no basis for declaring the land privately owned, the
authorities decided not to plant on the area. Further, they agreed to a continuation of agricultural cultivation being carried out on the site by the petitioner.[11] According to the documents no other claims were presented to the
appeals committee, and thus the Justice Ministry informed the Civil Administration that planting was permitted everywhere on the slope except for the

---

[8] Israel Defense Force [Civil Administration, Infrastructure Division], 1029–1091–85, September
10, 1987.

[9] JNF, 3300/2724 (Shai/289–3), December 14, 1987.

[10] Civil Administration of Judea and Samaria, Infrastructure Division, 2853–2794, February 11,
1988.

[11] Civil Administration Ramallah District, KMA 72–37, October 16, 1988. This decision was
made by Albeck, who in addition to her role as legal advisor, is an authority on land issues and
a central figure in the drafting and application of land policy.

twenty-dunam enclave previously discussed.[12] The lack of appeals does not signify a lack of claim to ownership of the land, however, and this is hinted at by a reference to a "lack of cooperation on the part of the [villagers]," resulting in the removal of all barriers to planting.[13] Lack of cooperation is a way of saying that the villagers were unable or chose not to engage the system.

The Villagers' Version of Events

The conflict over afforestation of the Beit Iksa slope is viewed quite differently by the villagers involved in the issue. The people of Beit Iksa have claims to the land being afforested on the slope, as well as to part of the area within the Ramot neighborhood of Jerusalem, and the agricultural land south of the village used by Israeli moshavim. They report that between one-half and two-thirds of the village lands were lost in 1948.[14] Since that time the vast majority of Beit Iksa's citizens have not been resident in the village. Some return in their old age, but fewer than 10 percent of those whose family origins are in the village actually reside there.

The villagers point out that most of the land that the village has lost since 1948 belongs to the outside residents. As a result, their land is under the authority of the Custodian for Abandoned Property, and the disposition of that land generally cannot be contested. In the wake of the 1967 War, the villagers saw absentee land opposite the village planted by the JNF, and subsequently they watched the Ramot neighborhood replace much of that forest. Some of this land was in a no-man's zone prior to 1967, and much of the rest along the former armistice line, and thus a military area. The villagers say that they were not issued *Tabu* deeds for their land, despite the payment of taxes to Jordan.[15]

Such was the status of the land described by the family of Abdel Hadi Khalil Ghayth, the petitioner in the Beit Iksa slope case described above. According to the family, the plot in question was not twenty dunams, but rather fifty dunams. They admit that their documentation was for twenty dunams of land, and explain that the plot size was underreported since Ottoman times in

[12] Ministry of Justice, 15/1390/232, April 2, 1989.

[13] Letter from Daniel Kramer, advocate to the Civil Administration, Infrastructure Division, March 29, 1989. In fact, another barrier remained. During the preparatory work an archaeological site was discovered in the area slated for afforestation. All development and construction in Israel and the territories is subject to the approval of the Department of Antiquities. Though not relevant to this discussion, the JNF had an ongoing problem with getting permission for planting because of incursions and damage to the area under the supervision of the archaeological officer of the Civil Administration.

[14] Interview with Lutfi Suliman, January 4, 1991.

[15] This was the only West Bank village studied in which residents reported tax payments to the Jordanians for agricultural land. In the other villages specific mention was made that the Jordanians did not collect such taxes.

order to decrease tax payments.[16] Thus, despite the fact that they had a *melia* for only twenty dunams, their claim to the JNF and Israeli authorities was for the full fifty dunams, and not the twenty dunams reported in the Israeli documents on the case. Half of this area was traditionally worked with olives and grapes, according to the family, and the other half was planted with cereals.

As far as the villagers know, there was no prior notification of plans for the resumption of the afforestation of the area in the 1980s, and the matter came to light only with the appearance of JNF work crews on the slope. When the family protested and asked the Palestinian work crew to stop the preparations, they were directed by the Israeli area supervisor to produce documentation for their claim to the land. In the eyes of the villagers, the JNF was a part of the government, and thus such requests were viewed as demands, backed by legal authority and supported by threat of enforcement.[17] The villagers thus presented their documents to the head of the work crew, and were told that the military governor would be summoned to the area.

According to the Ghayth family, a tour of the site was conducted in the presence of the military governor, though they do not recall the presence of Albeck, the legal advisor, at that time. At the conclusion of the survey, they understood that the JNF was ordered to desist from planting the area, but one week later the planting resumed.[18] A letter concerning the dispute, referred to above, was sent by Abdel Hadi Khalil Ghayth to the government. No notice of the receipt of that letter was offered by the government, nor were the villagers aware of any follow-up to it. In the absence of a governmental response the family concluded, in part correctly, that the issue had been decided against them.

Moreover, the villagers contend that there was never any indication on the part of the JNF or anyone else that the twenty disputed dunams would remain free of forest trees. Instead, they claim that the area was planted along the lines of the original plan.[19] At the bottom of the slope there are mature fruit and olive trees, being worked by villagers from both Beit Iksa and Beit Surik. These trees have not been challenged by the JNF. It is the high ground, including the land claimed by the Ghayth family, that is being afforested.

---

[16] Interview with Khalid Ghayth, January 4, 1991.

[17] In fact, Jordanian laws give wider latitude to governmental forestry workers to enforce the law than do Israeli regulations. Such powers do not accrue to JNF staff, however, who must enlist the aid of authorized members of the respective security forces to deal with those suspected of transgressions.

[18] The villagers are quite vague about specific dates, and sometimes confused about the sequence of events, and, thus, no effort will be made to compare the Israeli and Palestinian versions of events in this regard.

[19] An examination of the site was inconclusive. JNF officials were vague about the exact location of the twenty dunams in question, as were the villagers. While there are small patches of land being worked in the area, neither side seemed able to specify boundaries.

Other villagers have claims in this area, and, according to the village version, many of them sought to protect their land. As in the Ghayth case, however, they state that there has been no response to or recognition of their claims.

In the course of these events, villagers uprooted a section of the land being planted by the JNF, and the area was subsequently replanted with forest trees. The forest was also subjected to more than twenty incidents of arson, an aspect of the conflict which will be discussed below. In March 1991, Abdel Hadi Khalil Ghayth went once again to confront the JNF crews and ask them to stop planting on his land. He was turned away from the area, and he reports that he was warned by the JNF crew that if he set foot on the land again, he would be sent directly to jail.

Currently the villagers fear an extension of the forest to the north, beyond the boundaries of the previous planting. They also are suspicious that a settlement will be constructed at the northern edge of the forest. Their concern is based in large part on an incident not directly related to tree planting. One of the village landowners died recently, after selling a portion of his land located not far from the forest edge. Some months after his death, the home of his widow was ransacked and burned. The only thing taken from the home were documents relating to the land remaining in the widow's possession. In the wake of the theft, claims by other villagers have begun to emerge for some of that land. Another figure in these claims is a known land seller from a nearby village who has served in the past as a straw man for Israeli contractors. In light of these events, the villagers anticipate an increase in land activity in their area.[20]

Reprisals against the Trees

As noted, the Beit Iksa forest was the site of repeated arson, which, though the cumulative damage was limited, was considered a serious problem by the JNF. The Palestinian watchman managed to apprehend perpetrators on only one occasion, out of more than twenty separate incidents. Because the forest is in a relatively isolated location, the effort and expense in fire fighting was considerable. In the opinion of the JNF, responsibility for the bulk of the arson falls on villagers from Beit Surik rather than Beit Iksa.[21] While the forest is much closer to the latter than to the former, some of the areas adjacent to the bottom of the forest, in the direction of Beit Surik, are worked by residents of that village.

In fact, the trees worked there by residents of Beit Surik have been subjected to damage, allegedly by Israeli settlers. As with other cases of tree de-

---

[20] On a number of occasions settlers have attempted to create a settlement at nearby Nebi Samuel. On each occasion the settlers have been removed by the army, despite claims that there is legal justification and earlier (Likud) government decisions supporting the settlement.

[21] Interview with M. Ovadia, JNF area supervisor, January 12, 1990.

struction in the West Bank, a number of Palestinian organizations in Jerusalem called attention to the damage, and protested it in strong terms. One of them, the Land and Water Institution for Studies and Legal Services, stated that it

> condemns this campaign which is carried out by the enemies of trees in Beit Surik and in the Occupied Territories and calls upon all the international organizations and committees to reveal this policy and to stop these aggressions which are carried out by the settlers with the full knowledge of the Israeli authorities.
>
> This importance stems out [sic] from the fact that the issue of agriculture, is one of the most crucial bases of the Palestinian economy in the West Bank and Gaza Strip. And this might have direct relation with the systematic aggression against our people in an attempt to uproot them from their homeland and replace them with incoming settlers.[22]

The villagers of Beit Surik, on the other hand, while lamenting the loss of their trees, understood the destruction completely. They explained that it came in response to the growing number of forest arsons carried out by village youth, and they were not surprised or particularly outraged by what they perceived as an understandable reprisal. This was not the first case of reciprocal destruction that Beit Surik had been involved in. The village has a history of friction with the Jewish community located in Har Adar, most of which has been directly related to local land conflicts.[23] In that dispute, the village suffered the loss of many trees, while land within Har Adar was burned by the villagers.[24]

Beit Surik

Like many other villages near the Green Line, Beit Surik[25] lost much of its land in 1948. Some of this land, under the direction of the custodian for abandoned land and other governmental bodies, was used for a variety of purposes. As a result, Beit Surik is currently bracketed by a combination of Jerusalem suburbs, kibbutzim and moshavim, JNF forests, and other West Bank villages. In addition to the disputed land in the direction of Beit Iksa, the village has ongoing problems with Har Adar and emerging problems

---

[22] Land and Water Institution for Studies and Legal Services, Press Statement no. 1, undated.

[23] The community of Har Adar began adjacent to but within the Green Line. Since the 1967 War, Har Adar has expanded beyond the Green Line, bringing it into conflict with Beit Surik. Since it straddles the Green Line, Har Adar fits the dual classification of community and settlement.

[24] Palestine Human Rights Information Center, "Human Rights Update: September, 1990," vol. 3, no. 10 (September 1990): 416.

[25] Currently there is very little JNF activity on Beit Surik land, thus there are few documents relating to afforestation near this village. Other aspects of the village's land issues are documented by the Civil Administration, but access to those documents is not available at this time. Similarly, the villagers are willing to exhibit documents for private review, but do not agree to have them cited or published.

with the suburb of Mevasseret Tzion. The dispute with Mevasseret Tzion is reflected in the decrease in distance between the two communities caused, in part, by the extension of planting by both villagers and the JNF (fig. 7). While Har Adar is a nonagricultural community, the growth of its residential area has an impact on the land and trees of Beit Surik.

Land associated with the village and now used by Israel has been alienated in three ways. The first and greatest factor in alienation was the absence of the owners, which brought their land under the supervision of the Israeli custodian. A second manner of alienation has been through the sale of Beit Surik land. Land sales are not recent, however, nor are they considered by the villagers to be legitimate.

The land sale most commonly referred to took place in 1976. At that time a collaborator from outside the village sold 240 dunams of land in the area of Mevasseret Tzion. The land was not his to sell, and the villagers objected. They relate that the seller was apprehended in 1983, convicted, and sentenced to seven years in prison. Before his term elapsed, however, he was paroled and allowed to go to the United States. There, according to the villagers,

> People from Beit Surik found this man in Chicago. They went to him and confronted him over the land he had sold. He told them he didn't do it, but the people knew the truth and they killed him. The police say that he was killed during a robbery, but we know that he was dealt with by people from here.[26]

No recent cases of land sale are mentioned by the villagers, though there was controversy over the willing transfer of land for use by residents of the portion of Har Adar which extends beyond the Green Line, and by the JNF. According to the villagers, five men from Beit Surik were approached by officials of the government concerning an access road for the JNF. The road was intended to allow them a direct route to forests inside the Green Line that are most easily linked with other area forests by a line running through Beit Surik's agricultural land. The initial representation was for a dirt road, three meters in width, which would be for the use of the JNF, the residents of Har Adar, and the villagers. In fact, the road was intended to provide access to some of the village's more remote fields, and thus was initially viewed with some favor. It was to be located halfway up a hillside, beyond most of the village orchards.

Of the five men asked to give their approval for the road, three were mukhtars and two were landowners who would be directly affected since the road would be on their land. Two of the men, both mukhtars, avoided signing by making themselves unavailable to the government. The remaining

---

[26] Interview with Omar Mohammed Ali Jamal, mukhtar of Beit Surik, January 2, 1991.

Fig. 7. Competitive planting in Beit Surik. Mature trees are at the bottom and left; expanding village orchards can be seen on the slope opposite. New JNF seedlings have been planted in the remaining space.

three villagers did give their consent, however.[27] When the road was completed, the expansion of Har Adar proceeded to encroach on the land between the new road and the hilltop. The villagers state that this land was used for cultivation of wheat and barley by a number of families who now live in Jordan, and supported a number of orchards as well. When the village protested the expansion of Har Adar in the direction of their fields, they were told that the signatures provided by the villagers related to all of the land in question, and not just the section used for the road.[28] They were also told that the area was state land. The people of Beit Surik dispute this, contending that except for a former Jordanian military post on the summit totaling ten dunams, the hillside is not state land.

An additional problem for the village has emerged from the expansion of Har Adar in the direction of the new road. Sewage from the community has been seeping down the hill and affecting between three and four hundred dunams of the village orchards. Illness has been traced to the fruit from the trees in this orchard, thus lowering the price that the villagers receive. And, while the olive trees planted there are able to withstand the polluted water, the plum trees have been perishing. Since plums are the main crop of Beit Surik, the damage caused by the sewage results in severe economic hardship.

Some of the villagers have constructed channels to lead the sewage away from their trees, but not all of the farmers can afford to do this.[29] And, in times of heavy rain, the ditches fail to contain the flow, and the orchards are flooded. The mukhtar has complained repeatedly about the problem, approaching the administration anew each time there is a change in personnel. He reports that promises are made on each occasion, but nothing is done to alleviate the problem.[30] In the mean time, villagers are planting along the slopes rather than in the valley bottom, thus protecting their new trees from exposure to the sewage.

The villagers believe that the flow of sewage through their orchards is a deliberate act on the part of Har Adar and the Civil Administration. They base their suspicion on the following explanation:

> Some people from Adar came and they were interested in purchasing the land where these orchards are. They said something about making a road from

---

[27] One of those who gave consent for the road was arrested during a subsequent visit to Amman. He was held for a number of months on suspicion of land sales to Jews. However, with testimony from the village as to the course of events, he was later released.

[28] The road was later paved, and served both the village and Har Adar. With the outbreak of the Intifada, however, security concerns led Har Adar to place a fence at the downhill edge of the road, which is not far from the community's homes. As a result, the road no longer provides access for the residents of Beit Surik to their adjacent fields.

[29] Interview with Abu Rashid, November 12, 1990.

[30] Interview with Omar Mohammed Ali Jamal, January 2, 1991.

the settlement to the main Tel Aviv highway, and the shortest way is through our trees. We told them we didn't want to sell the land. Not long after that we began having the problem with the sewage.

We went to them to complain. They said that they would purchase land to place a pipe to carry away the sewage. They wanted a path twenty meters wide! We thought that on that path they'll build their road, and we wouldn't sell it. We said that we could sell them land for a place to collect these waters, but they didn't want that. Then we said that we would give them land for this thing, and they didn't want that either. So they don't have our land, but we have their sewage.[31]

In this atmosphere of suspicion, the villagers of Beit Surik have begun to act in ways that they hope will protect their land from current and future challenges. The configuration of Har Adar is such that it provides them with ongoing motivation. The highest trees belonging to the village thrust up beyond the three-meter road, into the area of housing constructed long after the trees were planted. It is clear to the villagers that were the trees not there, housing would have been constructed on that land as well. With tangible evidence that tree planting can be effective in preventing encroachment, the villagers have decided to broaden the use of a proven tool (fig. 8).

To do so, they are currently reclaiming previously unused land by expanding their area of cultivation. Where they lack the material resources to grow crops, they give the soil a crude plowing to demonstrate use. Villagers are also beginning to build walls or fences around the land they are working, as well as around land that they intend or hope to work, in order to prevent alienation. Such methods were initially implemented by individuals, with the rest of the village waiting to observe the outcome. When particular tactics were deemed a success, the villagers met with the mukhtar to review the situation and, through a process of informal learning and discussion, the ideas spread and took hold. Today, the farmers state unequivocally that, without such methods, they will lose their land, while, with them, they are protected from encroachment. As a result, they are working intensively to bring into use and protect the land nearest to Har Adar and Mevasseret Tzion. Those farmers who lack the resources to protect their land are seeking loans in order to make the desired improvements.

Though the village is very aggressive in protecting its land, the picture is not one of unblemished success, nor is it a picture of unified effort in the face of Israeli challenges. A current dispute within the village revolves around the question of how to confront the suspicion concerning plans for the further expansion of Har Adar. In late 1990 the Civil Administration invited village notables to examine plans for an extension of housing within the West Bank portion of the community. The delegation from Beit Surik was assured that the growth would not affect village land. The hearing was

---

[31] Interview with Abu Nabil, October 10, 1990.

Fig. 8. Blocking expansion of Har Adar. The olive trees of Beit Surik stop the settlement from continuing down the slope. The plum trees lower down absorb the sewage run-off, which contaminates their fruit.

informal, however, and the notables asked that a date be set for a formal review of the plans.

A date was fixed, but it fell during the period of the Gulf War, and, as a result of a curfew in the West Bank, the villagers were prevented from attending the meeting. The proceeding was not rescheduled, and the notables were prepared to forego the formality, based on their impression that the expansion was not a threat to the village. A minority faction in the village pressed for further clarification. Their fears, based on the experience with the three-meter road, made it impossible for them to trust the veracity of the Civil Administration. The issue has become internalized, dividing the village. Though it is difficult to determine the composition of the two opinion groups, the split is clearly within extended family groups, and there is some indication that it is generational in nature.

It seems to be the youth of the village who are in favor of pressing the issue, seeking clarification from the government, and instituting a lawsuit if necessary.[32] The older residents seem to favor a quiet continuation of the aggressive land practices described above. These same elders lament the lack of interest their children exhibit in continuing to work the land as their ancesters have, preferring instead to seek wage labor. Particularly painful for them is the employment of Beit Surik youth in the construction of Israeli housing in Har Adar, Mevasseret Tzion, and Ramot.

There is a logic, however, in this generational orientation. The older villagers come from a tradition of avoiding rather than seeking contact with the government, and there is little in their relationship with Israel that would indicate a reason for them to change their view. Their experience is with the land, and their nature is to continue working it in the face of challenge.

The younger generation has a different approach, one that is more political in nature. They are more literate, militant, and conversant with the ways of aggressive occupation than their parents' generation. It is precisely the exposure to Israeli culture through the interactions of the job market which equip them to engage Israeli bureaucracy. It is also a sign of their relative modernity that they are willing to enlist outside help, such as legal aid, research, assistance organizations, and other nontraditional forms of action, in advancing their cause.

It is important to note the differences between Beit Iksa and Beit Surik in terms of the efforts made to prevent land alienation. While Beit Surik retains a greater percentage and a broader representation of its population than

---

[32] To this end they retained a Palestinian lawyer, but dissatisfied with his efforts, they replaced him in 1992 with an Israeli lawyer. Though no suit has been implemented, research has indicated that damages can be sought in the millions of dollars. As a result of the Israeli lawyer's efforts, a certain amount of media attention to the case has already been generated.

Beit Iksa, it too suffers from land loss resulting from absentee owners. The primary distinction, cutting across all sectors of the two villages, seems to be a marked difference in attitude and orientation toward the land dispute. Beit Iksa remains largely passive, and in the cases where action is taken, it is reactive. Beit Surik is proactive, seeking to secure the land not only for current needs, but for future use as well. Of the cases included in this study, and for the area of the green belt as a whole, these two neighboring villages represent the extremes in terms of failure and relative success.

10

The Village of Abu Dis

One day they came to make a garbage dump beside our village. The man from the army in Bethlehem, Eli, came and he knew the name of the land they wanted, but not where it was. They asked for an old man who could show them this land, and I was sent for. They said, "Show us the land that is called Wadi Beida" [the Egg Wadi] because it was not on their map. But Wadi Beida is on the left side very close to the village, and they told me it was on the right side. I thought it was a mistake, and I asked them, "Wadi Beida? Wadi Beida?" They said yes, on the right side. I told them "I will take you." I led them out, along the right side, but further from the village than Wadi Beida was on the left side. I took them to Wadi Obeid [the White Wadi] instead. They said "Wadi Beida?" I said "Wadi Obeid" they said "Wadi Obeida?" and I said "Wadi Obeid," we all looked at the place, and today the garbage is there.[1]

Abu Dis, located east of Jerusalem, is one of the larger villages in the area and, more than many others, functions primarily as a bedroom suburb of the city.[2] Though historically the village has relied primarily on nonagricultural income, land remains an important issue for the villagers. Abu Dis currently faces a number of challenges to its customary landholding practices: the maintenance of a municipal dump, as indicated above, the construction and expansion of the Ma'aleh Adumim and Kedar settlements, and the planting activities carried out by the JNF on and around the aforementioned sites, all of which are on land claimed by the villagers.

The areas in question, both those actively contested and those not, fall into a number of categories that, together with the type of Israeli use of them, shape the nature of the dispute. For the most part, Israel views the land dis-

---

[1] Interview with Abu Yusuf of Abu Dis, January 10, 1990.

[2] Israel Kimche et al., *Arab Settlement in the Metropolitan Area of Jerusalem* (Jerusalem: Jerusalem Institute for Israel Studies, no. 16, 1986), p. 86 [Hebrew].

cussed as state land. Where issues of private ownership arise, land has changed hands through commercial transactions, though these, too, are problematic. The discussion of the land issues of Abu Dis will be divided into two sections. The first focuses on the area of Ma'aleh Adumim, and the second deals with the municipal dump and the road to Kedar. In both cases, the area is entirely within the West Bank, and entirely outside the Jerusalem municipal boundary (fig. 9). In theory, this would suggest that the JNF and the Jerusalem municipality would not be direct actors in this dispute, but, as will be shown, this is not the case.[3]

Village Background

As noted, Abu Dis has not been known for its agricultural activity. Accounts of the village dating back several centuries indicate that its population was always large in comparison to other area villages. Income, however, was primarily drawn from the Jerusalem-Jericho traffic rather than from agriculture. Cultivation has always been sparse, limited by the rainfall, which averages 300 millimeters annually. Hutteroth's figures for Abu Dis reveal a grain tax payment just over twice that of Sur Baher, while the population is three times that of Sur Baher.[4] Notable, too, is that the taxation on olive trees, fruit trees, and vineyards in Abu Dis amounts to half that of the smaller village.

The income in Abu Dis came initially from robbing the traffic between Jerusalem, Jericho, and points beyond the Jordan River. In the nineteenth century, however, the Ottoman government came to terms with the residents of the village, and the activity along the road was converted from crime to protection, with the extraction of toll formalized and approved. There are suggestions that the population of Abu Dis was at that time part of a larger bedouin tribe, and that the village served as its base of operations.[5]

Village lore recalls a history of extensive pastoralism, certainly a characteristic compatible with the suggestion of bedouin origin. One traveler reported that during the off-season when income from the road diminished, the villagers occupied themselves with mat weaving using reeds taken from the banks of the Jordan River.[6] It is interesting that the villagers would have

---

[3] The limitation on municipal participation stems from the technical and legal complications of acting in the West Bank. The same is true of the JNF, in terms of the funding sources for its work, as detailed in previous chapters.

[4] Wolf-Dieter Hutteroth and Kamal Abdulfattah, *Historical Geography of Palestine, Transjordan, and Southern Syria in the Late Sixteenth Century* (Erlangen: Selbstverlag der Frankischen Geographischen Gesellschaft in Kommission bei Palm & Enke, 1977).

[5] For this and additional information on travellers' accounts relating to Abu Dis see Yehoshua Ben-Arieh, *A City Reflected in Its Times: New Jerusalem —The Beginnings* (Jerusalem: Yad Izhak Ben-Zvi, 1979), p. 71 [Hebrew].

[6] Ibid., p. 71, citing F. Rosen, *Oriental Memoirs of a German Diplomat* (London, 1930), pp. 28–29.

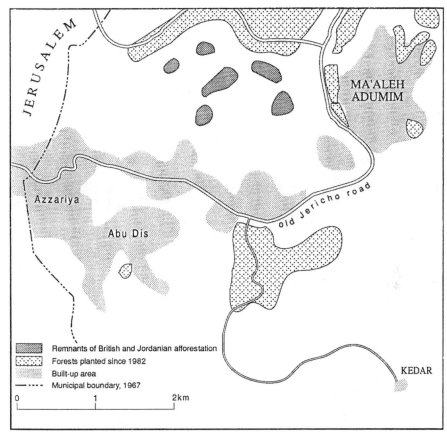

Fig. 9. Afforestation near Abu Dis and Ma'aleh Adumim. Village houses and land use extends beyond the built-up core in the direction of JNF planting.

income based on a resource taken from the river's edge, roughly twenty-four kilometers to the east, in light of the claims that the lands of the village descend in a continuous corridor to the Jordan. The vast majority of the land between the village and the river is unsuitable for cultivation because of the degree of aridity. Thus, not far beyond the eastern perimeter of the settled area, cultivation is limited to the slopes and bottoms of the wadis, which hold a greater share of the winter precipitation and collect the topsoil carried away by the rains. During all but the brief spring season, the area contains little vegetation beyond the thorny desert plants that provide food for the grazing flocks.

Today, land is not a significant element in the livelihood of the residents of Abu Dis. Rather than draw income from the traffic of tourists, Abu Dis has increasingly come to house laborers who earn their living in Jerusalem and, since 1967, inside Israel. The one element of the economy that has developed locally is related, as in earlier times, to the Jericho road. Along this road there is a commercial strip, dominated in large part by garages that house a large number of mechanics. Business on this commercial strip, like the rest of the village economy, is largely dependent on its proximity to Jerusalem.

The original village core was some distance away from Jordanian municipal Jerusalem, but village growth was consistently in the direction of the city, that is, to the northwest. Through the advance of the municipal border eastward in 1967, and the continued expansion of the built-up village area, Abu Dis now has a common boundary with Jerusalem in the west. In the north Abu Dis has begun to mesh with the adjacent village of Azzariya, which also extends along its length.

Much of the growth in Abu Dis has taken place on land within the built-up area of the village itself. Thus, in addition to covering a relatively large area, the population density of Abu Dis is quite high.[7] Unlike most other villages in the West Bank, even those close to Jerusalem, much of Abu Dis lacks even a semblance of an agricultural character. The urban atmosphere that dominates the village is strengthened by the proximity to the built-up area of Azzariya and the village of Silwan, a nonagricultural community, now a neighborhood of Jerusalem. To the south and east of Abu Dis there is open land, primarily used by the villagers for grazing, as noted above. It is over this land that the conflicts are unfolding.

Use of Abu Dis Land and the Construction of Ma'aleh Adumim

The settlement of Ma'aleh Adumim is the largest Jewish community in the West Bank and the anchor of the settlement ring being constructed around Jerusalem. It is located approximately two kilometers east of the built-up areas of Azzariya and Abu Dis, along a ridge that dominates the road to Jericho. Though it is northeast of the core of Abu Dis, traditional land claims suggest that it falls within the area customarily associated with the village.

Such designations are problematic, however. A map produced by the West Bank Data Project seems to supports this claim, at least in part.[8] Palestinians from a number of different villages lay claim to part of the land of Ma'aleh Adumim, and each village tends to deny or minimize the claims of others. Whatever the various opinions may be, the residents of Abu Dis lay firm claim to this land. When touring the area, they point out vague sections of land upon which there is general agreement, among the elders, as to the customary name assignations.

---

[7] Kimche, p. 86. Benvenisti and Khayat's *West Bank and Gaza Atlas* lists the village size as 2,210 dunams and its population in 1987 as 5,368 people. In terms of built-up area this makes Abu Dis one of the larger villages in the West Bank. Meron Benvenisti and Shlomo Khayat, *The West Bank and Gaza Atlas* (Jerusalem: West Bank Data Project, 1988).

[8] Ibid., p. 76.

Further, they identify water sources and other landmarks that they permit bedouin in the area to use, in exchange for an annual fee.[9] As indicated earlier, there is a measure of agriculture on the wadi bottoms and slopes. Often this work too is carried out by bedouin, with a similar arrangement for the payment of a fee. Usually such cultivation consists of a simple plowing, followed by the sowing of wheat or barley. In years of sufficient rainfall, the crop is harvested and sold. In times of little rainfall, the herds are brought to graze on whatever manages to grow.

In terms of the amount of land claimed by the villagers, the area in occasional cultivation is insignificant. It is limited to the village periphery and the wadi courses. The cultivation ceases in the east as a result of two barriers. One of these is physical: the amount of rain and runoff diminishes before it reaches the eastern portion of the hilly area.[10] The second is administrative: the Israeli military has closed off much of the eastern part of the highlands for the purpose of military training and live-fire areas.[11]

According to the villagers, cultivation was carried out on part of the restricted area prior to the commencement of the military activities. Seemingly they were instructed to stay away from the unused land, but were permitted to continue working those areas in cultivation. However, the lands were abandoned out of fear of the military training.[12] Also common in the area was grazing of the village herds. However, since 1967, and the turn to wage labor, the size of the village's flocks has decreased dramatically. The peak amount of land in use by the villagers, for residence, cultivation, and primarily grazing, was thought to be 150,000 dunams.[13]

---

[9] The fee is symbolic, as is the entire arrangement. Many of the areas in question are never visited by the nominal owners, who lack the means and motivation to be in the area. Many of the sites are far removed from easy access and are of little practical significance to anyone but pastoralists.

[10] Or, conversely, the runoff takes the form of flash floods, making agriculture equally if not more problematic.

[11] A map of the restricted military area can be found in Benvenisti and Khayat's atlas, p. 97.

[12] Interview with Ibrahim Abu Hilal, January 1, 1990. Some villagers say that they continued to cultivate in the areas forbidden, but were frightened off by warnings from the army. Each year a number of people, both Arabs and Jews, are injured in accidents involving military training areas or explosive devices that remain on the ground at the conclusion of training exercises. Areas restricted for training by the army sometimes operate on a periodic basis, with civilian use of the land allowed by permit and monitored by the army. The claim by the villagers that they were permitted to maintain their activities on cultivated sites is unusual.

[13] There was a small debate among the villagers before this figure was reached. The initial suggestion was that the village owned 15,000 dunams of land. Younger men protested that this figure was too small, and after some consultation a zero was added, and the corrected figure received unanimous agreement. Of course an exact figure for the amount of land owned would be an impossibility for the villagers owing to the inexactitude of terms and boundaries. The concept that the village owns land all the way to the Jordan River is more in keeping with the larger figure than the smaller.

As noted, the settlement of Ma'aleh Adumim and a number of related developments fall within the area claimed by the villagers of Abu Dis, with individuals reporting the loss of up to 1,000 dunams of their land to the settlement.[14] Ma'aleh Adumim was established in 1975, and in its first decade the settlement's population topped 10,000, more than twice that of the next largest settlement in the territories. As indicated, it is located on a ridge above the old Jerusalem-Jericho road, just east of where the new by-pass road from north Jerusalem links up with the earlier route (eliminating the need to pass through Azzariya and Abu Dis). The settlement is not immediately bordered by permanent communities, though a number of bedouin groups live in close proximity to it. In 1969–70, the Ma'aleh Adumim Forest was initiated on the site, which is not far from the hilltops on which the remnants of British and Jordanian afforestation can be found.

Since the settlement and the nearby military and industrial installations provide little relief from the harsh landscape, the creation of gardens and parks within and afforestation around these areas has been given high priority. And, as in other areas, the afforestation has additional purposes. The slopes below Ma'aleh Adumim are steep and barren, making them prone to dangerous erosion. The stabilization of these slopes is, thus, necessary for the continuation of construction on the ridge. A further purpose of afforestation is to dominate open land (fig. 10). In part, this is to allow for future expansion of Jewish residential areas, and, along with this, to prevent the encroachment of Arab land use close to the settlement.

As the settlement took shape, the need for afforestation became increasingly apparent. With funding provided by the Ministry of Housing, planting resumed in 1980. By 1984, approximately 500 dunams had been planted in and around Ma'aleh Adumim.[15] The rate of construction outpaced that of planting, however, and the local council pressed for an increase in the scope of planting. The initial concentration of planting was located at a site on the settlement's periphery. A priority was also given to planting between the settlement and the Jerusalem-Jericho road, covering the slope along a stretch of nearly two kilometers, a swath that in some places was several hundred meters wide. As these trees mature they are transforming the look of this sizable strip of land, converting it from the common wilderness landscape to one of solid afforestation.

With the planting on this slope progressing, work spread to the remaining slopes that surround the settlement.[16] To this end, a master plan

---

[14] Field Survey with Abu Khalil, December 26, 1989.

[15] JNF, 643/Judea and Samaria, August 30, 1984.

[16] Extensive work has also continued to the north of Ma'aleh Adumim, with trees being planted in the framework of the Tzofim Forest discussed in chapter 7. Linking with this forest, Ma'aleh Adumim composes the southeast terminal of the green belt.

Fig. 10. The greening of the wilderness near the municipal dump. Among the rocks in the foreground, and across the slope beyond, trees have been planted that will soon bring a radical change in the landscape, while effectively dominating the land.

for planting in Ma'aleh Adumim was drafted with the coordination of the local council, the Ministry of Housing, and the JNF. The goal of the master plan
was the afforestation of between three and four hundred dunams annually,
primarily along the settlement's slopes.[17] Part of this master plan was devoted
to the afforestation of the nearby industrial and military sites mentioned
above. In this, as well as in the work carried out for Ma'aleh Adumim itself,
the JNF was a significant contributor to the afforestation budget.[18]

As indicated, the land on which Ma'aleh Adumim has been constructed is claimed by residents of Abu Dis. The settlement is more than two
kilometers from the village core, however, and the land in question was used
for grazing rather than cultivation. The claims are, therefore, undocumented,
at least in terms of specific title to specific pieces of land. And, as opposed to
contested areas closer to the village core, no paper work was offered by the villagers to illustrate the issue. According to one resident of Abu Dis, compensation for the land of Ma'aleh Adumim was offered in 1987, at the rate of six
shekels per dunam,[19] but this was refused. Currently expansion of Ma'aleh
Adumim and the adjunct developments is taking place. Some of the increase
in residential use is in the direction of Abu Dis, and afforestation is likely to
push beyond the area of construction.[20] Whatever the legal status of the area
used for the expansion, it is sure to be claimed by the surrounding villagers.

The Municipal Dump and the Kedar Settlement

As indicated in this chapter's opening quotation, the Jerusalem municipal dump is located on land near Abu Dis, though the exact name of the site
remains somewhat unclear. According to the government, the dump is located on state land, while the local version contends that the land belongs to
the village.[21] The area, totaling three thousand dunams, was officially designated as state land only on September 2, 1988,[22] some four years after plan-

---

[17] Ma'aleh Adumim Local Council, 2–12/608, Protocol: JNF–Ma'aleh Adumim, December 28,
1988.

[18] Ibid., p. 3. Ma'aleh Adumim Local Council 3412–467–PC, January 8, 1989. JNF, 643/Judea and
Samaria, August 30, 1984.

[19] Interview with Abu Mohammed, January 1, 1990. Six shekels per dunam, a few dollars only,
is an inconceivable sum in relation to the range of market value for a dunam of land.

[20] See chapter 7, note 30.

[21] At one point the villagers reported that the government claimed to have purchased the land
from someone in the village. I was asked to discover from Israeli sources who had sold land
that did not belong to him, at least as far as the villagers were concerned. When asked what
would happen if the "seller" was identified, they answered, "We would only want to talk to
him." This seemed highly unlikely, given the frequent violent outcome of land disputes, and
therefore I ignored the request.

[22] Civil Administration of Judea and Samaria, Infrastructure Division, 1436–2106–85, October
18, 1988.

ning for the planting to accompany the dump began.[23] Afforestation is a factor in the dispute because of the attempt by the municipality and the JNF to alleviate some of the negative environmental influence of the dump by way of afforestation around the site. The ramifications of afforestation "around" the site, as this is interpreted by the participating bodies, serve as the focus of this section.

The area of the dump lies east southeast of the village core and is over a kilometer away from the closest permanent dwelling associated with Abu Dis. Access to the dump, however, is along a route that diverges from the main Jerusalem-Jericho road just two hundred meters from the village periphery. Initially, this route was of low quality and changed from asphalt to packed dirt after less than a kilometer. With the construction of the dump, the paved section of the road was increased. Signs posted near the beginning of the road indicate that it is not for public use. An extension was later added with the construction of the hilltop settlement of Kedar, and the road was upgraded along its length. The dump is northeast of the settlement, and not within eyesight, being more than a kilometer distant.

Despite this, afforestation was conceived for the site to solve partially the problem of the view of the dump in the landscape, while simultaneously contributing to the control of "air pollution."[24] The planting was to take place adjacent to the active dump, on land that had been filled with garbage several years earlier and subsequently covered with soil.[25] Earlier experimentation on the site had demonstrated that such planting was feasible, and would contribute to the amelioration of conditions in the surrounding area. Unofficial explanations of the purpose of the afforestation also include the "beautification" of the road to Kedar.[26] In fact, it is along this road, beginning with the section closest to the village and continuing to the settlement of Kedar, that the dispute is taking place.

Preparation for planting in the framework of plans for the dump began in the fall of 1988, though afforestation on other sites in the area had taken place in previous years. In the first year of work on the dump project, 350 dunams were slated for planting. The funding for the work was divided equally between the Jerusalem municipality, the ILA, and the JNF.[27] In that first year, the work was carried out in the southern portion of the dump site, and thus did not draw particular attention from the villagers.

---

[23] JNF, Greater Jerusalem File, unnumbered, "Balance of Afforestation Areas for the Year 83/84 and Planning for the Year 84/85," July 26, 1984.

[24] JNF, 3300/577, June 13, 1988.

[25] Civil Administration of Judea and Samaria, Infrastructure Division, 1436–2106–85, October 18, 1988. JNF, 3300/504, August 11, 1986.

[26] Field Survey with G. Sopher, November 8, 1989.

[27] JNF, 3300/879, August 25, 1988.

In the following year, however, preparatory work began for planting along the road leading to the dump and Kedar, not far from the village itself. Part of this area was "designated for the dump and . . . the burying of trash or quarrying is not expected."[28] The area of planting was clearly outside municipal territory, despite the fact that the general location was serving as a municipal facility, a factor of organizational and administrative significance.[29]

Because the site was in the West Bank, all work carried out required the authorization of the Civil Administration. The JNF thus made a formal request for permission to work on the site, and this was granted in October 1988, with the stipulation that "the execution of all work in the area and every entrance to the area be coordinated with the Civil Administration in the Bethlehem District."[30] In fact, once the project was approved by the Civil Administration, the supervision of the work carried out was formal, but at the same time perfunctory.

As a result, there was little contact between the villagers and the government once the work commenced. Official notices of the declaration of state land, on the various occasions when that had taken place, had been delivered to the village mukhtar. The mukhtar was directed to inform the villagers of the order, and to instruct them concerning the process of appeal. According to the villagers, the mukhtar refused on principle to carry out this task and, as a result, on a number of occasions the villagers remained uninformed of declarations of land status and impending action. They were, therefore, completely surprised when JNF crews appeared on the village periphery and began preparing the land for planting.[31]

Planting and the Village Response

Despite their surprise at the appearance of the crews, the villagers had a firm idea of what the implication of the JNF activity was. Their impression was that "this Keren Keyemet comes and plants trees and, after the trees,

---

[28] JNF, 3300/87, February 25, 1988.

[29] ILA, Division of Planning and Development, Jerusalem District, March 17, 1988. The ILA reminded the JNF that the area of the dump "in Azzariya [sic] is outside the municipal area of Jerusalem, and therefore it is under the care of the Judea and Samaria section of the ILA, and not the Jerusalem District."

[30] Civil Administration for Judea and Samaria, Infrastructure Division, 1436–2106–85, October 18, 1988.

[31] While it seems accurate that the villagers were surprised by the appearance of the JNF work crews, the question of notification concerning declarations of state land is a bit more murky. There is a clear sense that on some occasions the villagers were not informed about legal proceedings, but there is also a good deal of confusion as to who was informed about what, and when. A refusal on principle to inform the villagers on the part of the mukhtar is a political statement, and must be weighed with a measure of caution concerning its validity.

comes to sell the land for the Jewish. It's a big company, a government."[32] When the first preparations were taking place near the main road, a number of residents from nearby homes came out to speak with the work crew (composed of West Bank Palestinians) and object to the work. The crew moved several hundred meters away and resumed their digging.[33] Thus, between the closest homes and the area of afforestation, there is a gap of some four hundred meters, some of which is in the form of a small depression.

In the area prepared nearest to the village, the JNF opened pits for the seedlings, sprayed herbicide, manually weeded, and created a number of new access routes, in the form of dirt roads scraped clean of stones by earth movers and bulldozers. The villagers affirm that, for as long as they can remember, no trees have grown in the area prepared by the JNF. On those portions that were not entirely rocky, intermittent cultivation took place, though without much effort and only irregularly.[34] There is some indication that such activity had not taken place for quite some time, and when the land was worked, it was only to provide additional income, and the villagers did not "actually live from this."[35] The area was, however, included in the land traditionally used by the village for grazing sheep and goats.

As the preparation for planting proceeded, the villagers began to assess their situation. They were determined to oppose the JNF efforts, but were unsure as to the most effective course of action. A lawsuit some years earlier, for an unrelated parcel of land, had cost them a lot of money, and not brought satisfactory results.[36] Nonetheless, the use of the courts was the most commonly suggested method of responding to the challenge. However, a number of factors mitigated against the success of this response.

To begin with, the villagers were unable to collect enough money to hire a lawyer experienced in land cases. Instead, a lawyer from the village agreed to take the case at a discount price. Despite this, quite a few villagers did not have or did not want to provide their part of the fee necessary to have standing in the case. As a result, not all of the families with a land claim became part of the legal efforts. And, with hired representation participating in the case, the poorer families were less likely to have access to legal aid groups, which usually do not join forces with private lawyers in such cases.[37]

---

[32] Interview with Abu Yazzid, January 10, 1990.

[33] The area that the workers left, not more than ten dunams all told, has yet to be planted.

[34] The cultivation consisted of sowing grains and depending on the rainfall, described above.

[35] Interview with Abu Yazzid, January 10, 1990.

[36] The village explanation for this was that the lawyer hired was a West Bank Palestinian who was not adept at navigating through the Israeli legal process.

[37] The issue of legal aid was primarily a hypothetical one. The villagers did not have a working knowledge of such groups, and when specific organizations were mentioned the response was that they would take help from anybody who could provide it. Few of the villagers

The villagers also began planting activities of their own which, though they did not know it at the time, were ultimately successful in maintaining possession of a portion of the land intended for JNF planting. Villagers had attempted to maintain use of the land that was being prepared for planting since the JNF workers first appeared on the site. Their activities—in particular their grazing of goats—were quickly observed.

Since the JNF anticipates resistance in such cases, a guard was assigned to supervise the site.[38] One of the tasks the guard has, in addition to protecting the seedlings, is to report illegal activity on the land. The villagers had been instructed that certain parts of the area were strictly off-limits to their herds. Within these areas were a number of traditional watering sites, and the villagers attempted to continue using them. They were warned that, if they did so, their animals would be confiscated. They were permitted to bring water to the flock from the wells, but not to bring the herd to the water.

In addition to the attempts to continue grazing on the land, a number of families planted new olive trees in two principal areas. One was in the decline between the village houses and the road. The trees closest to the village were older than the plans for planting. As the JNF manifested its presence, however, the planting of olive trees increased in the direction of the dump. While the scope of this planting was not great, its results were efficient, and therefore significant.

Interestingly, JNF fieldworkers seem much more aware than the villagers of the impact that this planting has had in terms of land rights. They indicate that where trees have been standing for three years, they cannot be removed, except by court order. Since this is time-consuming and expensive, the JNF would rather avoid such disputes whenever possible. The villagers contend that the olive trees near the area being prepared and planted by the JNF were six years old. The JNF held that they were only two years old. In either case, in 1989 a decision was taken in the field to leave the trees standing, and the legitimacy of the claim to the land on which they were planted was not pursued.[39]

---

had any concept of how to enlist the aid of such groups, and none became involved with these issues.

[38] The guard is an unarmed Palestinian. At times the guards employed are local, and the JNF believes that the stronger the standing of the guard in his own and neighboring villages, the more effective he will be in his task. In this case the guard was from the Hebron area. When villagers accompanied me to the site, we were immediately challenged and instructed to leave the area. A brief discussion ensued wherein the villagers asserted their claim to the land, and questioned the guard's national loyalties. The guard indicated a grudging willingness to carry a verbal petition to JNF workers on the site (on this day, a crew of demobilized soldiers), but returned with firm orders to leave the area. These were disregarded, and the groups observed one another tensely while at the same time maintaining a circumspect distance.

[39] Field survey, November 1989.

The villagers of Abu Dis fail to articulate an appreciation for the success of this method in preventing land alienation, yet they carry out tree planting in such a way as to convince the JNF that they are cognizant of the significance of planting in terms of establishing legal rights and frustrating Israeli plans. The JNF directs its planting and road clearing to cut off or interdict the path of expansion of the villagers' olive groves, and indicates that success is achieved by both sides in this contest. The villagers, on the other hand, seem unaware of the value, and the potential, of this tactic, even when prompted by questions concerning the success of what has already been done.

In part, this may be the result of their planting effort near Kedar. In this case, the villagers planted near the perimeter, outside the fence that marked the boundary of the settlement. In the same month that hundreds of olive saplings were planted on the northwest side of the settlement, and while villagers were tending the area, a number of armed people (soldiers, according to some of the villagers) came out and uprooted all the olives that had been planted. Not long after, the fence of the settlement was moved to include the area that had been planted by the villagers. The settlement is some distance from the village, however, whereas the area along the road being planted by the JNF is within eyesight of the villagers, and is thus of more immediate worth to them.

Proof of Possession

Despite the fact that the land along the road has not been worked recently, and never with particular intensity, it is, nonetheless, quite familiar to the village elders. As children, they covered this land on foot, tending to the flocks of the village, and, in the course of their herding, they learned the traditional divisions of property along family lines. As a result of the move away from agricultural work among the younger generations, it is only the older villagers—men and women—who are familiar with the units of land and their traditional names. The older generation laments the decline in interest in the land, and see it as an additional outcome of Israel's influence on Palestinian life.

With the young showing little interest in the details of landholding,[40] the elderly have maintained formal ownership and continue to possess whatever documentation there may be to support their claims. This is not true of all landowners, though most seem to appreciate the importance of having something on paper. Often these documents relate to different periods of rule—Ottoman, Jordanian, and Israeli—and have been passed down through at least two generations. That documents are in Ottoman Turkish,

---

[40] As indicated elsewhere, this is beginning to change as a result of a number of factors related in part to the Intifada, and in part to developments in the political and economic situation in Israel and the territories.

English, Arabic, Hebrew, or combinations of any or all of these, does not facilitate their interpretation on the part of the villagers, some of whom are illiterate in any case. Compounding the difficulty for the villagers is the poor state
of many of the documents, and the lack of clarity resulting from the sloppy
handwriting of government officials.

Despite all this, a number of villagers in Abu Dis possess documents
that they believe support their claims. While some of the villagers are too
poor to participate in the legal cases, others use these papers as a major portion of the evidence that they present. Whether or not the documents are
submitted as evidence, the villagers are convinced of their validity, and of
their constitution of irrefutable proof of claims to the land. Naturally, the
older the document, the more it is valued by the holder. At the same time,
anything in Hebrew which is believed to confirm landownership is seen as
ultimate proof of the truth of the claim. Thus, the connection between something in writing and the disposition of the ruling powers is clearly perceived,
as is the relative merit of documents in terms of historical weight and current
applicability.

There is also a degree of appreciation for the different land categories
and the implications thereof, though this is tempered by a lack of awareness
of details and confusion concerning terms and conditions. Nonetheless, the
villagers use the Ottoman land terminology in their attempts to disprove Israeli declarations of state land. They deny, for example, that the area today occupied by Ma'aleh Adumim is *miri* land, as they suggest was claimed by the
Israelis. Rather, they contend that it was *mewat* land intended for grazing.
They justify this claim by explaining that they paid tax for the land during the
Ottoman and British periods.[41] However, they seem unaware that the tax they
mention was taken for cultivated areas, rather than grazing areas. Further,
the villagers equate payment of land tax with formal land settlement, an
understandable but potentially catastrophic error for those unfamiliar with
the bureaucracy of landholding.

Some of the villagers are aware that they lack formal and full title to
their land. The realization of this is not new, but the degree of vulnerability
they feel has increased since 1967 and the advent of Israeli rule. Since that
time Israel has canceled all incomplete registration proceedings, while simultaneously carrying out the alienation of West Bank land. Many villagers were
unable to afford the process of registration during previous administrations,
its cost often equaling the total income of a year of labor, sometimes more.
For the area in question this was not even a possibility, as the Jordanian settlement process was not completed this far south. Currently, the villagers are
loathe to initiate any procedure with the government involving land, where

---

[41] This type of land was not taxed during the Jordanian period, and is not taxed under Israeli
rule.

such possibility exists or is technically compulsory, for fear of complications, expenses, and unexpected surprises that will be to their detriment.

Emischalib

One thing is certain: when Israel puts land in the West Bank to use, Palestinians demand to use, or to continue to use, that same land. Such is the case with the land currently being afforested near Abu Dis. A portion of that land, to the east of the road leading to the dump, is called by the traditional name Emischalib. The section totals seventy-three dunams, is stony, and has never had trees growing on it. The villagers who claim ownership of the land are among those too poor to participate in legal action against the JNF and its partners.

Part of Emischalib is tacitly ceded by the owner to government control, with the explanation that for some sections of the land "the majority of it is rock. And according to the law, according to the Ottoman law, the land which has one-third of it as rocks, it belongs to the government. And Israel is the government instead of Jordan."[42] In spite of the articulation of this codicil, the land—in its entirety—and the surrounding area is claimed by the Chaish clan, and other families. Some family members explain the lack of utilization of the land by saying that trees cannot be planted there because of the quantity of stones covering the ground. Other family members point to the JNF planting and say, "We can plant trees. They *are* planting trees. Now, we can do it ourselves."[43]

In fact, the most cultivable portion of Emischalib is not being used for planting. Rather, it is the places free of stones that the JNF is using for the creation of their working roads. The villagers perceive this as a deliberate strategy, in that the stony ground is in any case unworkable, so that what little space they have for planting is lost to the road clearing. Since the first planting season, this work has spread to both sides of the road to the dump, and thus the JNF planting is being carried out even closer to the village. In the depression that separates the village edge from the area of afforestation additional olive trees are being planted, such that little room remains between villagers' olives and the JNF's pines. To date, none of the olive planting in this area has been challenged by the JNF.

Documents of Ownership

The area that has been planted with olives is currently secure as far as the villagers are concerned, though they have little confidence in what the future may bring. It is the area of JNF planting which is the object of their attention, and the legal attempts to regain control of the land. The case is still in

---

[42] Interview with Abu Yazzid, January 10, 1990.

[43] Interview with Ibrahim Abu Hilal, January 10, 1990. Emphasis is the speaker's.

the phase of preparation, and the outcome will not be expressly predicted here. Rather, the types of proof that the villagers bring to their case will be briefly described.

Perhaps the most common piece of evidence presented, at least in Abu Dis, and one of the most compelling as far as the villagers are concerned, is the revenue tax receipt issued by the Mandatory Government of Palestine. These receipts are numbered, dated, and signed by the tax collector. The form itself is written in English, Arabic, and Hebrew, with the notation for taxation in Abu Dis handwritten in Arabic. While these forms typically fail to indicate to which district and subdistrict they relate, the village name Abu Dis is clearly listed, as is the volume and folio number for the tax registers.

The main portion of the tax form has listings for different types of property tax, and the entry listed on the forms held by the villagers lists a sum to be paid for "rural property tax," the Hebrew phrasing of which clearly indicates "agricultural property tax." On the forms presented as evidence of possession of the area being planted by the JNF there were notations only in this tax category. At the bottom of the form the name of the tax official appears along with the date (all of the forms viewed were dated in the 1940s), the amount collected, and the name of the person paying. As indicated, the villagers present such forms to support their claim of ownership of Emischalib and the surrounding area.

A number of problems exist which detract from the evidentiary weight of these documents. First and foremost, there is no indication on the form of the location of the land for which tax has been paid, other than the general village designation.[44] The clarification of location frequently remains problematic even with accompanying survey maps. These maps often indicate the dimensions and shape of the land in question, the orientation to the north, and sometimes the names of adjacent properties or their owners (though often the signatures of those owners are lacking). What they fail to do, however, is place the land being surveyed clearly within the areal context, with the result that the exact location of the parcel remains obscure. While the boundary representations may be fairly precise, the locational drawings are often crude and inaccurate.

During the period of Jordanian rule the same forms of evidence were used as are common under Israeli administration, though Jordanian standards were more lax. Acceptable forms of evidence include the tax receipts and survey maps discussed above, the testimony of neighboring landowners, and the support of the village mukhtar. At my request, the material offered by the people of Abu Dis was assessed by a former Jordanian land settlement of-

---

[44] As pointed out earlier, even when the Israeli High Court accepts a claim of landownership, if the exact location of the land cannot be proven the owner may lose rights to the particular disputed area, and be granted an equal amount of land in another location.

ficer whose area of responsibility was not far from the village. His determination was that the documents held by the villagers were a good indication of land possession, but did not constitute proof of a claim to any particular piece or amount of land. His conclusion was based on the lack of specificity in the documents outlined above.[45] It seems unlikely that documents deemed questionable by a Jordanian land official, in relation to this particular claim, will suffice to convince the Israeli judicial system that the land is owned by the residents of Abu Dis.

What is more likely is that the land in question will remain in government hands, and the planting by the JNF will continue. The afforestation around Ma'aleh Adumim will compose the eastern extremity of the green belt, at least for as long as the land planted is not converted to alternative use. The trees in the area of the municipal dump, and particularly those along the road leading to it and Kedar, will form another portion of the green belt. This forest will be the link between Ma'aleh Adumim and the afforested areas within the municipal boundary in the southeastern sector of the city: the Peace Forest, Jabel Mukaber, and Sur Baher. In the arid landscape of the Judean Wilderness, these stands of trees clearly set the city apart in the landscape, and help to fill in the green belt around Jerusalem.

---

[45] Interview with Suliman Aiyoub, January 16, 1990.

11

An Overview: The Politics of Planting

At the heart of the Israeli-Palestinian conflict is the contention of two national groups for control of the same space. This study examined that conflict as it is being played out between the Israeli government, primarily acting through the JNF, and the residents of Palestinian villages in and around the Jerusalem municipality. The relationship between these two protagonists is fundamentally determined by the basic attitude of each toward the landholding status of the other. The government's approach during the period of the Likud government has been that all land not proven to belong to a resident is at the disposal of the state.[1] Crudely put, "What's not yours is ours," with the power to define terms residing with Israel. The Palestinians contend that Israel has no rights to the land, whether individual ownership has been proven or not.

What is illustrated through the studies presented here is the basic conflict in attitudes concerning landownership, a conflict that is related to cultural and historical orientation, in addition to modern political considerations. In keeping with the murky tradition of documentation stemming from the Ottoman period, strengthened by a proclivity to avoid government whenever possible, and drawing upon the power of local custom, the Palestinian

---

[1] Though the Labor-led government elected in June 1992 professes a radically different settlement policy for the West Bank, its philosophy on the nuances of landholding remain to be seen. As far as the area of the study is concerned, it falls entirely within the area of "Greater Jerusalem," an area also considered by the new government as an indivisible entity including but going beyond the municipal boundaries. Thus, Israeli settlement activity in the study area survived the transition from the Likud to the Labor-led government. See Shaul Ephraim Cohen, "Political Factors in the Determination of Jerusalem's Territorial Framework," in *Politics and Society in Jerusalem*, edited by Ifrach Zilberman (Jerusalem: Jerusalem Institute for Israel Studies, in press).

villagers largely view landholding according to their own terms, and in their own vernacular. An example of this is in Abu Dis, where the elders of the village can concur on ancestral plot names, but are vague concerning locations, boundaries, and sizes.

In contrast to local custom, Israel applies standards that draw upon the latest technology, on the one hand, and pre-existing legal doctrines, on the other. The attitudes, policies, and activities promulgated in the West Bank are often inconsistent with the manner in which a largely inherited system was applied by previous administrations. Moreover, the current application of land law in the West Bank is radically different in spirit and consequence from that of any previous administration. Within the Israeli frame of reference, however, and in terms of a more Western legal orientation, the policies applied coincide with the explicit dictates of land regulation.

As a result, there is a chronic failure to communicate: each side imposes the burden of understanding on the other, thereby exacerbating the already intense competition for land. At the same time, there are subtleties in the field which suggest that monolithic characterizations of the two sides are quite problematic. While the Israeli government is indeed in pursuit of land in the West Bank, the bodies involved in land policy and the implementation of that policy are, at some levels, sensitive to the complexity of legal and human factors. As a result, there are opportunities in the system for flexibility in cases where it would not be expected, such as in the villages of Sur Baher and Beit Iksa.

The Palestinian Planting

From material presented in the historical chapters, it is clear that Palestinians have a proclivity for the planting of olive trees, and that the olive represents to them something more than other fruit-bearing trees. Long a major element of the local economy, the olive has taken on symbolic characteristics, which the Palestinians present as an image of themselves. And while the politicization of this imagery is particularly evident since the inception of Israeli rule, the spread of olive cultivation is a cyclical phenomenon, and was clearly present during the period of the British Mandate.

Landholding has long been problematic for the Palestinian peasant, and any method that enhances solvency will contribute to the ability of individuals to maintain their land. Olive planting has been carried out beyond the logical dictates of sound economic practice, however, and sometimes in the face of it. When the British supplied subsidized olives, it was extremely difficult to meet the demand. Today, with the olive market glutted, Palestinians continue to prefer planting olives, rather than switch to a more profitable alternative. The tradition of planting the olive is deeply ingrained, and constitutes a fundamental way in which Palestinians choose to use their land, and to protect it.

In three of the four villages studied, this continues to be the case. In Beit Iksa, there is a minor amount of new olive planting, but the location does not correspond to the area of immediate Israeli pressure on the land. In the other villages studied, the expansion of the Israeli presence provoked the planting of new trees, both as extension of existing groves, and in areas previously unworked. Moreover, where Israeli trees were planted, Palestinians expressed a desire to plant that same land for themselves, even where they had not done so in the past. Another factor present in the green belt is preemptive planting. This takes place along roadways, near Jewish neighborhoods and settlements, and on isolated plots of land where there is no real imminent threat, but where the Palestinians plant anyway, in order to be prudent.

The extent of new Palestinian planting in the area is minor compared to the scope of afforestation that has been carried out since the inception of Aronson's plan for the green belt. Nonetheless, in many places where there has been large-scale afforestation by Israel, there has been small-scale planting by the Palestinians. As a result, the pine and the olive often meet in the landscape, indicating that use gives rise to use.

Though the amount of open space in the green belt is rapidly diminishing, the use of tree planting as a landholding tactic by the Palestinians may be on the rise. This makes sense in that recognition of the problem increases as more land is alienated. By the same token, there is less land left to protect from alienation; thus in many cases, the coincidence of a willingness to act, possession of the resources necessary, and knowledge of a viable tactic has come too late.

There is, however, a growing cadre of Palestinians who are actively working to slow the pace of Israeli expansion. Those of greatest interest to this study are the agronomists and agricultural engineers who are offering their services to the villagers. Their goal is to foster the development of an independent Palestinian agricultural and economic infrastructure, while simultaneously working for the protection of Palestinian land. As indicated above, these goals have been prioritized, with long-range economic and agricultural planning giving way to the pressures of the land conflict.[2]

As a result, Palestinian groups are supplying subsidized olive saplings to villagers whose land is thought to be in danger of alienation by Israel. The groups attempt to introduce other fruit trees to fulfill this need, but the villagers resist, often taking olives or nothing at all. At times it is the villagers who approach these self-help and advisory groups, but more often, it is active outreach on the part of the professionals which brings the information and the assistance to the villages.

---

[2] This work has its own internal politicization, and competition between Palestinian self-help groups, both independent and politically affiliated, is having a detrimental effect on their usefulness.

Thus the ideology of *sumud*, or steadfastness, seems to be a factor for only some of the villagers, some of the time. Moreover, the actions taken by the villagers appear to be primarily directed by instinct and experience, rather than guided by political concepts or strategies. At the local level, the struggle is for hegemony over the adjacent field or orchard, rather than for the construction of political entities. In portraying the peasant as the conscious bearer of the nationalist banner, the literature concerning this element of the land conflict appears to exaggerate current circumstance or anticipate potential developments, rather than accurately reflect the attitudes and actions of those working the land. The Palestinian villagers, like many other peasants, are struggling to get by. In terms of the Israeli-Palestinian conflict, their primary concern is how they will be affected in the most basic and immediate sense.

Israeli Planting

While the green belt will never form a continuous ring around Jerusalem, it has done much to dominate a significant amount of land both east and west of the city. Earlier afforestation, such as that in the area of the Ramot neighborhood, has not withstood the pressure of residential expansion within the municipal boundary. More recent planting, such as that near Ma'aleh Adumim and Kedar, accompanies the growth of Israeli settlement in the West Bank, and, in places, preserves land for future extension of residential and industrial use.

A clear function of Israeli planting which is visible in the landscape, and supported by the documentation cited herein, is to prevent the spread of Palestinian land use to areas heretofore unused. Forests are also used in those areas that may have been, or in the future might be, used by Palestinians, but that are currently vulnerable to the application of Israeli control. The decision concerning the location of particular planting projects stems from a number of different considerations.

Within the Israeli government, there are several ministries or ministerial subunits that make and implement land policy in the West Bank. The most aggressive is the Ministry of Housing, which has authority over the ILA. The Ministry of Housing is a primary actor in much of the afforestation taking place in the green belt, through the provision of funding, land, bureaucratic support, and political backing.

The other primary actor, of course, is the Forestry Division of the JNF. The goals of the JNF at times coincide with those of the Ministry of Housing, at least in terms of controlling land, but its motivation is quite different. Though it seems simplistic to say, the primary goal of the Forestry Division is to create forests. The various functions of the forests figure into their motivations, as does income earned by subcontracting to the government for forest planting in the West Bank. The goal of this division, however, is the creation of as much forest on as much land as possible for as long as possible. Thus, if presented with the choice of more or less land to plant, the choice of the division would be for the greater amount, irrespective of location or political consideration. Similarly, the Forestry Division would prefer to plant a forest inside the Green Line which would not be converted to alternate use, rather than a larger forest in the West Bank which would be cut down at some point to allow for construction.

At the same time, the JNF workers are alert to what they perceive as Palestinian encroachment on state land, and they act to prevent it when they can. Israeli afforestation in the green belt is therefore directed from both the higher and lower echelons. The net result is acute familiarity with the land, and intense pressure on those areas designated for planting, according to the variety of needs and functions the forests fulfill. Though the record is not unblemished, the green belt forests have, for the most part, accomplished their tasks. Those in the lower echelons are aware, however, that the amount of land available is decreasing, and that the Palestinians are having a measure of success with their planting as well.

There is also an antithesis to the planting of trees. By examining planting as a tactic to control land, I have focused on one of the more constructive (or less destructive) elements of the Israeli-Palestinian conflict. However, I could not ignore the effort and energy each side invests in hindering the planting of the opponent. At times such activities can be benign and even unintentional, while more often they are calculated and malicious.

Lessons from the Village Studies

The areas detailed in this research present a range of the characteristics that mark the Palestinian villages of the green belt. Sur Baher is within the municipal boundary, it maintains a modicum of agriculture, it is being pressured by Israeli expansion, and it has had much of its land expropriated. Because of its location, the residents of Sur Baher are subject to Israeli law and the authority of the Jerusalem municipality.

Abu Dis is in the West Bank, yet involved in a dispute in which the municipality, through the dump, is a major actor. It also has land disputes with the Ma'aleh Adumim and Kedar settlements. Like Sur Baher, it has found little relief through the appellate and judicial systems, and has therefore not gained or maintained title to the land in question. While Abu Dis has never engaged in extensive cultivation, trees have been planted in recent years, and grazing continues on and beyond the contested land.

Beit Iksa and Beit Surik present an additional case of West Bank villages under pressure, from a Jerusalem neighborhood in the case of the former, and a settlement and suburb, in the latter. In one of the villages, the residents confronted the administration with little success, and retreated from the conflict and from their land. In the other, agriculture has been maintained, and even expanded, with a measure of tangible benefit.

The clear message from these village studies is that, in general, planting does serve to protect land from the advances of the other side. The success seems due to a combination of practical and legal considerations. On the Israeli side, the planting prevents Palestinian land use and the establishment of new claims to the land. On the Palestinian side, the planting can establish rights, and, in any case, serves notice to Israelis in the field that the process of alienating the planted land will likely require litigation and expense. As a result, except in the case of outright expropriation, Israel prefers to avoid land on which the Palestinians are maintaining orchards.

Thus in Beit Surik, Abu Dis, and even to a small extent in Beit Iksa, the presence of Palestinian orchards has prevented or limited the extent of Israeli land use. In these villages, Israeli tree planting has similarly limited Palestinian land use. The unusual case is Sur Baher, which, as a result of a legal expropriation of land, should have been the most straightforward. Instead, the government's attempt to convert orchards to forest was met with resistance not just by the villagers, but by Israeli neighbors as well. Government planting was met with planting by the villagers, and neither side achieved its goals. Each side interfered physically with the planting of the other. After a court battle, the disposition of the land remained as it was prior to the dispute, and only a portion of the newly planted trees remained.

Were it not for the Intifada, this case would have continued along an interesting line. The proposal by the villagers and the neighbors that the JNF plant olives that could be used by the Palestinians did not come to its anticipated fruition. Nonetheless, the model remains, and has merit. Without changing the landownership status, the JNF, Jerusalem municipality, ILA, and the villagers could have achieved a modus vivendi. Under the current system, tree planting confers rights, but it also preserves rights. Land that is disputed in the West Bank could be left in dispute, while its future use is protected through the planting of trees, which serve ongoing functions. In effect, tree planting can be a tool to minimize the damage caused by the conflict, and help stabilize relationships that have been exacerbated during the period of the Intifada.

The Significance of the Green Belt

While Israel is the dominant force in and around Jerusalem, the future of political control of the city and its surroundings is still a question. When the population of the Jerusalem region is examined as a whole, Israeli numerical superiority is much less significant than that which holds within the municipal boundary. As each side presses its claim for control of Jerusalem, the balance between the two populations will continue to be an issue.

Because of this, the struggle for control of land in and around the city has tremendous significance. If unchecked, the Palestinian villages and towns around Jerusalem will maintain their rapid rate of growth, and quite possibly create a Palestinian majority in the Jerusalem region. The planting of new trees by the Palestinians lessens the likelihood of Israeli use and protects land for agriculture and additional housing. For this reason, Israel is seeking to block Palestinian expansion, on the one hand, and increase Israeli settlement, on the other. The planting of forests by the JNF creates a reserve for future Israeli building.

There is also a landscape function to the green belt, which sets Jerusalem apart from the surrounding area. The alteration of the landscape has a number of nonpolitical motivations, such as creating recreation areas and improving the environment. At the same time, Jerusalem is being visibly severed from the West Bank. Where the green belt is adjacent to Israel, the forest continues beyond the green belt, serving as a link with the Israeli interior. In contrast, the West Bank portion of the green belt stands out sharply from the surrounding wilderness. The visible stamp in the landscape is that Jerusalem is different from and distinct from its Palestinian hinterland.

While not exhaustive, the village studies provided here present a range of the issues confronting Palestinian villagers and Israeli land agencies, and some of the outcomes of their competition for land in the Jerusalem region. The material detailing land, legal, and planting histories for the participants is intended to reveal the patterns observed in these particular villages, though their outlines can be found throughout the area of the Israeli-Palestinian conflict. The anomalies of the cases included here are the consequence of particular conditions that apply to the land conflict in the villages selected, and as a result of proximity to Jerusalem, and all that has occurred to and in the city since 1948, and especially since 1967.

It was not the goal of this research to determine the "truth" in the disputes included herein. Rather, it was an attempt to examine the relationship of Palestinians and Israelis to the land in competition, and the way each side adopted and adapted patterns and modes of landholding to its own ends. It is in this context that the current tactics, particularly tree planting, can be more fully appreciated. While the contextual discussion is indicative of the salience of these issues beyond the confines of the study area, the focus on the Jerusalem region lends the issues addressed in the research even greater pertinence. As the attempts to find a resolution for the Israeli-Palestinian conflict begin to concentrate on the issue of the future of Jerusalem, the lines being drawn through current tree planting and the land control that it confers will be a significant component of that discussion.

Bibliography

Books

Aamiry, M. A. *Jerusalem: Arab Origin and Heritage*. London: Longman, 1978.

Al Fakia, Muhammed Abu Zaideh, and Ali Muhammed Salem Hoshia. *Katana between Yesterday and Today*. Jerusalem: n.p., 1990. [Arabic]

Al Hambali, Abu Al-Yaman Mujjeer al-Din. *The History of Jerusalem and Hebron*. Beirut: n.p., n.d. [Arabic]

Alterman, Rachel. *Expropriation of Land for Public Needs According to the Law of Planning and Construction: In Anticipation of Re-evaluation*. Haifa: Center for Research of the City and Region, *Technion*, 1983. [Hebrew]

Al 'Uqbi, Nure and Jamal Talab. *Olive Trees under Occupation*. Jerusalem: Arab Studies Society, 1987. [Arabic and English]

Aresvik, Oddvar. *The Agricultural Development of Jordan*. New York: Praeger Publishers, 1976.

Baer, Gabriel. *A History of Land Ownership in Egypt: 1800–1950*. London: Oxford University Press, 1962.

Beaumont, Peter, et al. *The Middle East: A Geographical Study*. Chichester: John Wiley and Sons, 1976.

Ben-Arieh, Yehoshua. *A City Reflected in Its Times: New Jerusalem—The Beginnings*. Jerusalem: Yad Izhak Ben-Zvi, 1979. [Hebrew]

Benvenisti, Meron. *City with a Wall in Its Heart*. Israel: HaKibbutz Hameuchad, 1981. [Hebrew]

_____. *Opposite the Closed Wall: Jerusalem Divided and Jerusalem United*. Jerusalem: Weidenfeld and Nicolson, 1973. [Hebrew]

_____. *The West Bank Data Project: A Survey of Israel's Policies*. Washington: American Enterprise Institute for Public Policy Research, 1984.

Benvenisti, Meron, and Shlomo Khayat. *The West Bank and Gaza Atlas*. Jerusalem: West Bank Data Base Project, 1988.

Bigelman, Shimon, ed. *Jerusalem Statistical Yearbook 1988.* Jerusalem: Municipality of Jerusalem and Jerusalem Institute for Israel Studies, 1988.

Burckhardt, John Lewis. *Travels in Syria and the Holy Land.* Association for Promoting the Discovery of the Interior Parts of Africa. London: John Murray, 1822.

Cohen, Amnon. *Economic Life in Ottoman Jerusalem.* Cambridge: Cambridge University Press, 1989.

_____. *Palestine in the Eighteenth Century: Patterns of Government and Administration.* Jerusalem: Magnes Press, 1973.

Cohen, Eliyahu. *Registration and Transactions in Israeli Land Law.* Jerusalem: Law and the Judgement, 1988. [Hebrew]

Davies, W. D. *The Territorial Dimension of Judaism.* Berkeley: University of California Press, 1982.

Doukhan-Landau, Leah. *The Zionist Companies for Land Purchase in Palestine 1897–1914.* Jerusalem: Yad Izhak Ben-Zvi, 1979. [Hebrew]

Efrat, Elisha. *Jerusalem and the Corridor: Geography of City and Mountain.* Israel: Achiasaf, 1967. [Hebrew]

Eisenman, Robert H. *Islamic Law in Palestine and Israel: A History of the Survival of Tanzimat and Shari'a in the British Mandate and the Jewish State.* Leiden: E. J. Brill, 1978.

FAO. *Mediterranean Development Project: The Integrated Development of Mediterranean Agriculture and Foresty in Relation to Economic Growth: A Study and Proposal for Action.* Rome: Food and Agriculture Organization, 1959.

Garon, Meir. *Changes in the Face of the Forest in Eretz Yisrael from the Beginning of the New Jewish Settlement and until Today.* M.A. thesis, Hebrew University of Jerusalem, 1971. [Hebrew]

Gatje, Helmut, ed. *The Qur'an and Its Exegesis: Selected Texts with Classical and Modern Muslim Interpretations.* London: Routledge and Kegan Paul, 1971. [Translated 1976]

Gerson, Allan. *Israel, the West Bank, and International Law.* London: Frank Cass, 1978.

Gibb, Sir Hamilton, and Harold Bowen. *Islamic Society and the West: A Study of the Impact of Western Civilization on Moslem Culture in the Near East,* vol. 1. London: Oxford University Press, 1950.

Goitein, S. D. *Studies in Islamic History and Institutions.* Leiden: E. J. Brill, 1968.

Government of Palestine, Office of Village Statistics. *Village Statistics.* 1938, 1945.

Guha, Ramachandra. *The Unquiet Woods: Ecological Change and Peasant Resistance in the Himalaya.* Berkeley: University of California Press, 1989.

Halabi, Usamah, et al. *Land Alienation in the West Bank: A Legal Spatial Analysis.* Jerusalem: West Bank Data Project, 1985.

Hashimoni, Schwied, Hashimoni. *Jerusalem Master Plan 1968.* Jerusalem: Municipality of Jerusalem, 1972.

Hutteroth, Wolf-Dieter, and Kamal Abdulfattah. *Historical Geography of Palestine, Transjordan, and Southern Syria in the Late Sixteenth Century.* Erlangen: Selbstverlag der Frankischen Geographischen Gesellschaft in Kommission bei Palm & Enke, 1977.

Israel National Section of the International Commission of Jurists. *The Rule of Law in the Areas Administered by Israel.* Tel Aviv: Israel National Section, 1981.

Issawi, Charles. *The Fertile Crescent 1800–1914: A Documentary Economic History.* London: Oxford University Press, 1988.

Jerusalem Media and Communication Centre. *Bitter Harvest: Israeli Sanctions against Palestinian Agriculture during the Uprising.* Jerusalem: Jerusalem Media and Communication Centre, 1989.

Johnson, Nels. *Islam and the Politics of Meaning in Palestinian Nationalism.* London: Kegan Paul International, 1982.

Kahan, David. *Agriculture and Water Resources in the West Bank and Gaza (1967–1987).* Jerusalem: West Bank Data Project and *Jerusalem Post,* 1987.

Kendall, Henry. *Jerusalem the City Plan 1948: Preservation and Development during the British Mandate 1918–1948.* London: His Majesty's Stationery Office, 1948.

Kimche, Israel, et al. *Arab Settlement in the Metropolitan Region of Jerusalem.* Jerusalem: Jerusalem Institute for Israel Studies, no. 16, 1986. [Hebrew]

_____. *Greater Jerusalem Region: Alternative Municipal Frameworks.* Jerusalem: Jerusalem Institute for Israel Studies, 1990. [Hebrew]

Kimmerling, Baruch. *Land, Conflict, and Nation Building: A Sociological Study of the Territorial Factors in the Jewish-Arab Conflict.* Jerusalem: Hebrew University Department of Sociology and Social Anthropology, 1976.

Kretzmer, David. *Israel and the West Bank: Legal Issues.* Jerusalem: West Bank Data Project, 1984.

Kutcher, Arthur. *The New Jerusalem: Planning and Politics.* London: Thames and Hudson, 1973.

Lambton, Ann. *Landlord and Peasant in Persia: A Study of Land Tenure and Land Revenue Administration.* London: Oxford University Press, 1953.

Lehn, Walter, in association with Uri Davis. *The Jewish National Fund.* London: Kegan Paul International, 1988.

LeStrange, Guy. *Palestine under the Moslems: A Description of Syria and the Holy Land from A.D.650 to 1500 Translated from the Works of the Medieval Arab Geographers.* Beirut: Khayat, 1965.

Liebovitz, Yeshiahu. *Faith, History, and Values.* Jerusalem: Hebrew University of Jerusalem, Student Union, 1978. [Hebrew]

Lustick, Ian. *State-Building Failure in British Ireland and French Algeria.* Berkeley: Institute for International Studies, University of California, 1987.

Ma'oz, Moshe. *Ottoman Reform in Syria and Palestine 1840–1861: The Impact of the Tanzimat on Politics and Society.* Oxford: Clarendon Press, 1968.

Mishal, Shaul, with Reuben Aharoni. *Speaking with Stones: The Words behind the Palestinian Intifada.* Tel Aviv: HaKibbutz HaMe'uchad, 1989. [Hebrew]

Morris, Benny. *The Birth of the Palestinian Refugee Problem, 1947–1949.* Cambridge: Cambridge University Press, 1987.

Ongley, F., trans. *The Ottoman Land Code.* London: William Clowes and Sons, 1892.

Orni, Ephraim. *Afforestation in Israel.* Jerusalem: HaKeren Keyemet L'Yisrael, 1975.

_____. *Agrarian Reform in Israel.* Jerusalem: HaKeren Keyemet L'Yisrael, 1975. [Hebrew]

_____. *Land of Israel: History, Policy, Management, and Development.* Jerusalem: HaKeren Keyemet L'Yisrael, 1980. [Hebrew]

Owen, Rodger. *The Middle East in the World Economy 1800–1914.* London: Methuen and Co., 1981.

Rechess, Eli. *Israeli Arabs and the Expropriation of Land in the Galilee: Background, Occurrences, and Projections.* Tel Aviv: Shiloach Institute for Research of the Middle East and Africa, 1977. [Hebrew]

Reichman, Shalom, et al. *Jewish Non-Agricultural Settlement in Judea and Samaria: Survey and Principal Findings.* Department of Geography and Institute for Urban and Regional Studies, Hebrew University of Jerusalem, 1980. [Hebrew]

Reiter, Yitzhak. *The Waqf in Jerusalem*. Jerusalem: Jerusalem Institute for Israel Studies, 1992. [Hebrew]

Sack, Robert David. *Human Territoriality: Its Theory and History*. Cambridge: Cambridge University Press, 1986.

Said, Edward W. *Orientalism*. New York: Random House, 1979.

Schmelz, U. O. *Modern Jerusalem's Demographic Evolution*. Jerusalem: Institute of Contemporary Jewry, Hebrew University of Jerusalem, and Jerusalem Institute for Israel Studies, 1987.

Sharon, Ariel, with David Chanoff. *Warrior: The Autobiography of Ariel Sharon*. New York: Simon and Schuster, 1989.

Shiloni, Tzvi. *The Keren Keyemet L'Yisrael as a Factor in Shaping the Colonized Landscape of Eretz Yisrael from the Time of Its Foundation to the Outbreak of World War I, 1897–1914*. Ph.D. thesis, Hebrew University of Jerusalem, 1987. [Hebrew]

Shiskin, Arieh, and Moshe Gilayi. *Report of the Public Committee: An Examination of Land Policy Goals*. Tel Aviv: Professional Evaluation Committee, 1986. [Hebrew]

Shlaim, Avi. *Collusion across the Jordan: King Abdullah, The Zionist Movement, and the Partition of Palestine*. Oxford: Clarendon Press, 1988.

Smith, George Adam. *Jerusalem: The Topography, Economics, and History from the Earliest Times to A.D. 70*. London: Hodder and Stoughton, 1907.

Sokobolski, Avraham, et al. *Judea and Samaria: Land Rights and Israeli Law*. Tel Aviv: Borsi, 1986. [Hebrew]

Stein, Kenneth W. *The Land Question in Palestine, 1917–1939*. Chapel Hill: University of North Carolina Press, 1984.

Thirgood, J. V. *Cyprus: A Chronicle of Its Forests, Land, and People*. Vancouver: University of British Columbia Press, 1987.

————. *Man and the Mediterranean Forest*. London: Academic Press, 1981.

Twain, Mark. *The Innocents Abroad; or, The New Pilgrims' Progress*. New York: Heritage Press, 1962. [Original publication 1869]

Weitz, Yosef [Joseph]. *Afforestation Policy in Israel*. Israel: Jewish National Fund, 1950.

————. *Forest and Afforestation in Israel*. Israel: Massada, 1970. [Hebrew]

————. *My Diaries and Letters to My Sons*. Israel: Massada, 1973. [Hebrew]

Zamir, Eyal. *State Land in Judea and Samaria: The Legal Status*. Jerusalem: Jerusalem Institute for Israel Studies, no. 12, 1985. [Hebrew]

Ziadeh, Farhat J. *Property Law in the Arab World: Real Rights in Egypt, Iraq, Jordan, Lebanon, Libya, Syria, Saudi Arabia, and the Gulf States*. London: Graham and Trotman, 1979.

Articles and Chapters from Books

Abbady, I. A., ed. "The Jewish National Fund and the New Jerusalem." *Jerusalem Economy*. Jerusalem: Jerusalem Chamber of Commerce, 1950. [Hebrew]

Abu Kishk, Bakir. "Arab Land and Israeli Policy." *Journal of Palestine Studies* 11, no. 1 (1981): 124–135.

Bar-Sela, Yoram. "Law Enforcement in the Eastern Sector of Jerusalem." In *Jerusalem: Aspects of Law*. Jerusalem: Jerusalem Institute for Israel Studies, Discussion Paper no. 3, 1983.

Bereck, P., and A. Levy. "Land Distribution in Israeli Moshavim." *American Journal of Agricultural Economics* 68, no. 3 (1986): 605–611.

Bobek, Hans. "The Main Stages in Socio-Economic Evolution from a Geographical Perspective." In *Readings in Cultural Geography*, edited by Philip L. Wagner and Marvin W. Mikesell. Chicago: University of Chicago Press, 1962.

Cattan, Henry. "The Question of Jerusalem." *Arab Studies Quarterly* 7, nos. 2–3 (1985): 131–158.

Cohen, Justice Haim. "The Status of Jerusalem in the Law of the State of Israel." In *Twenty Years in Jerusalem 1967–1987*, edited by Yehoshua Prawer and Ora Ahimeir. Israel: Ministry of Defence and Jerusalem Institute for Israel Studies, 1988. [Hebrew]

Dakkak, Ibrahim. "The Transformation of Jerusalem: Juridical Status and Physical Change." In *Occupation over Palestine*, edited by Naseer H. Aruri. Belmont, Mass.: Association of Arab-American University Graduates, 1983.

Drori, Moshe. "The Israeli Settlements in Judea and Samaria: Some Legal Aspects." In *Judea, Samaria, and Gaza: Views on the Present and Future*, edited by Daniel E. Elazar. Washington: American Enterprise Institute for Public Policy Research, 1982.

Giordano, Guglielmo. "The Mediterranean Region." In *A World Geography of Forest Resources*, edited by Stephan Haden-Guest et al. American Geographical Society Special Publication no. 33. New York: Ronald Press Co., 1956.

Goren, Shlomo. "Preservation of Plantations in Light of the Religious Law." In *Tree and Man*, edited by Gedalia Ginzburg. Kfar Etzion: Kfar Etzion Field School, 1975. [Hebrew]

Graham-Brown, Sarah. "Agriculture and Labour Transformation in Palestine." In *The Rural Middle East*, edited by Kathy Glavanis and Pandeli Glavanis. London: Zed Books and Bir Zeit University, 1990.

Grossman, David. "Employment Potential of the Arab Agricultural Sector in the Occupied Territories." *Karka: Journal of the Land Use Institute* 30 (September 1988). [Hebrew]

Hutteroth, Wolf. "The Pattern of Settlement in Palestine in the Sixteenth Century: Geographical Research on Turkish Defter-i Mufassal." In *Studies on Palestine during the Ottoman Period*, edited by Moshe Ma'oz. Jerusalem: Magnes Press, 1975.

Israel National Section of the Commission of International Jurists. "Public and Private Lands." *The Rule of Law in the Areas Administered by Israel*. Tel Aviv: Commission of International Jurists, 1981.

Jiryis, Sabri. "Domination by the Law." *Journal of Palestine Studies* 11, no. 1 (1981): 67–92.

Kark, Ruth. "Land and the Idea of Land Redemption in Traditional Cultures and in Eretz Yisrael." *Karka* 33 (December 1989). [Hebrew]

_____. "Historical Sites: Perceptions and Land Purchase: The Case of Modi'in, 1882–1931." *Studies in Zionism* 9, no. 1 (1988): 1–18.

Kerr, Malcom H. "The Changing Political Status of Jerusalem." In *The Transformation of Palestine: Essays on the Origin and Development of the Arab-Israeli Conflict*, edited by Ibrahim Abu-Lughod. Evanston: Northwestern University Press, 1971.

Khalidi, Rashid. "Palestinian Peasant Resistance to Zionism before World War I." In *Blaming the Victims: Spurious Scholarship and the Palestinian Question*, edited by Edward W. Said and Christopher Hitchens. London: Verso, 1988.

Kimmerling, Baruch. "Sovereignty, Ownership, and 'Presence' in the Jewish-Arab Territorial Conflict: The Case of Bir'im and Ikrit." *Comparative Political Studies* 10, no. 2 (July 1977): 155–176.

Kislev, Ran. "Land Expropriations: History of Oppression." *New Outlook* 19, no. 6 (1976): 22–31.

Kollek, Teddy. "Present Problems and Future Perspectives." In *Jerusalem Perspectives*, edited by Peter Schneider and Geoffrey Wigoder. London: Rainbow Group, 1976.

Kroyanker, David. "The Face of the City." In *Twenty Years in Jerusalem 1967–1987*, edited by Yehoshua Prawer and Ora Ahimeir. Israel: Ministry of Defence and Jerusalem Institute for Israel Studies, 1988. [Hebrew]

Lazarus-Yaffe, Hava. "The Sanctity of Jerusalem in Islamic Tradition." In *Jerusalem in the Modern Period*, edited by E. Shaltiel. Jerusalem: Yitzhk Ben-Zvi, 1981. [Hebrew]

Liskovski, Aharon [Layish]. "The 'Present Absentees' in Israel." *HaMizrach HeHadash* 10, no. 3 (1960): 186–192. [Hebrew]

Lustick, Ian. "Israel and the West Bank after Elon Moreh: The Mechanics of De Facto Annexation." *Middle East Journal* 35, no. 4 (1981): 557–577.

Matar, Ibrahim. "Israeli Settlements and Palestinian Rights." In *Occupation over Palestine*, edited by Naseer H. Aruri. Belmont, Mass.: Association of Arab-American University Graduates, 1983.

————. "Israeli Settlements in the West Bank and Gaza Strip." *Journal of Palestine Studies* 11, no. 1 (1981): 93–110.

Mooney, H. F. "Southwestern Asia." In *World Geography of Forest Resources*, edited by Stephan Haden-Guest et al. New York: Ronald Press Co., 1956.

Murphy, Alexander B. "Historical Justifications for Territorial Claims." *Annals of the Association of American Geographers* 80, no. 4 (1990): 531–548.

Piron, Mordechai. "Prohibition on the Cutting Down of Trees." In *Tree and Man*, edited by Gedalia Ginzburg. Kfar Etzion: Kfar Etzion Field School, 1975. [Hebrew]

Poliak, A. N. "Classification of Lands in the Islamic Law and Its Technical Terms." *American Journal of Semitic Languages and Literatures* 57, no. 1 (1940): 50–62.

Reichman, Shalom. "A Map of Landownership in Jerusalem, 1947." In *Jerusalem in Zionist Vision and Realization*. Jerusalem: Zalman Shazar Center for Jewish History, 1989. [Hebrew]

Rishmawi, Mona. "Planning in Whose Interest? Land Use Planning as a Strategy for Judaization." *Journal of Palestine Studies* 16, no. 2 (1987): 105–116.

Rubenstein, Daniel. "The Jerusalem Municipality under the Ottomans, British, and Jordanians." In *Jerusalem Perspectives*, edited by Peter Schneider and Geoffrey Wigoder. London: Rainbow Group, 1976.

Sabri, Mahsan. "The Legal Status of Israeli Arabs." *Legal Studies* 3, no. 2 (1973–74). [Hebrew]

Shehadeh, Raja. "The Law and a Palestine Settlement." *Middle East International* 221 (1984): 13.

————. "Some Legal Aspects of Israeli Land Policy in the Occupied Territories." *Arab Studies Quarterly* 7, nos. 2–3 (1985): 42–61.

Shuqeir, Adnan. "The Role of Forests and Nature Reserves in the West Bank in Advancing Internal Tourism." *Shu'un Tanmawiyyeh* 2, no. 2 (Spring 1992). [Arabic]

Sluglett, Peter, and Marion Farouk-Sluglett. "The Application of the 1858 Land Code in Greater Syria: Some Preliminary Observations." In *Land Tenure and Social Transformation in the Middle East*, edited by Tarif Khalidi. Beirut: American University of Beirut, 1984.

Sofer, Naim. "The Political Status of Jerusalem in the Hashemite Kingdom of Jordan, 1948–1967." *Middle Eastern Studies* 12, no. 1 (1976): 73–94.

Stendal, Ori. "Changes in the Arab Population," In *Twenty Years in Jerusalem 1967–1987*, edited by Yehoshua Prawer and Ora Ahimeir. Israel: Ministry of Defence and Jerusalem Institute for Israel Studies, 1988. [Hebrew]

Stern, David. "Population Distribution in an Ethno-Ideologically Divided City: The Case of Jerusalem." *Urban Geography* 13, no. 2 (1992): 164–186.

Talhami, Ghada. "Between Development and Preservation: Jerusalem under Three Regimes." *American Arab Affairs* 16 (1986): 93–107.

Tamari, Salim. "From the Fruits of Their Labour: The Persistance of Share Tenancy in the Palestinian Agrarian Economy." In *The Rural Middle East*, edited by Kathy Glavanis and Pandeli Glavanis. London: Zed Books and Bir Zeit University, 1990.

Tannous, Afif I. "The Village in the National Life of Lebanon." *Middle East Journal* 3 (1949): 151–163.

Toledano, Ehud. "Sanjak Jerusalem in the Sixteenth Century: Village Settlement and Aspects of Demography." In *Chapters in the History of Jerusalem at the Beginning of the Ottoman Period*, edited by Amnon Cohen. Jerusalem: Yad Izhak Ben Tzvi, 1979. [Hebrew]

Tress, Madeline. "The Role of the Peasantry in the Palestine Revolt, 1936–1939." *Peasant Studies* 15, no. 3 (1988): 161–190.

Udovitch, A. L. "Technology, Land Tenure, and Rural Society: Aspects of Continuity in the Agricultural History of the Pre-Modern Middle East." In *The Islamic Middle East 700–1900*, edited by A. L. Udovitch. Princeton: Darwin Press, 1981.

Warriner, Doreen. "Land Tenure Problems in the Fertile Crescent in the Nineteenth and Twentieth Centuries." In *The Economic History of the Middle East 1800–1914*, edited by Charles Issawi. Chicago: University of Chicago Press, 1966.

Zohari, Michael. "The Flora and Vegetation in the Jerusalem Landscape." In *The Book of Jerusalem: The Nature, History, and Development of Jerusalem from Her Earliest Days until Our Times*, edited by Michael Avi-Yona. Jerusalem: Bialik, 1956. [Hebrew]

Index

THE UNIVERSITY OF CHICAGO
GEOGRAPHY RESEARCH PAPERS
(Lithographed, 6 x 9 inches)

Titles in Print

127. GOHEEN, PETER G. *Victorian Toronto, 1850 to 1900: Pattern and Process of Growth.* 1970. xiii + 278 p.

131. NEILS, ELAINE M. *Reservation to City: Indian Migration and Federal Relocation.* 1971. x + 198 p.

132. MOLINE, NORMAN T. *Mobility and the Small Town, 1900-1930.* 1971. ix + 169 p.

133. SCHWIND, PAUL J. *Migration and Regional Development in the United States, 1950-1960.* 1971. x + 170 p.

134. PYLE, GERALD F. *Heart Disease, Cancer and Stroke in Chicago: A Geographical Analysis with Facilities, Plans for 1980.* 1971. ix + 292 p.

136. BUTZER, KARL W. *Recent History of an Ethiopian Delta: The Omo River and the Level of Lake Rudolf.* 1971. xvi + 184 p.

139. McMANIS, DOUGLAS R. *European Impressions of the New England Coast, 1497-1620.* 1972. viii + 147 p.

142. PLATT, RUTHERFORD H. *The Open Space Decision Process: Spatial Allocation of Costs and Benefits.* 1972. xi + 189 p.

143. GOLANT, STEPHEN M. *The Residential Location and Spatial Behavior of the Elderly: A Canadian Example.* 1972. xv + 226 p.

144. PANNELL, CLIFTON W. *T'ai-Chung, T'ai-wan: Structure and Function.* 1973. xii + 200 p.

145. LANKFORD, PHILIP M. *Regional Incomes in the United States, 1929-1967: Level, Distribution, Stability, and Growth.* 1972. x + 137 p.

148. JOHNSON, DOUGLAS L. *Jabal al-Akhdar, Cyrenaica: An Historical Geography of Settlement and Livelihood.* 1973. xii + 240 p.

149. YEUNG, YUE-MAN. *National Development Policy and Urban Transformation in Singapore: A Study of Public Housing and the Marketing System.* 1973. x + 204 p.

150. HALL, FRED L. *Location Criteria for High Schools: Student Transportation and Racial Integration.* 1973. xii + 156 p.

151. ROSENBERG, TERRY J. *Residence, Employment, and Mobility of Puerto Ricans in New York City.* 1974. xi + 230 p.

152. MIKESELL, MARVIN W., ed. *Geographers Abroad: Essays on the Problems and Prospects of Research in Foreign Areas.* 1973. ix + 296 p.

154. WACHT, WALTER F. *The Domestic Air Transportation Network of the United States.* 1974. ix + 98 p.

160. MEYER, JUDITH W. *Diffusion of an American Montessori Education.* 1975. xi + 97 p.

162. LAMB, RICHARD F. *Metropolitan Impacts on Rural America.* 1975. xii + 196 p.

163. FEDOR, THOMAS STANLEY. *Patterns of Urban Growth in the Russian Empire during the Nineteenth Century.* 1975. xxv + 245 p.

164. HARRIS, CHAUNCY D. *Guide to Geographical Bibliographies and Reference Works in Russian or on the Soviet Union.* 1975. xviii + 478 p.

165. JONES, DONALD W. *Migration and Urban Unemployment in Dualistic Economic Development.* 1975. x + 174 p.

166. BEDNARZ, ROBERT S. *The Effect of Air Pollution on Property Value in Chicago.* 1975. viii + 111 p.

167. HANNEMANN, MANFRED. *The Diffusion of the Reformation in Southwestern Germany, 1518-1534.* 1975. ix + 235 p.

168. SUBLETT, MICHAEL D. *Farmers on the Road: Interfarm Migration and the Farming of Noncontiguous Lands in Three Midwestern Townships. 1939-1969.* 1975. xiii + 214 p.

169. STETZER, DONALD FOSTER. *Special Districts in Cook County: Toward a Geography of Local Government.* 1975. xi + 177 p.

172. COHEN, YEHOSHUA S., and BRIAN J. L. BERRY. *Spatial Components of Manufacturing Change.* 1975. vi + 262 p.

173. HAYES, CHARLES R. *The Dispersed City: The Case of Piedmont, North Carolina.* 1976. ix + 157 p.

174. CARGO, DOUGLAS B. *Solid Wastes: Factors Influencing Generation Rates.* 1977. 100 p.

176. MORGAN, DAVID J. *Patterns of Population Distribution: A Residential Preference Model and Its Dynamic.* 1978. xiii + 200 p.

177. STOKES, HOUSTON H.; DONALD W. JONES; and HUGH M. NEUBURGER. *Unemployment and Adjustment in the Labor Market: A Comparison between the Regional and National Responses.* 1975. ix + 125 p.

181. GOODWIN, GARY C. *Cherokees in Transition: A Study of Changing Culture and Environment Prior to 1775.* 1977. ix + 207 p.

183. HAIGH, MARTIN J. *The Evolution of Slopes on Artificial Landforms, Blaenavon, U.K.* 1978. xiv + 293 p.

184. FINK, L. DEE. *Listening to the Learner: An Exploratory Study of Personal Meaning in College Geography Courses.* 1977. ix + 186 p.

185. HELGREN, DAVID M. *Rivers of Diamonds: An Alluvial History of the Lower Vaal Basin, South Africa.* 1979. xix + 389 p.

186. BUTZER, KARL W., ed. *Dimensions of Human Geography: Essays on Some Familiar and Neglected Themes.* 1978. vii + 190 p.

187. MITSUHASHI, SETSUKO. *Japanese Commodity Flows.* 1978. x + 172 p.

188. CARIS, SUSAN L. *Community Attitudes toward Pollution.* 1978. xii + 211 p.

189. REES, PHILIP M. *Residential Patterns in American Cities: 1960.* 1979. xvi + 405 p.

190. KANNE, EDWARD A. *Fresh Food for Nicosia.* 1979. x + 106 p.

192. KIRCHNER, JOHN A. *Sugar and Seasonal Labor Migration: The Case of Tucumán, Argentina.* 1980. xii + 174 p.

194. HARRIS, CHAUNCY D. *Annotated World List of Selected Current Geographical Serials, Fourth Edition. 1980.* 1980. iv + 165 p.

196. LEUNG, CHI-KEUNG, and NORTON S. GINSBURG, eds. *China: Urbanizations and National Development.* 1980. ix + 283 p.

197. DAICHES, SOL. *People in Distress: A Geographical Perspective on Psychological Well-being.* 1981. xiv + 199 p.

198. JOHNSON, JOSEPH T. *Location and Trade Theory: Industrial Location, Comparative Advantage, and the Geographic Pattern of Production in the United States.* 1981. xi + 107 p.

199-200. STEVENSON, ARTHUR J. *The New York–Newark Air Freight System.* 1982. xvi + 440 p.

201. LICATE, JACK A. *Creation of a Mexican Landscape: Territorial Organization and Settlement in the Eastern Puebla Basin, 1520-1605.* 1981. x + 143 p.

202. RUDZITIS, GUNDARS. *Residential Location Determinants of the Older Population.* 1982. x + 117 p.

204. DAHMANN, DONALD C. *Locals and Cosmopolitans: Patterns of Spatial Mobility during the Transition from Youth to Early Adulthood.* 1982. xiii + 146 p.

206. HARRIS, CHAUNCY D. *Bibliography of Geography. Part II: Regional. Volume 1. The United States of America.* 1984. viii + 178 p.

207-208. WHEATLEY, PAUL. *Nagara and Commandery: Origins of the Southeast Asian Urban Traditions.* 1983. xv + 472 p.

209. SAARINEN, THOMAS F.; DAVID SEAMON; and JAMES L. SELL, eds. *Environmental Perception and Behavior: An Inventory and Prospect.* 1984. x + 263 p.

210. WESCOAT, JAMES L., JR. *Integrated Water Development: Water Use and Conservation Practice in Western Colorado.* 1984. xi + 239 p.

211. DEMKO, GEORGE J., and ROLAND J. FUCHS, eds. *Geographical Studies on the Soviet Union: Essays in Honor of Chauncy D. Harris.* 1984. vii + 294 p.

212. HOLMES, ROLAND C. *Irrigation in Southern Peru: The Chili Basin.* 1986. ix + 199 p.

213. EDMONDS, RICHARD LOUIS. *Northern Frontiers of Qing China and Tokugawa Japan: A Comparative Study of Frontier Policy.* 1985. xi + 209 p.

214. FREEMAN, DONALD B., and GLEN B. NORCLIFFE. *Rural Enterprise in Kenya: Development and Spatial Organization of the Nonfarm Sector.* 1985. xiv + 180 p.

215. COHEN, YEHOSHUA S., and AMNON SHINAR. *Neighborhoods and Friendship Networks: A Study of Three Residential Neighborhoods in Jerusalem.* 1985. ix + 137 p.

216. OBERMEYER, NANCY J. *Bureaucrats, Clients, and Geography: The Bailly Nuclear Power Plant Battle in Northern Indiana.* 1989. x + 135 p.

217-218. CONZEN, MICHAEL P., ed. *World Patterns of Modern Urban Change: Essays in Honor of Chauncy D. Harris.* 1986. x + 479 p.

219. KOMOGUCHI, YOSHIMI. *Agricultural Systems in the Tamil Nadu: A Case Study of Peruvalanallur Village.* 1986. xvi + 175 p.

220. GINSBURG, NORTON; JAMES OSBORN; and GRANT BLANK. *Geographic Perspectives on the Wealth of Nations.* 1986. ix + 133 p.

221. BAYLSON, JOSHUA C. *Territorial Allocation by Imperial Rivalry: The Human Legacy in the Near East.* 1987. xi + 138 p.

222. DORN, MARILYN APRIL. *The Administrative Partitioning of Costa Rica: Politics and Planners in the 1970s.* 1989. xi + 126 p.

223. ASTROTH, JOSEPH H., JR. *Understanding Peasant Agriculture: An Integrated Land-Use Model for the Punjab.* 1990. xiii + 173 p.

224. PLATT, RUTHERFORD H.; SHEILA G. PELCZARSKI; and BARBARA K. BURBANK, eds. *Cities on the Beach: Management Issues of Developed Coastal Barriers.* 1987. vii + 324 p.

225. LATZ, GIL. *Agricultural Development in Japan: The Land Improvement District in Concept and Practice.* 1989. viii + 135 p.

226. GRITZNER, JEFFREY A. *The West African Sahel: Human Agency and Environmental Change.* 1988. xii + 170 p.

227. MURPHY, ALEXANDER B. *The Regional Dynamics of Language Differentiation in Belgium: A Study in Cultural-Political Geography.* 1988. xiii + 249 p.

228-229. BISHOP, BARRY C. *Karnali under Stress: Livelihood Strategies and Seasonal Rhythms in a Changing Nepal Himalaya.* 1990. xviii + 460 p.

230. MUELLER-WILLE, CHRISTOPHER. *Natural Landscape Amenities and Suburban Growth: Metropolitan Chicago, 1970-1980.* 1990. xi + 153 p.

231. WILKINSON, M. JUSTIN. *Paleoenvironments in the Namib Desert: The Lower Tumas Basin in the Late Cenozoic.* 1990. xv + 196 p.

232. DUBOIS, RANDOM. *Soil Erosion in a Coastal River Basin: A Case Study from the Philippines.* 1990. xii + 138 p.

233. PALM, RISA, AND MICHAEL E. HODGSON. *After a California Earthquake: Attitude and Behavior Change.* 1992. xii + 130 p.

234. KUMMER, DAVID M. *Deforestation in the Postwar Philippines.* 1992. xviii + 179 p.

235. CONZEN, MICHAEL P., THOMAS A. RUMNEY, AND GRAEME WYNN. *A Scholar's Guide to Geographical Writing on the American and Canadian Past.* 1993. xiii + 751 p.

236. COHEN, SHAUL EPHRAIM. *The Politics of Planting: Israeli-Palestinian Competition for Control of Land in the Jerusalem Periphery.* 1993. xiv + 203 p.